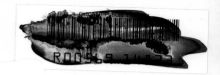

DATE			

COGNITION, STRESS, AND AGING

JAMES E. BIRREN and JUDY LIVINGSTON, Editors

Andrus Gerontology Center
University of Southern California

and

Donna E. Deutchman, Editorial Coordinator

Prentice-Hall, Inc., Englewood Cliffs, New Jersey 07632

Library of Congress Cataloging in Publication Data

Main entry under title:
Cognition, stress, and aging.

   Based on research by Fellows of the Andrew Norman
Institute at the Andrus Gerontology Center, University
of Southern California.
   Includes bibliographies and index.
   1. Aged—Diseases—Psychosomatic aspects.
2. Cognition. 3. Stress (Psychology) 4. Aging—
Psychological aspects. I. Birren, James E.
II. Livingston, Judy. III. Ethel Percy Andrus
Gerontology Center.
RC952.5.C59 1985   618.97'08   84-13296
ISBN 0-13-139825-3

Editorial/production supervision: Colleen Brosnan
Cover design: Lundgren Graphics, Ltd.
Manufacturing buyer: Barbara Kelly Kittle

Printed in the United States of America.

10 9 8 7 6 5 4 3 2 1

ISBN 0-13-139825-3 01

Prentice-Hall International, Inc., *London*
Prentice-Hall of Australia Pty. Limited, *Sydney*
Editora Prentice-Hall do Brasil, Ltda., *Rio de Janeiro*
Prentice-Hall Canada Inc., *Toronto*
Prentice-Hall of India Private Limited, *New Delhi*
Prentice-Hall of Japan, Inc., *Tokyo*
Prentice-Hall of Southeast Asia Pte. Ltd., *Singapore*
Whitehall Books Limited, *Wellington, New Zealand*

This book is dedicated to the memory of George Olincy.
His personal commitment to the development
of progressive ideas and support of inquiry
and scholarship inspired us all.

CONTRIBUTORS

James E. Birren, Ph.D., (Chapter 1) is the Executive Director of the Ethel Percy Andrus Gerontology Center, Director of the Andrew Norman Institute for Advanced Study in Gerontology and Geriatrics, and Professor of Psychology at the University of Southern California. Dr. Birren is also currently a member of the World Health Organization's Expert Advisory Panel on Health of Elderly Persons. He is past President of the Gerontological Society of America, the Western Gerontological Society, and the Division on Adult Development and Aging of the American Psychological Association. In addition, he is a Fellow of the American Psychological Association, the Gerontological Society, the American Geriatrics Society, and the American Association for the Advancement of Science. His many awards include the Brookdale Foundation Award for Gerontological Research, an Honorary Doctorate from the University of Gothenburg, and the Gerontological Society Award for Meritorious Research.

Jerome P. Heckenmueller, Ph.D., (Chapter 5) is currently a Professor of Psychology at Aquinas College, Grand Rapids, Missouri where he is investigating psychophysiological mechanisms involved in the relationship between cognitive control and stress reactions across the life span. He is experimenting with age integrated learning in order to test whether the college classroom can serve as a positive social support (eustress) that can facilitate the development of cognitive control in all ages resulting in increased independence, enhanced educational outcomes, and improved psychosocial adjustment. Dr. Heckenmueller's interest in gerontology was cultivated when, in 1981, he was awarded a National Science Foundation grant to study with Dr. James E. Birren, Director of the Ethel Percy Andrus Gerontology Center at the University of Southern California, where he also served as a charter Fellow of the Andrew Norman Institute for Advanced Study in Gerontology and Geriatrics and wrote his chapter for this volume.

James P. Henry, M.D., Ph.D., (Chapter 2, 4) is currently a Research Professor of Psychiatry at Roma Linda University Medical School and Staff Physician at the Jerry L. Pettis Veterans' Hospital. He is also an Associate Fellow of the Andrew Norman Institute for Advanced Study in Gerontology and Geriatrics at the Andrus Gerontology Center, University of Southern California. His area of special interest is the mechanisms by which emotional arousal can lead to disease. Publications include *Stress, Health and Social Environment* and related articles in professional journals.

Deborah D. Newquist, M.S.W.-M.P.A., (Chapter 6) is a Senior Staff Associate at the Andrus Gerontology Center, University of Southern California. Her research interests are the health characteristics and behavior of older adults, disability, and cross-cultural aging. She is a past Co-Editor of *Generations,* the quarterly journal of the Western Gerontological Society. One of her most recent publications is *Health and Extended Worklife,* a special report to be published by the U.S. House of Representatives Select Committee on Aging. She is a Ph.D. Candidate in Anthropology at the University of California, Los Angeles.

Gary T. Reker, M.A.Sc., Ph.D., (Chapter 3, 7) is Associate Professor of Psychology at Trent University, Peterborough, Ontario, Canada. His two chapters in this volume were written while on sabbatical leave as a Fellow of the Andrew Norman Institute for Advanced Study in Gerontology and Geriatrics at the Andrus Gerontology Center, University of Southern California in Los Angeles. Dr. Reker has published in the areas of cognitive complexity, forensic psychology, program evaluation and psychological test construction. His primary research interests include life-span developmental psychology, the relation of mental attitudes (optimism, meaning in life) to well-being in the elderly, and the holistic approach to life.

Donald R. Shupe, Ph.D., (Chapter 8) is Professor of Psychology and Chairman of the Gerontology Department, Central Washington University, Ellensburg, Washington. He has published articles in psychology, research methodology, aesthetics, and behavioral medicine. His current research interests include psychological parameters of nursing home design and function, perceived control in the elderly, and behavioral slowing with age.

Joan B. Stoddard, Ph.D., (Chapter 4) is currently engaged in private consultation work. She received her degree from the University of Southern California, and her interests in the social aspects of aging experience led to her appointment as chair of the Task Force on Older Women, a project for a division of the Gerontological Society of America. Her research includes a content analysis of verbal behavior among women of differing career experience, and an investigation of the effects of media role models on the self-esteem of older women. Work on the latter project was funded by the National Study Grant Award, Phi Delta Gamma.

Paul T. P. Wong, Ph.D., (Chapter 8) is Professor of Psychology, Trent University, Peterborough, Ontario, and Fellow of the Canadian Psychological Association. He has published extensively on frustration and persistence. Recent publications in social psychology include "When People Ask Why Questions" (with B. Weiner) in the *Journal of Social and Personality Psychology* and "An Attribution Analysis of Locus of Control" (with C. F. Sproule) in H. Lefcourt's *Research on the Locus of Control Construct.* Current research interests focus on coping behavior and well-being in the elderly.

Judy Maes Zarit, Ph.D., (Chapter 1) is currently Coordinator of Gerontology Services at Didi Hirsch Community Mental Health Center in Los Angeles. Recent publications include a series of booklets for older patients instructing them in doctor-patient communication called *How to Talk to Your Doctor.* Dr. Zarit's special areas of interest are intervention strategies for caregivers of senile dementia patients, neuropsychological assessment of Alzheimer's disease and its correlation with post-mortem pathology, and cognitive-behavioral psychotherapy with older patients.

CONTENTS

PREFACE

The concern with the effect of cognitive schemas as mediators of stress, and the resultant changes in health status with age, is a relatively new concern in the field of gerontology, and one which of necessity involves extremely complex and overlapping interactions. This volume is an attempt to begin the integration of information and development of theory necessary to expand our understanding of the health of an increasing older population. Few of the chapters deal equally with all three areas of the general theme; this is a result of the research to date in the field, which tends to focus on two of the areas—for example, age and health relationships, or the effects of perceptual frameworks on health—rather than all three. However, these chapters taken together raise many of the basic issues and begin what will be a continuing examination of an important area for future research.

This volume is the first in an annual series which will be devoted to special topics in the field of aging and produced by scholars from the United States and other countries who are Fellows of the Andrew Norman Institute for Advanced Study in Gerontology and Geriatrics at the Andrus Gerontology Center. These books take a multidisciplinary approach to issues in the field of aging which are complex and not yet totally understood but which often have important implications for the development of national policy in this country and abroad. This volume will be followed by others on Age, Health and Employment; Dementing Illnesses: Policy and Management; Aging and Education; and Theories of Aging.

The chapters in this volume address various issues related to age and health with particular emphasis on cognitive processes, emotions, attitudes, and psychosocial factors which may affect health with advancing age. In some areas the literature was so large that the authors had to be selective, and the reference lists do not necessarily include "everything" on a particular topic. In other areas data are sparse and conceptualization was and is necessary as a prelude to organized inquiry. The book is not intended as a definitive reference work for the entire field; rather it selects a number of representative and important topics to examine critically, suggests some new models, and indicates profitable directions for future research. It is intended primarily for use by researchers, professionals, and graduate students with interests in health and aging.

In some ways the books, and the very existence of an Institute for Advanced Study in Gerontology and Geriatrics, represent the "coming of age" of the field of gerontology. During its developmental years, work in the field was concentrated on the collection of data in a wide variety of areas and on establishing the validity of methodologies and topics of study. We are now in a position to undertake the development of theory and the building of basic models, as well as continuing to gather more sophisticated data. Also, we are beginning to look at complex problems where disciplines overlap and where that overlap must be dealt with in order to move toward greater understanding. These volumes will increasingly represent the effort to bridge a variety of disciplines, to suggest basic models, and to provide current reviews of research in ground-breaking areas.

The Andrew Norman Institute for Advanced Study in Gerontology and Geriatrics was established in 1981 at the Andrus Gerontology Center of the University of Southern California, funded by an initial grant from the Andrew Norman Foundation. Fellows of the Institute spend ten months at the Andrus Center doing work related to the year's special topic, meeting in a weekly seminar, and preparing papers for the annual book, as well as pursuing individual research projects.

The goals of the Institute include furthering research in gerontology and geriatrics and encouraging the exchange of information and the development of collaborative research among scholars from the United States and other countries. The "aging of societies" is one of the most important issues facing all nations in the world today; and the field of gerontology is at a point to benefit greatly from cross-cultural and multi-national exchanges of information and approaches to issues related to aging.

We would like to thank Drs. Frank Beaudet, Vern Bengtson, Jacqueline Goodchilds, Iseli Krauss, William Lammers, Joseph Matarazzo, Jaak Panksepp, Val Remnet, Warner Schaie, Richard Schulz, Ray Steinberg, Joan Stoddard, Ezra Stotland, Michael Taussig, Judith Treas, Ingrid Waldron, Robert Wiswell, and Diana Woodruff for their assistance in reviewing chapters for this volume. Dr. Judy Zarit, Research Assistant for the ANI, assisted the authors in collecting and evaluating published materials, and Dr. Joan Stoddard served as Acting Program Administrator for a portion of the year. Ms. Judy Pinal typed many of the manuscripts. Ms. Donna Deutchman has done an outstanding job as Editorial Coordinator for this series.

In addition to the generous support from the Andrew Norman Foundation, we gratefully acknowledge the financial assistance of Dr. Armand Hammer and the Metropolitan Life Insurance Foundation. The Andrus Gerontology Center has supported this effort both financially and through the generous assistance of many of its staff and resources.

Finally, we would like to state our appreciation for the vision and leadership demonstrated by George and Virginia Olincy of the Andrew Norman Foundation, who saw the value of an Institute for Advanced Study in Gerontology and Geriatrics and helped to make it a reality.

CONCEPTS OF HEALTH, BEHAVIOR, AND AGING

James E. Birren and Judy M. Zarit

The purpose of this chapter is to discuss concepts and issues surrounding current concerns with the health of an increasingly older population. The chapters that follow will deal with specifics of the relationships between health and behavior in the adult years. While most authors assume that these terms—health, behavior and aging—are well understood, in fact, there are no widely agreed-upon definitions. We will, therefore, attempt to define these key concepts before discussing them.

The health sciences have undergone major changes in the second half of this century. Emphasis has shifted from infectious diseases to chronic diseases, from acute care to long-term care, from curative medicine to health promotion, and from high-technology medicine to holistic health. Boundaries between the allied health professions have become blurred to the point where, according to the head of one of the largest medical libraries, "we no longer know where medicine begins and ends." We have gone from a primarily industrial society to one in which most workers are now involved in generating and distributing information (Naisbitt, 1982). We have also shifted from a preoccupation with the needs of the child to those of the mature and older adult. An important area of need for the older population is health care.

Because many aspects of health are age associated, it is necessary to ask: What is the nature of the process we call aging? Contemporary thought suggests that it is a complex phenomenon with no single controlling mechanism, and that many social and behavioral factors can modify the way in which we age. Studies show, for example, that social class and educational level are related to mortality rates. To attribute our state of health solely to heredity or to the condition of our immune system is simplistic; the view that social and behavioral contributors are primarily responsible is equally naive (Finch & Hayflick, 1977). It is increasingly recognized, therefore, that how well we live, how long we live and our satisfaction with life can be accounted for by heredity *and* the interaction of myriad factors in our physical and social environments (Birren & Bernstein, 1978). This point of view runs contrary to the way health professionals and researchers are trained, i.e., as biologists or social scientists. With these thoughts in mind, this chapter will define and discuss concepts of health, behavior and aging. While precise definitions and careful use of terms cannot replace research, it can identify and clarify the implied theoretical framework constructed in earlier stages of research.

BEHAVIOR

Although the term *behavior* is usually used without definition or explanation, its meaning can vary depending on the theoretical orientation of the writer and the context. At its most general, behavior is "the manner of conducting oneself in the external relations of life," "a course of action toward or to others," or "the manner in which a thing acts under specified conditions or circumstances, or in relation to other things" (Oxford English Dictionary, 1933).

Each contemporary school of psychology views behavior from the standpoint of its own particular theory. To behaviorists, it is central; to psychoanalysts it is more peripheral; the neuroscientists are concerned with brain-behavior relationships; and the cognitive psychologists focus on covert behavior, such as memory and thinking. Some synthesis in viewpoint may be possible after examining the definitions presented below.

1. The grandfather of behaviorists, John B. Watson, saw a similarity between response and behavior, i.e., both are under the control of a stimulus and both depend upon reinforcements (Rychlak, 1973). 2. For B. F. Skinner, the basic dictum was simply an observed correlation between stimulus and response. When the observed correlation is very high, a behavior is a reflex. Skinner felt that psychologists were not sophisticated enough to concern themselves with events that could not be seen, and therefore should not concern themselves with underlying mechanisms (Bolles, 1975). 3. Modern behaviorists are not quite so restrictive. Indeed, the electrochemical firing of a single cell in the nervous system is now considered a discrete behavior (Craighead, Kazdin, & Mahoney, 1976).

This view of behavior as largely under stimulus control led to careful empirical study; the resulting theory had mainly to do with how behavior is learned. Behavior therapy adopted learning principles and the experimental approach to attempt to change human behavior. Behavior, when reduced to antecedent and consequent conditions, theoretically should be lawful and modifiable (Goldfried & Davison, 1976). To the complete behaviorist, a symptom can be taken as the illness, as the observable maladaptive behavior to be removed. Wolpe defines behavior as essentially "a change of state or of spatial relations to other things" (Rychlak, 1973).

The behaviorist and behavior therapist use the terms "stimulus," "response," "reinforcement," and "behavior" loosely and inconsistently to describe psychological phenomena that cannot be contained within a simple terminological system, and they tend to ignore motivation and drives, which cannot be directly observed.

However, this emphasis on observable behavior has led to the successful treatment and/or control of smoking, obesity, chronic pain, hypertension and an assortment of other problems which were formerly considered to be "medical," and to the establishment of health psychology or behavioral medicine, a bridge between psychology and medicine.

Psychoanalytic Theory

Psychoanalysis is biological in its orientation, because Freud was a medical doctor as well as a neurologist, and saw mental illness as a disease that could be treated. While behavior itself is not a major concern of psychoanalytic theorists, they do believe that it is regulated in accordance with certain basic principles. For example, according to the pleasure-pain principle, human behavior is designed to pursue pleasure and to avoid pain. The reality principle allows a rational determination of behavior, which includes a willingness to tolerate current discomfort in order to achieve future pleasure (MacKinnon & Michels, 1971). Behavior, then, is guided by principles that allow explanation in terms of nonobservable phenomena. In fact, Freudians distrust that which is too obvious. They see it as evidence of defense mechanisms—from which true motivations can only be inferred. Thus behavior is secondary in importance to the meaning behind it.

Neuropsychology

Neuropsychology is beginning to play an important role in explaining the relationship between the brain and behavior. While in the past the brain has been viewed as a telephone exchange or control panel, it is now seen as a complex and uniquely constructed functional system. A. R. Luria provides one of the most complete neuropsychological definitions of behavior:

> It has become abundantly clear that human behaviour is active in character, that it is determined not only by past experience, but also by plans and designs formulating the future, and that the human brain is a remarkable apparatus which cannot only create these models of the future, but also subordinate its behaviour to them (Luria, 1973, p. 13).

Luria was dissatisfied with explanations of behavior that relied solely on past learning and experience. Further, he found the reflex arc unacceptable as a concept of elementary behavior because there is such a wide range of human movement. He believed that certain behaviors—such as putting into effect intentions, plans or programs, which constitute the greater part of human activity—were controlled by the future. He thought that the two concepts of brain and behavior required a broader explanatory framework, which included social history as well as a scheme for the construction of motor tasks. A motor task may be constant or invariant, but it is fulfilled by varying sets of movements according to the intent of the performer (Luria, 1973).

Charles Golden has made strides to quantify Luria's qualitative method for studying brain-behavior relationships as they relate to neuropathology. This endeavor has been criticized as reductionistic, however, because it attributes a neuropsychological sign to a lesion in a given area of the brain (this is a major weakness of the Halstead-Reitan neuropsychological battery). Golden, Ariel, McKay, Wilkening, Wolf, and MacInnes (1982) defend themselves by pointing out that their method is deductive and at best allows an inference to be drawn from test performance. The trend in current neuropsychology is towards complex rather than simple explanations of behavior.

Cognitive Theories

While strict behaviorists emphasize observable responses, there has been a growing move to include covert, nonobservable variables, e.g., emotions and implicit verbalizations, in current neobehavioral and cognitive-behavioral research. Both approaches rely upon operationally defined, clearly specified variables (Rimm & Masters, 1979). However, cognitive theorists would explain health behavior in terms of the individual's beliefs and thoughts as evidenced by verbalized thoughts and actual behavior. Cognition, in extreme cases, is believed to alter health directly, as when a cancer patient is able to visualize and mentally reduce a tumor.

Cognitive behaviorists are the first to agree that there is no commonly accepted definition of behavior therapy. While strict behaviorists confined themselves to the study of overt behavior, neobehaviorists developed a mediational stimulus-response model, which allowed them to apply principles of conditioning to abnormal behavior by adding the mediating constructs of, for example, fear or anxiety. This led to a social learning theory which posited three different ways behavior could be organized: Events controlled by external stimuli are classically conditioned; events determined by external reinforcement are operationally conditioned; and cognitive mediational processes are needed to explain the reciprocal interaction between behavior and the environment (Wilson, 1978).

Cognitive behavioral research is done according to the standards of operational and observable anchors. This means that any discussion of cognitive processes must be defined in terms of the operations used to measure them and that all cognitive behavior must be anchored to observable behavior (Craighead, Kazdin, & Mahoney, 1976).

There are certain orienting assumptions to this broader conception of behavior. All behavior is believed to be determined, whether by personality needs, structures, or situational determinants. Behavior also has plasticity; that is, learning occurs. People react not only to internal and external stimuli, but, because behavior is motivated and goal directed, they are also proactive. Behavior is centrally regulated and adaptive. It tends toward problem solving, growth and optimal functioning in the healthy individual, even in the face of stress (Korchin, 1976). An expanded definition of behavior might include any kind of reaction, including complex patterns of feeling, perceiving, thinking and willing, in response to internal or external, tangible or intangible stimuli (Kaluger & Kaluger, 1974).

Behavior can be defined narrowly or broadly. For the purposes of this chapter a definition that includes both observable behaviors and cognitions may be the most useful.

HEALTH

Health cannot be defined without also considering disease and illness, as evidenced by the following definitions. In 1946, the World Health Organization defined health as "a state of complete physical, mental and social well-being and not merely absence of disease or infirmity." In recent years that definition has been expanded to include "a *modus vivendi* enabling imperfect men to achieve a rewarding and not too painful existence while they cope with an imperfect world" (Dubos, 1977). These positive approaches to health are in contrast to the common notion that health is simply the absence of illness and that gradations within health are irrelevant. Science and medicine have historically been more concerned with treating "what went wrong" than with clarifying the complex elements necessary to promote and support health (Butler & Lewis, 1982).

Health can also be defined in positive terms such as "soundness of body" and "spiritual, moral or mental soundness or well-being" (Oxford English Dictionary, 1933). This has led to the concept of preventive medicine, i.e., taking steps to remedy or assuage the vulnerabilities before an illness occurs.

When the individual and his or her biological, psychological and social components are viewed as a complex system, good health depends upon the orderly functioning of all parts of that system as well as the interaction between its components. Disease in one part of the system may affect all parts.

What then is a disease and how does it differ from illness? While dictionaries consider disease and illness synonymous (Oxford English Dictionary, 1933; Webster's New World Dictionary, 1970), they also have different connotations. Disease can be seen as "a particular destructive process in the body—with a specific cause and characteristic symptoms" (Webster's New World Dictionary, 1970), which implies a serious organic or psychic malady, such as cancer or insanity (Dubos, 1977). In this context, disease is an entity separate from and superimposed on an organism, and refers to abstract and impersonal issues, such as physiological mechanisms, socially causal factors or structural components.

The term illness, on the other hand, has a sociocultural context (Fabrega, 1980). In modern usage, it is used to describe the manner in which people perceive, organize and express disability, regardless of origin, and is embedded in behavior. For example, illness can be viewed as a deviation from social norms. Once an individual assumes a "sick role" certain prescribed behaviors are expected. The incapacity is seen as involuntary (no one *wants* to become ill!) and is considered a legitimate basis for exemption from normal obligations. However, the individual still has the obligation to get well and to seek help for the condition (Lieban, 1977).

Persons at all ages may have subclinical degrees of disease, but as long as they do not "act" ill, e.g., take medicine or consult a physician, they will describe themselves as healthy. There seems to be a threshold of clinical deficiency beyond which one no longer considers oneself well. In younger people, this threshold may be fairly high, because it is possible to compensate by using resources from other parts of the body. For the elderly, the threshold may be lower, and the ability to compensate may be slowed or impaired. A good example can be seen in the neurological examination. Reaction time and reflexes are known to be slower and more variable in older persons. The neurologist must distinguish, then, between normal slowing with age, individual differences, and disease. This is normally done by differentiating the signs within the context in which they appear (Drachman, 1980).

Concepts of illness, disease and health are inextricably bound to social behavior. Presenting oneself to a physician is a type of social behavior that represents a conscious decision. Not all patients have complaints that can be recognized as biological. Some present with complaints that appear to be rooted in and defined by social variables, although many people with these complaints do not present themselves for medical treatment at all or seek other types of help (Fabrega, 1980).

Physicians tend to divide the patient population into two groups: those who are "truly medically ill," and those who were first thought to be ill, but for whom there are no explanatory organic defects. At the end of the 1930s, psychosomatic medicine came into existence to provide explanations for cases in which there was palpable organic detritus, but psychological factors were so prominent they could not be ignored. This was not a departure from the traditional medical model, but provided a psychological explanation for the etiology of symptoms.

In its first issue, *Psychosomatic Medicine* (1939) stated that the object of psychosomatic medicine was "to study in their interrelation the psychological and physiological aspects of all normal and abnormal bodily functions and thus to integrate somatic therapy and psychotherapy." This branch of medicine was seen as a method of approach to the problems of etiology and therapy, rather than a delimitation of the area, and, significantly, the idea of a distinction between mind and body was rejected. Franz Alexander (1939) viewed psychosomatic medicine as a revival of old prescientific views in a new scientific form. He felt that the fundamental philosophical postulate of modern medicine was that the body and its functions could be understood in terms of physical chemistry; he believed that an acceptance of this postulate would allow for tremendous advances in medical research. But "the greatest accomplishments of the past become later the greatest obstacles against future development" (Alexander, 1939); continuing to hold this postulate ultimately led to a widening chasm between mind and body that stood in the way of understanding the complexity of the interaction.

Psychosomatic medicine was conceived of as the science of human life phenomena, which attempts to bring together the organismic and the psychosocial modes of abstraction (Lipowski, 1967). Gestalt psychologists contributed to this view with their thesis that the whole is not the sum total of its parts, but something different from them, and that from the study of the parts alone the whole system never can be understood. Medicine had been moving in the direction of increased understanding of separate parts of the body with a specialized technician for each, but psychosomatic medicine attempted to counter this by providing a bridge between psychology and medicine.

Psychosomatic disorders are believed to be caused by arousal of negative emotions in response to stressful situations; when these emotions are not dealt with adequately, the patient will show resulting response stereotype and chronic arousal resulting in damage to a particular organ system.

There seem to be biological factors that contribute to an individual's predilection for psychosomatic disorders. Genetics play a part, e.g., a family's tendency toward asthma, hypertension, cardiovascular disorders, etc. There appear to be differences in autonomic system reactivity: some people will react with an upset stomach, others undergoing the same stress might have an elevated pulse rate. The choice of affected system is probably influenced by heredity, illness and prior trauma to that particular system. Both classical and operant conditioning occur in the autonomic nervous system. An asthmatic whose attacks are provoked by roses may not wheeze when first entering a room full of roses. Rather, he may become anxious at finding himself in the situation and then wheeze. When biofeedback has been used to treat an emotional reaction, the number and/or severity of attacks has been reduced (Fried, 1974).

The sociocultural aspect of psychosomatic disorders cannot be underestimated. Classic psychosomatic illnesses, such as arthritis, asthma, peptic ulcers, colitis, migraine headaches, hypertension, eczema, and heart attacks, are nearly absent in primitive groups until they are exposed to social change (Kidson & Jones, 1968; Stein, 1970). Even in industrialized nations, patterns of psychosomatic disorders change when there is severe stress. For example, in Japan the tremendous social changes since World War II have been accompanied by great incidence of bronchial asthma and colitis among the young, and increased hypertension and heart attacks among adults (Ikemo et al., 1974).

Traditionally, psychosomatic medicine focuses on disorders that can clearly be linked to some psychological etiology. Behavioral medicine takes the slightly different approach that there is no fundamental epistemological difference between mind and body. Therefore, all illness has effects that are at the same time physiological and psychological (Melamud & Siegel, 1980). Conversely, behavioral factors are seen as important in maintaining good health. Behavioral medicine differs from psychosomatic medicine in that the emphasis is on learning principles, rather than on understanding the etiology of the problem. Its basic thesis—that what can be learned that is maladaptive can be relearned in a positive way—applies to all illness, regardless of whether the origin is physiological or psychological. Scoliosis, for example, is clearly a physiological ailment. But behaviorists would focus upon the faulty learning involved. Miller (1978) showed remarkable success in avoiding surgery and years of wearing a body cast with a device that delivered a mild electric shock when the patient's posture deviated from normal.

This discussion of health, disease, and illness has only touched the surface of complex issues. As in the case of behavior, a definition of health depends upon the perspective of the writer and the particular situation being examined. These considerations should be kept in mind when reading subsequent chapters in this volume.

AGING

At its most general, *to age* means "to cause to ripen or become mature over a period of time under fixed conditions" (Webster's New World Dictionary, 1970). Textbooks usually differentiate among biological, psychological and social aging. There has been a great deal of research on all these aspects; each discipline tends to focus on its own model and to disregard the others. Biologists, for instance, have a decremental model, while psychologists use several models including incremental and homeostatic ones. However, because it is possible to experience increments and decrements simultaneously, with psychological insight compensating for physical decline, focusing on only one model has caused researchers to overlook important interrelationships. But before proceeding to an interactive approach, we will define biological, psychological and social aging.

Biological Aging

The underlying concern of biological aging is to understand why a particular organism has a finite life span. Each species has a characteristic length of life. A distinction should be made between the maximum life potential of a species and the average length of life of its members (Sacher, 1977). The average length of life is a central tendency of a population of animals, around which are distributed individual differences. In mammals, this average can vary from two to three years for a mouse or rat, to about 73 years for humans. Other animals fall in an intermediate range. The maximum life potential, in contrast, is that tendency of a survival curve to show an upper limit of age with an asymptotic value (Fries, 1980).

The most important predisposing factors for longevity are heredity and environment. As a species, humans carry a genetic message that influences the length of life, but each individual also carries genetic information concerning maximum life potential. Further, environmental support, or assault and adaptation to it, directly relates to actual longevity. The maximum life potential for animals in the wild, for example, might be increased if they lived in a more protected environment. Basically, however, the fundamental concept behind the biological point of view is that the probability of dying increases with the age of the animal after maturity.

Handler's (1960) definition of biological aging is typical: "Aging is a deterioration of a mature organism resulting from time dependent, essential irreversible changes intrinsic to all members of the species such that, with the passage of time, they become increasingly unable to cope with the stresses of the environment, thereby increasing the probability of death."

Comfort (1956) similarly defined aging, but preferred the term "senescence": "Senescence is a change in the behavior of the organism with age, which leads to a decreased power of survival and adjustment." Cowdry (1942) presents a more complex biological definition: "Since almost all living organisms pass through a sequence of changes characterized by growth, development, maturation and finally senescence, aging presents a broad, biological problem." He distinguished between endogenous changes in tissues and fluid that lead to vulnerability in the cells of organ systems with the passage of time, and the effect of exogenous factors, such as trauma, infection or nutritional inadequacies, which result in degenerative changes and susceptibility to disease.

Papilia and Olds (1981) exemplify this dualistic notion of biological aging with their definition. Biological aging is seen as both a program process, reset for every species and subject to only minor modifications, and the result of accumulated insults to the body. On a cellular level, Medvedev (1964) believes that aging is caused by damage to the genetic information involved in the formation of cellular proteins and by errors in the transmission of information from the DNA to the final protein product.

Busse (1969) speaks of *primary* and *secondary* aging: primary aging being the result of inherited biological processes which are time dependent and detrimental to the survival of the organism; secondary aging being caused by the decline of function due to chronic diseases or other damage to the organism.

Biological aging is often defined according to the point of view of a discipline. Physicians, for instance, tend to view aging exogenously as a product of disease and trauma; underlying this viewpoint is the tacit assumption that organisms would be reasonably perfect were it not for disease. This leads to the optimistic belief that when medical science unlocks the mystery of disease there will be no limit to longevity. Osler (Woodruff & Birren, 1975) believed that aging was closely related to the state of blood vessels in the body. Thus from this perspective, if medical science can discover how to maintain blood vessel functioning, the problem of aging would be solved.

Clearly, biological definitions of aging that ignore either endogenous or exogenous factors fail to explain important variations in longevity. A comprehensive definition might therefore be: biological aging, senescing, is the process of change in the organism, which over time lowers the probability of survival and reduces the physiological capacity for self-regulation, repair, and adaptation to environmental demands.

Psychological Aging

Psychology deals with behavior that is a product of both the biological and social systems. The paucity of attempts to define psychological aging reflects the limited ability of psychology to deal with phenomena associated with increasing age.

Birren and Renner (1980) have defined psychological aging as "the regular changes that occur in mature, genetically represented organisms living under representative environmental conditions as they advance in chronological age." While more specific than most, this definition overlooks persons who deviate from the population norms, either in terms of disease or environmental conditions. Psychologists study capacities, abilities and endogenously based, as well as culturally determined, behaviors. Psychological aging refers to changes that occur in the ability of the organism to adapt its capacities, e.g., sensation, perception, memory, learning, intellectual abilities, drives, and motivation, to alterations in the social and physical environment and within the organism itself.

Social Aging

The social sciences are prone to focus on methodology for studying aging, rather than on finding a precise definition. They also tend to emphasize the social problems and disabilities that occur with age. However, there are elucidating concepts defined in passages such as the following excerpts from Maddox and Wiley (1976):

> . . . the early discussion of aging as a social problem identified most of the contemporary issues in the social scientific study of human aging: the social and cultural as distinct from the biological meaning of age; age as a basis for the allocation of social roles and resources over the lifespan, the basis of social integration and adaptation in the later years of life; and the special methodological problems of studying time-dependent processes over the life cycle and interpreting observed stability and change. . . . techniques for sorting out the relative importance of cohort, environmental and aging effects on behavior in late life. . . . the personal troubles commonly associated with late

life were being described frequently as a social problem and the aged as a problem group in the United States.

A related aspect of social aging is the process of adapting to the age roles assigned by society.

Sociology, anthropology, economics, psychology and political science each employ different research paradigms, with the result that age can be treated as an independent, dependent or confounding variable. This diversity among the social sciences may account for the lack of a precise definition of the aging process. Birren and Renner (1977), therefore, constructed the following definition of social age to help bridge the gap:

> Social age refers to the roles and social habits of an individual with respect to other members of a society. Compared with the expectations of his group and society, does an individual behave younger or older than one would expect from his chronological age? Since the basis of age-graded expected behavior is a product of one's culture, both biological and psychological characteristics of individuals enter the societal norms and the values of society.

This definition, however, does not recognize the dynamic properties of aging or of change with time.

Summary

Biological aging refers to physiological decline and reduced capacity for self-regulation and tissue compensation. Psychological aging refers to the individual capacity for self-regulation and adaptation to changes in the relationship between self and environment; and social aging refers to the process of adjustment to societal norms. Biological aging tends to describe a process of gradual decline, while both psychological and social aging allow for decline, increment or homeostasis. Each of these definitions represents a particular perspective; none explains aging completely.

THEORIES OF DEVELOPMENT AND AGING

Biological theories of aging fall into two categories: (1) the theory that aging is the result of genetic damage; and (2) the theory that there is damage which leads to increasing disease with age. Since aging is not manifested until puberty, the question arises as to how a genetic basis for aging can evolve since it is beyond the reach of selective pressures.

Parents who are long lived increase the likelihood of survival of their offspring. In prehistoric days, the long-lived member, because of his or her experience and wisdom, also improved the survival chances of the tribe. Thus tribes with elders had a selective genetic advantage. This led Birren to theorize that if there is genetic control over aging it must arise as a counterpart to development. That is, aging must be a manifestation of characteristics of development which were present at the time of reproduction. This counterpart theory suggests a pathway through which a genetic substrate can evolve, and may explain the emergence of complex behavioral characteristics, such as wisdom in late life (Clayton & Birren, 1980).

Given the fact that most of the genetic material in a cell is not used during the early life of the organism, it is possible that there is release of genetic expression in later life; that is, previously unexpressed genetic characteristics are activated. The late-life appearance of genetic diseases is indeed a puzzle. For example, in the case of senile dementia, the disease may not appear until the eighth or ninth decade. For other points of view in biological theories of aging, readers are referred to Finch and Hayflick (1977).

Development as a concept refers to the changes in the young organism in size, form and function. As the fetus grows, it changes in appearance and size and becomes capable of increasingly complex physiological functions. In turn, the new-born child grows taller and heavier. His or her body takes on different proportions. With development, the individual becomes increasingly self-regulating from a physiological point of view; that is, variations in the environment have lesser consequences to life-sustaining functions. This increasing capacity for self-regulation is expressed in the declining mortality curve from birth to early adolescence. In terms of form, it is easy to distinguish differences in proportion between the young child and the adult. Indeed, Leonardo da Vinci many years ago described the principles of drawing people of different ages.

Individuals continue to expand their capacity for self-regulation after reaching physical and physiological maturity. This increasingly complex behavior can be called adult development.

Birren and Schroots (1980) defined development as the process of achieving biological and behavioral self-regulation and control over the social and physical environment as capacities and resources are increasing. After adulthood, individuals continue to increase their control over the environment and their capacity for self-regulation, even in the face of stable or decreasing resources. Is this process of continued change or differentiation in the later years development, or is it aging?

Paradoxically, it seems that at the same time that the older adult organism is suffering some involution of biological self-regulation, it may be reaching a higher level of behavioral mastery over the environment. Birren and Schroots (1980) suggest that an ontogenetical point of view that incorporates both development and aging allows us to embrace both the child and adult phases of life.

The somewhat contradictory nature of the simultaneously developing and aging organism is exemplified by the nervous system. With age, the organism may show diminished capacity under stress to regulate important bodily functions which ultimately may affect survival, such as temperature, blood pressure and glucose levels. Increased knowledge of the neuroendocrine functions of the brain indicates that the endocrine functions of the organism are under the regulatory control of the hypothalamus. In a sense, the aging process may begin early in adult life when our physiological capacity to maintain optimum equilibrium states is reduced. But this will not affect survival unless certain limits are exceeded.

Concurrent with the reduction in homeostatic capacity is the increased ability to master complex behavior which improves the probability of survival. The older worker or motorist, for example, has a lower accident rate and therefore a higher ability for survival than the young person whose physiological capacity for self-regulation may be higher, but whose behavioral self-regulation leads to risk taking.

At the 1962 meeting of the Gerontological Society some of these issues were discussed. Birren (1964) made the point that "somewhat more is known about growth and development than about senescence, yet much of development has been studied without regard to the context of the whole life span. This gives rise to intriguing and important questions about the late-life consequences of the biological, psychological and social conditions of early life. The forces affecting the individual over the life span are complex, yet it is not useful to merely say they are complex and let matters rest. The task of the scholar and researcher is to specify how they are complex based upon studies of man and organism." The symposium examined biological, psychological and social processes over the life span. In retrospect it is apparent that the symposium's understanding of how complex systems operated was limited.

Recently, Yates (1982) proposed an organismic biology, which may make it possible to integrate development and aging. He suggested an index of complexity to meet the need to describe an organism as a function of age. Yates describes the human organism as comprised of interrelated systems. Each system functions within some parameters, which he calls band widths, that are dynamically regulated. He believes that homeostasis occurs when there is a stable relationship between systems, particularly in the area where band widths overlap. Variation in the stability of regulation can be large. Yates's approach may make it possible to integrate many different levels of psychological, physiological and social observation about the organism.

One advantage of the systems model is that it favors holism and integration over reductionism and mechanism. Yates does imply a hierarchical ordering of systems from simple to complex that is not often used in describing the psychological aspects of behavior. Rather, the principles of simple behavior are assumed or considered irrelevant to more complex behavioral sequences.

According to Yates's theory, the subsystems are not continually interacting despite their dynamically regulated nature. In one sense the systems function autonomously until the band width has been exceeded. At that point an interaction occurs between the systems and new relationships are imposed. There is considerable variation within and between individuals as to when these interactions will occur. One example is the interrelationship between physical and psychological disability of the functioning of an individual. The band width could be expected to be somewhat less with age, so that physical and psychological systems would begin to overlap sooner. There may not be another system within the individual to compensate for physical and/or psychological loss, so it would become necessary for the individual to interact with other people or to develop a social support system. Using Yates's model, the capacity of the individual would have been exceeded, necessitating interaction with a larger, more complex system.

The foregoing discussion implies that the purpose of the organism is to establish dynamic self-regulation. Furthermore, it implies that there are hierarchical systems within the organism ranging from simple to complex. The more simple systems require maturation before the complex processes can begin. Development is accompanied by progressive differentiation of the cells and tissues of the organism, and with age there is an increase in heterogeneity in the morphology, physiology and behavior of the organism. One of the advantages of adopting the language and theoretical point of view of Yates is that it enables us to deal more effectively with concepts of health. His theory that the healthy organism has wider band widths of functions in self-regulating subsystems and that more complex behaviors emerge hierarchically allows us to examine the mechanisms of deterioration or vulnerability.

The aging organism, while more vulnerable to environmental stresses, is also wiser and therefore more differentiated. The biologist, then, must recognize that while the older individual may have a higher probability of dying due to the deterioration of a vital subsystem, his or her ability to function effectively may be continually expanding.

Many researchers in child development have assumed that there is a close relationship between behavior development in the child and the adult. Therefore, they have an implicit belief in the continuity of behavior and personality over the life span. If, however, behavior is hierarchically organized and the level of functioning of the subsystem is superseded at the time that the complex behavior emerges, early development is only loosely related to the behavior of the adult. For this reason, the term *counterpart* is used to suggest a relationship but not a direct mapping of child ontogenesis upon adult ontogenesis.

SYSTEM APPROACH TO DEVELOPMENT AND AGING

A key issue in the study of aging is the treatment of time. Experimental scientists argue that time does not *cause* anything. It can, however, serve as a useful way of organizing facts. For example, in the early development of astronomy as a science, time was used to observe the periodicities and recurring patterns of stars and planets in space. Similarly, in the study of human evolution, time is an important organizer, which allows biologists and archeologists to retrace the sequence of events as they occurred in the past. In the inorganic world, the disintegration of a mass of radioactive atoms is a more accurate clock than sidereal time, which is based on the planetary system.

The strength or weakness of time as an organizing variable in a science depends upon the level of complexity of the phenomena being studied. It should be noted that time can be treated as an independent or dependent variable or used as an arbitrary index for organizing facts. Systems analysis may offer a bridge between nineteenth-century views of scientific phenomena and current concepts, similar to the conceptual innovation that was required to move from classical mechanics to quantum mechanics in physics. While in physics it is possible to predict the disintegration of a mass of radioactive atoms with great accuracy, it is not possible to state which atoms are likely to disintegrate. In a similar manner, the social sciences can predict the probability of dying with advancing age, but individuals do not necessarily fit simple deterministic models.

Systems analysis allows us to separate and study subsystems of the organism that may not be highly interdependent in the normal range of functioning. In this sense, the organism can be viewed as analogous to the solar system, which is organized, moves forward in time, and yet has subsystems that do not significantly affect the organism as a whole. Time direction can differ within the individual components (Reichenback & Mathers, 1959). A human organism may have one subsystem which is growing younger while another is growing older. Thus, there is a mean value for the age of the organism as a whole, but variations in subsystem age. If a critical subsystem fails, the whole organism can be limited in its survival. Therefore, predicting an organism's life potential is complex, particularly since the interdependencies of the subsystems may only exist at limiting values. An organism's subsystems may function largely autonomously until certain limits are exceeded.

Aging clearly involves the entire organism and the phenomena of biological, social and psychological aging can be viewed as the consequences of changes in subsystems. The mechanisms of aging may be due to interactions between—rather than within—subsystems. While this point of view is speculative, it may be a fruitful point of departure for future theory and research.

PROSPECTS FOR RESEARCH

Responsibility for Health

An issue that has direct bearing on aging and longevity is individual health behavior. In the early part of this century, an ill person who lacked economic resources and/or family support usually ended up a charity patient. During the second half of the twentieth century, society has become the principal care provider not only for the indigent, but also for workers at all levels, who receive medical insurance as a fringe benefit. As health care costs have risen, however, the role of the individual is becoming increasingly important.

It is now recognized that our health status is influenced by the manner in which we lead our lives. Certain behavior such as smoking, heavy drinking, abuse of prescription and nonprescription drugs and overeating has been correlated with increased incidence of certain diseases, e.g., emphysema, cirrhosis, and coronary artery disease. Those who indulge in poor health habits occupy a disproportionate number of hospital beds and incur a disproportionate amount of health care costs.

Society is being forced to absorb these costs for high risk individuals, so that the individual may be free of catastrophic and routine health costs. This has not only contributed to the increasing cost of medical care but has also separated the individual from the consequences of his or her behavior. Society no longer punishes for the presence of illness or blames the individual for the behavior that leads to the need for care. Even in the area of venereal disease, where there is a close link between self-initiated prevention methods and disease, the focus is on treating the individual and whomever he or she has had contact with, using the utmost discretion and imposing minimal financial strain.

In the case of lung cancer, no distinction is made between those who incurred the disease by a life-long practice of smoking and those who were exposed to a toxic by-product of an industrial environment. Just as there is no punishment for bad behavior, there is also no reward for the professional who encourages health habits that will minimize health care and its attendant costs. It is analogous to the situation of the conscientious pharmacist: good pharmacy practice may dictate that follow up with prescription drugs be encouraged, but profit is based solely on the volume of drugs sold.

Figure 1-1 illustrates one way of conceptualizing the varying contributors to poor and good health and the locus of responsibility. The circle in the center

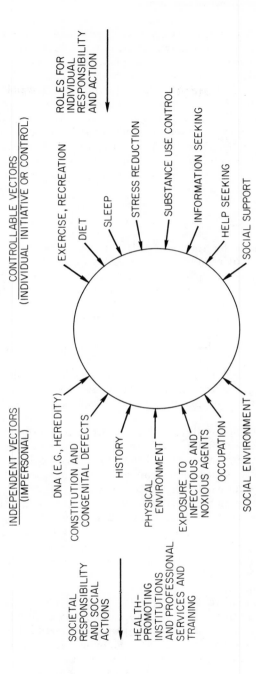

FIGURE 1-1. A graphic representation of individual well-being.

represents the individual. He or she can take responsibility for controllable vectors (exercise, diet, sleep, stress reduction, etc.) and increase chances of well-being. Independent vectors (heredity, history, occupation, environment, etc.) are factors over which the individual has no control, and while it can be argued that some of the independent vectors can be controlled—for instance that one can avoid toxic fumes—quite often the danger isn't identified before damage has been done. If the independent vectors predominate, the organism is likely to experience stress and perhaps illness. The controllable vectors represent ways in which the individual can fight back. If there are significant independent vectors, e.g., hereditary disease such as diabetes, maintaining good health becomes a delicate balancing act. If a person has good heredity, a low-stress occupation in a healthful environment, the odds are better.

Aging and Well-Being

Our past views of the healthy organism—i.e., one that is free of disease—does not aptly describe the older individual. Disease was regarded as an invasion of the organism by a foreign agent, such as a virus or bacterium. Very old people, however, are likely to have several concurrent diagnosable diseases, yet the character of these diseases is of a different nature in the sense that they are very close to being properties of the organism itself. If, then, an elderly individual were to feel that she is not herself because she is ill, the illness is close to being a part of the functioning system. Rather than doing battle with a foreign invasion, therefore, the task becomes to adjust the system so that it optimizes its functions.

Many of our metaphors about illness and aging derive from the period in our history when the major killers were infectious diseases. We must now shift to metaphors that embrace the concepts of an integrative physiology of the organism and chronic diseases.

The shift of metaphor also involves a shift of responsibility. In the case of an invasion by an alien bacterium, we look to the physician to give us an antibiotic to increase our defenses. On the other hand, if our heavy smoking is contributing to the high probability of developing coronary artery disease or lung cancer, then the active element is our own health-related behavior.

A healthy older person can be defined as one who has the capacity for self-regulation, physiologically, psychologically and socially, and who derives contentment from his or her existence. The purpose of the fertilized egg is to become a mature organism in size, form and function. Moving toward this goal implies that we have an increasing capacity for self-regulation. As we develop with age, we become more independent of environmental variations and can make appropriate adjustments to maintain relative autonomy.

It seems likely that we develop a broad band width of stability within which variations in the environment will not disturb our ability to function. The question then becomes, what happens to the capacity for self-regulation after the attainment of early adulthood? Some systems, like the immune system, remain efficient for a broad span of years, although later in life the organism may become increasingly susceptible to infectious disease. This suggests that the organism is highly buffered against change except change which is self-initiated, and further implies that a wide number of subsystems of the organism, biological, psychological and social, are essentially autonomous in their functioning until some variable exceeds the band width provided by the buffering capacity of the organism. Once this homeostatic or homeokinetic band width is exceeded, a new set of relationships holds (see Yates, 1982). In fact, at the boundary conditions of these band widths, nonlinear relationships enter and in many cases the organism becomes dominated by the system's repercussion. A fever may ensue from an infection or from exposure to some foreign substance. The fever leads to an inability of the nervous system to function in its normal way and the nervous system increasingly loses its ability to regulate the vegetative functions of the organism. Thus begins a cascading sequence of events, which if not interrupted or halted causes the organism to become increasingly incapable of functioning.

This line of reasoning suggests that we need more of a system or "one science" approach to the health of the older individual, which includes physiological, psychological and social interactions in the young adult organism. Because, in the young adult, subsystems may act autonomously over a wide range of variations, it does not follow that the subsystems may not be interacting in the old organism.

Conclusion

There are numerous prospects for research concerning the health and capacity for self-regulation of the older individual:

1. Updating our metaphors of illness will encourage individuals to take better advantage of health providers and to regulate their own behavior. This would enable the health provider to use the patient as a colleague in making alterations in the subsystems that determine the well-being of the organism. With this in mind:

2. It is necessary to explore why patients go to physicians and what models of health they have in mind. Clearly, in an interactive system of change, patients will assume more responsibility for self-regulation than if they simply go to a physician for the magic bullet that kills a foreign infectious invader. In turn, physicians, nurses and other health care providers have to be educated in a system or integrative approach to health and well-being that includes the patient as an active participant.

3. If we conceive of the brain as the primary integrative organ of the body, we need further knowledge about how social and behavioral inputs influence the effectiveness of the vegetative regulation of the organism. Current literature gives a great deal of attention to the older person's social network. Presumably, the older person who lives in a stimulating environment has more cushions against physical and social loss (one example of an interaction, of course, is bereavement, in which the loss of a loved one has physical as well as psychological impact on the well-being of the survivor).

The buffering capacity of social and psychological systems is an important element in maintaining independent functioning in an environment in which an individual can have access to up-to-date health information that will facilitate well-being. For the isolated individual, on the other hand, chronic disease and physical disability may disproportionately erode the capacity to function. Social networks cannot be judged solely by frequency of interaction with one's relatives, neighbors and friends. The degree of psychological attachment that exists between the individuals must also be taken into account. When exploring the social network of older persons, therefore, the elements to consider are: (1) the information content of the network; (2) the energy inputs of the network, i.e., who is helping a disabled person; and (3) psychological attachments.

SUMMARY

There have been many changes in American society which affect our views of behavior and aging. The average length of life has been extended, necessitating a greater emphasis on long-term care and chronic disease. Data from epidemiological studies show that social and environmental factors influence health and the way one ages. There is a trend toward holistic health along with an expectation that genetic research will soon result in a cure for now-prevalent diseases.

The rigid boundaries we have heretofore placed around the concepts of health, behavior and aging must give way to the recognition that many interesting factors are responsible for our well-being in the middle and later years of life.

Unfortunately, many researchers do not bother to specify what they mean by the term aging, although biologists do so more frequently than social scientists. In the behavioral and social aspects of life, there can be expansions of competence and functioning concurrent with biological deterioration.

This chapter has attempted to bring together different definitions of health, behavior, and aging to lay a groundwork for later chapters and to emphasize the importance of definition in the area to be discussed or researched. The main conclusion that we came to was that there are no commonly accepted and agreed upon definitions for these terms and that it is too early in our studies to begin to finalize definitions. Rather, we would suggest using operationalized definitions and limiting discussion of results to those directly related to the defined variables.

REFERENCES

ALEXANDER, F. (1939). Psychological aspects of medicine. *Psychosomatic Medicine, I,* 6–18.

BIRREN, J. E. (1964). *The psychology of aging.* Englewood Cliffs, NJ: Prentice-Hall.

BIRREN, J. E., & BERNSTEIN, L. (1978). Health and aging in our society: Perspectives on mortality. *Transactions of the Association of Life Insurance Medical Directors, 62,* 135–152.

BIRREN, J. E., & RENNER, V. J. (1977). Research on the psychology of aging. In J. E. Birren & K. W. Schaie (Eds.), *Handbook of the psychology of aging.* New York: Van Nostrand Reinhold.

BIRREN, J. E., & RENNER, V. J. (1980). Concepts and issues of mental health and aging. In J. E. Birren & R. B. Sloane (Eds.), *Handbook of mental health and aging.* Englewood Cliffs, NJ: Prentice-Hall.

BIRREN, J. E., & SCHROOTS, J.J.F. (1980, August). A psychological point of view toward human aging and adaptability. In *Adaptability and aging.* Proceedings of the 9th International Conference on Social Gerontology. Quebec, Canada, pp. 43–54.

BOLLES, R. C. (1975). *Learning theory.* New York: Holt, Rinehart & Winston.

BUSSE, E. W. (1969). Theories of aging. In E. W. Busse & E. Pfeiffer (Eds.), *Behavior and adaptation in late life.* Boston, MA: Little, Brown.

BUTLER, R. I., & LEWIS, M. I. (1982). *Aging and mental health.* St. Louis, MO: C. V. Mosby.

CLAYTON, B., & BIRREN, J. E. (1980). The development of wisdom across the life span: A reexamination of an ancient topic. *Life Span Development and Behavior, 3,* 103–135.

COMFORT, A. (1956). *The biology of senescence.* London: Routledge and Kegan Paul.

CRAIGHEAD, W. E., KAZDIN, A. E., & MAHONEY, M. J. (1976). *Behavior modification: Principles, issues and applications.* Boston, MA: Houghton Mifflin.

COWDRY, E. V. (Ed.). (1942). *Problems of aging.* Baltimore, MD: Williams & Wilkins.

DRACHMAN, D. A. (1980). An approach to the neurology of aging. In J. E. Birren & R. B. Sloane (Eds.), *Handbook of mental health and aging.* Englewood Cliffs, NJ: Prentice-Hall.

DUBOS, R. (1977). Determinants of health and disease. In D. Landy (Ed.), *Culture, disease and healing.* New York: Macmillan.

FABREGA, H., JR. (1980). *Disease and social behavior.* Cambridge, MA: M.I.T. Press.

FINCH, C. E., & HAYFLICK, L. (Eds.). (1977). *Handbook of the biology of aging.* New York: Van Nostrand Reinhold.

FRIED, J. J. (1974). Biofeedback: Teaching your body to heal itself. *Family Health, 6,* 18–21.

FRIES, J. F. (1980). Aging, natural death, and the compression of morbidity. *New England Journal of Medicine, 303,* 130–135.

GOLDEN, C., ARIEL, M., McKAY, J., & WILKENING, J. (1982). The Luria Nebraska Battery. *Journal of Consulting and Clinical Psychology, 50,* 291–300.

GURALNIK, D. B. (Ed.). (1970). *Webster's new world dictionary of the American language.* Englewood Cliffs, NJ: Prentice-Hall.

HANDLER, P. (1960). Radiation and aging. In N. W. Shock (Ed.), *Aging: Some social and biological aspects.* Washington, DC: American Association for the Advancement of Science.

IKEMI, Y., AGO, Y., NAKAGAWA, S., MORI, S., TAKAHASHI, N., SUEMATSU, H., SUGITA, M., & MATSUBARA, H. (1974). Psychosomatic mechanism under social changes in Japan. *Journal of Psychosomatic Research, 18,* 15–24.

KALUGER, G., & KALUGER, M. F. (1974). *Human development: The span of life.* St. Louis, MO: C. V. Mosby.

KIDSON, M. A., & JONES, I. (1968). Psychiatric disorders among aborigines of the Australian Western Desert. *Archives of General Psychiatry, 19,* 413–417.

KORCHIN, S. J. (1976). *Modern clinical psychology.* New York: Basic Books.

LIEBAN, R. W. (1977). The field of medical anthropology. In D. Landy (Ed.), *Culture, disease and healing.* New York: Macmillan.

LIPOWSKI, Z. J. (1967). Review of consultation psychiatry and psychosomatic medicine. *Psychosomatic Medicine, 29,* 153–171.

LURIA, A. R. (1973). *The working brain.* New York: Basic Books.

MacKINNON, R. A., & MICHELS, R. (1971). *The psychiatric interview in clinical practice.* Philadelphia: PA: W. B. Saunders Co.

MADDOX, G. L., & WILEY, J. (1976). Scope, concepts and methods in the study of aging. In R. H. Binstock & E. Shanas (Eds.), *Handbook of aging and the social sciences.* New York: Van Nostrand Reinhold.

MEDVEDEV, Z. A. (1964). The nucleic acids in development and aging. *Advances in Gerontological Research, 1,* 181-202.

MELAMUD, B. G., & SIEGEL, L. (1980). *Behavioral medicine: Practical applications in health care.* New York: Springer-Verlag.

MILLER, N. E. (1978). Biofeedback and visceral learning. *Annual Review of Psychology, 29,* 373-404.

MURRAY, J.A.H., BRADLEY, H., CRAIGIE, W. A., & ONIONS, C. T. (Eds.). (1933). *Oxford English dictionary.* Oxford: Oxford University Press.

NAISBITT, J. (1982). *Megatrends: Ten new directions transforming our lives.* New York: Warner Books.

PAPILIA, D. E., & OLDS, S. W. (1981). *Human development.* New York: McGraw-Hill.

REICHENBACK, M., & MATHERS, R. A. (1959). The place of time and aging in the natural sciences and scientific philosophy. In J. E. Birren (Ed.), *Handbook of aging and the individual.* Chicago: University of Chicago Press.

RIMM, D. C., & MASTERS, J. C. (1979). *Behavior therapy.* New York: Academic Press.

RYCHLAK, J. F. (1973). *Introduction to personality and psychotherapy.* Boston, MA: Houghton Mifflin.

SACHER, G. A. (1977). Life table modification and life prolongation. In C. E. Finch & L. Hayflick (Eds.), *Handbook of the biology of aging.* New York: Van Nostrand Reinhold.

STEIN, J. (1970). *Neurosis in contemporary society: Progress and treatment.* Belmont, CA: Brooks-Cole.

WILSON, G. T. (1978). Cognitive behavior therapy: Paradigm shift or passing phase? In J. P. Foreyt & D. P. Rathjen (Eds.), *Cognitive behavior therapy.* New York: Plenum.

WOODRUFF, D. S., & BIRREN, J. E. (Eds.). (1975). *Aging: Scientific perspectives and social issues.* New York: Van Nostrand Reinhold.

WORLD HEALTH ORGANIZATION. (1946). *Constitution of the World Health Organization.* Geneva, Switzerland: World Health Organization.

YATES, F. W. (1982). Outline of a physical theory of physiological systems. *Canadian Journal of Physiology and Pharmacology, 60,* 217-248.

2

PSYCHOSOCIAL FACTORS, DISEASE, AND AGING

James P. Henry

PSYCHOSOCIAL STRESS AND ORGANIC DISEASE

The Normal "Rectangular" Pattern of Aging Survival

If it were to be normal for humans to steadily deteriorate after their 40s with death from senility at 65 to 70, then their institutionalization would be the logical recourse for our society. Forty-year-olds who are caring for their own nuclear family will often have a hard time caring for a failing parent.

But it is not necessary for health to begin failing in one's 60s. It is increasingly recognized that the picture of gradual incapacitation after the 40s is due to various slowly acting processes, such as arteriosclerosis of the heart vessels, cardiomyopathy, high blood pressure, or chronic arthritis. These diseases do not necessarily affect persons in the 60- to 70-year-old age group. The mechanisms by which stress induced by the environment can lead to chronic disease and the role of psychosocial stress and behavior are being defined (Henry & Stephens, 1977; Weiner, 1977; Weiss, Herd, & Fox, 1981). There is a growing realization that deterioration

The author wishes to express his appreciation to the National Heart, Lung, and Blood Institute, National Institutes of Health, Bethesda, Maryland, for supporting this work under NIH Grant HL 25544, and to thank Dr. John P. Meehan for his collaboration in the development of Figure 2-6.

and death from these conditions in one's 50s and 60s is abnormal and may well be prevented by what Gentry, Chesney, Gary, Hall, and Harburg (1982) refer to as reduction of risk associated with socioecological stress by social actions that modify living circumstances appropriately. Today's pharmacotherapy and the success of programs based on modifying lifestyle indicate that important gains can be expected in the prevention of death and disability from heart attack and stroke, to mention only cardiovascular disease. Persons who avoid various risk factors, including Type A behavior, can already expect a better than 50:50 chance of a healthy active survival into their 80s (Andrews, Tennant, Hewson, & Vaillant, 1978; Berkman & Syme, 1979; Jacobson, 1964).

If it were the norm to survive in relatively good health until 80 to 85, by that time one's children would be in their early 60s and their children would be adults. Energy would then be available for the care of the 80- to 85-year-olds. By familial caring for parents at home, the otherwise inevitable institutionalization of the aged could be postponed until their final rapid decline, which Fries and Crapo (1981) argue is the norm for disease-free humans. They do not experience a steady decline from age 40 onwards, but a sudden sharp drop in the 80s, giving rise to the so-called rectangular curve as seen in the more recent survival data shown in Figure 2-1. According to the new view, high blood pressure, or coronary heart disease, or breast or lung cancer are not inevitable consequences of weakening body defenses due to aging; they are preventable diseases. Survival from birth to various ages for white males and females in the United States at successive periods during the past 140 years are shown in Figure 2-1 (Jacobson, 1964). The curves indicate that in modern society one's chances of survival only start to decline rapidly on reaching the later years. Even in 1960, half the males reached 80, and, in fact, the females did better. The mortality statistics have continued to improve still further during the past 20 years, and as the cardiovascular epidemic abates, the curve steadily becomes more rectangular.

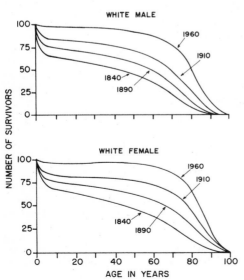

FIGURE 2-1.

Number of survivors from birth to successive ages for U.S. white males and females, analyzed by year of birth, between 1840 and 1960. Projections are indicated by broken lines. [Reprinted from Jacobson, P. H. (1964). Cohort survival for generations since 1840. *Milbank Memorial Fund Quarterly, 42,* 36–53, by permission of The MIT Press, Cambridge, MA.]

Disturbed Male-Female Bonding as a Source of Stress

Death rates of women differ so much from those of men, especially when broken down into marital status, as in Figure 2-2 (Berkson, 1962), that it is clear the role of social environment is important. The nuclear family and the husband-wife bond form a primary, protective, mutually supportive link. When this bond breaks down, the vulnerability of the male is increased, which is dramatically demonstrated by the higher mortality rates of widowers and divorcees as contrasted with those of married men (Helsing, Szklo, & Comstock, 1981). Because of the difficulty that persons with the Type A behavior pattern have with denial of emotion (Hackett, Cassem, & Wishnie, 1968), their spouses often feel lonely and deprived of warmth and interpersonal relationships. These individuals lack an awareness of feelings. Throughout their lives they have so consistently denied feelings, that they have failed to develop appropriate language and fantasies to cope with interpersonal affect and relationships. Helpless to describe emotions that only exist as affect of which they are not in control, they are forced to withdraw socially to conserve themselves. Lacking social interests and skills, they fail to develop a normal network of friends and mature psychological defenses. They are prone to yield to upsurges of affect and take impulsive action to correct situations perceived as getting rapidly out of control (Stern & Pascale, 1979). Such behavioral crises are accompanied by intense mobilization of the autonomic and endocrine systems. The various factors involved are also discussed by Stoddard and Henry (see Chapter 4 of this volume).

One important determinant of the older man's and the older woman's ca-

FIGURE 2-2. Death rates from all causes by marital status in the United States. [From Berkson, J. (1962). Mortality and marital status: Reflections on the derivation of etiology from statistics. *American Journal of Public Health, 52*(8), 1318–1329. Reproduced with permission of The American Public Health Association.]

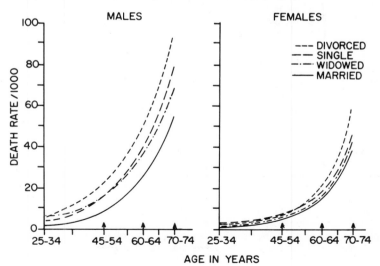

pacity to deal with the problems of life without experiencing devastating emotional arousal appears to be the quality of the emotional bonds they enjoy. The work of Medalie and Goldbourt (1976) indicates that a relationship of mutual support at home improves the man's capacity to endure the often impersonal competitive environment of a technological society. They have shown that husband-wife relationships perceived by husbands as nonsupportive are significantly more often accompanied by coronary heart disease, as exemplified by angina in the man, than those having less conflict.

In their study of the role of status relationships as risk factors in spousal conflict and abuse, Hornung, McCullough, and Sugimoto (1981) evaluated the educational and occupational attainments of individual marital partners. They used a scale of conflict tactics to measure abuse (see Table 2-1) and confirmed three distinct components of spousal violence.

The first component is psychological abuse as indicated by one partner insulting or swearing at the other; this was contrasted with mature tactics of discussing an issue calmly or of having someone else resolve the matter. They perceived the threat to throw things as the turning point in a further crucial step toward physical abuse. In their study of young couples from Kentucky, Hornung et al. (1981) found that psychological abuse was a very common event, but physical abuse was far less frequent. It was interesting that conflict was less when the wife stayed at home than when she went to work.

TABLE 2-1   Conflict Tactics Scale

	1. Discussed issue calmly.
	2. Got information to back up his/her side of things.
	3. Brought in or tried to bring in someone to help settle things.
	4. Insulted you or swore at you.
	5. Sulked or refused to talk about issue.
Psychological	6. Stomped out of room or house or yard.
Abuse	7. Cried.
	8. Did or said something to spite you.
	9. Threatened to hit you or throw something at you.
	10. Threw or smashed or hit or kicked something.
	1. Threw something at you.
	2. Pushed, grabbed, or shoved you.
Physical	3. Slapped you.
Aggression	4. Kicked, bit, or hit you with fist.
	5. Hit or tried to hit you with something.
Life-	1. Beat you.
Threatening	2. Threatened you with knife or gun.
Violence	3. Used knife or fired gun.

Each woman was asked how often each of the behaviors listed above were committed against her by her husband or male partner, and how often she committed each behavior against him during the past year. Responses were coded: never, once, twice, 3-5 times, 6-10 times, and more than 20 times.

[From C. A. Hornung, B. C. McCullough, & T. Sugimoto. (1981). Status relationships in marriage: Risk factors in spouse abuse. *Journal of Marriage and the Family,* *43* (August), 680.]

Hornung and McCullough (phone conversation, 1982) have found that men married to overachieving women are at high risk of heart attack in their 40s, but the risk declines in men in their 60s. The combination of financial problems, or lack of utilization of the man's capabilities on the job, and of higher achievement by the woman appears to them to be particularly stressful. Haynes and Feinleib's (1980) findings of high rates of heart attack among women in white-collar jobs married to men in blue-collar jobs appear to Hornung and McCullough to be an expression of this effect of occupational incompatibility which they found extended even to professionals.

Recently, Haynes et al. (1983) have arrived at similar conclusions. They used Framingham data to assess the effects of marital status inconsistency and incompatibility on the incidence of coronary heart disease in men, and found that men were over three times more likely to develop heart disease when married to women employed in white-collar jobs than when married to clerical workers, blue-collar workers, or homemakers. If the high-status wife had a nonsupportive boss, the effect was even more marked. In a later study by the same group, Eaker et al. (1983) report that Type A men are three to five times more vulnerable to coronary heart disease if their wives are working. In blue-collar families, Type A men married to Type B nonambitious women are almost six times more likely to develop heart disease than Type B men. The authors speculate that the combination of a working wife with high status based on educational level, who, despite her high achievement, is not ambitious greatly threatens the self-esteem of the Type A husband; this is especially true if the husband is of low status. When frustrated, the Type A hostility (Williams, 1980), achievement motivation, and dominance characteristics of the man lead to increasingly frenetic behavior (Ray & Bozek, 1980). This leads to chronic arousal of the neuroendocrine system and accelerating cardiovascular deterioration.

Life Changes and the Social Environment as Stressors

It is to be expected that the numbers of events involving marital conflict would increase during times of life changes demanding social readjustment. As Table 2-2 shows, typical examples of family experience as measured by the Holmes-Rahe Scale of Life Change Events include marital arguments, in-law troubles, changes in health, etc. (Henry & Stephens, 1977). Another set of problems that could lead to marital conflict are personal, such as changes in living conditions, sleeping or eating habits, major or minor illness. Finances can also lead to conflict; this set of problems includes mortgages and loans and other changes in financial affairs. Clearly the expenses involved in purchasing a home and maintaining it are a major source of potential problems. Yet another source of emotional interaction focuses around work. Included are retirement and change to a different line of work. The way in which retirement eventually does or does not lead to difficulties in maintaining an effective self-image depends on individual circumstances. For some, leisure may benefit domestic tranquility, but the effect may be the opposite for others. The intensity of ties that bond members of a family can make conflict particularly arousing. As a source of psychological and physical abuse, however, the social environment is of the greatest importance. This is true whether it involves the boss, customer, co-worker, or the mugging predator on the street.

TABLE 2-2   Holmes-Rahe Life Change Events for Seattle Adults

	LCU VALUES		LCU VALUES
Family		Personal (cont.)	
Death of spouse	100	Major revision of personal	
Divorce	73	habits	24
Marital separation	65	Change to new school	20
Death of close family member	63	Change in residence	20
Marriage	50	Major change in recreation	19
Marital reconciliation	45	Major change in church	
Major change in health		activities	19
of family	44	Major change in sleeping	
Pregnancy	40	habits	16
Addition of new family		Major change in eating habits	15
member	39	Vacation	13
Major change in arguments		Christmas	12
with spouse	35	Minor violations of the law	11
Son or daughter leaving home	29	Work	
In-law troubles	29	Being fired from work	47
Spouse starting or ending		Retirement from work	45
work	26	Major business adjustment	39
Major change in family		Changing to different line	
get-togethers	15	of work	36
Personal		Major change in work	
Detention in jail	63	responsibilities	23
Major personal injury or		Trouble with boss	23
illness	53	Major change in working	
Sexual difficulties	39	conditions	20
Death of close friend	37	Financial	
Outstanding personal		Major change in financial state	38
achievement	28	Mortgage or loan over	
Start or end of formal		$10,000	31
schooling	26	Mortgage foreclosure	30
Major change in living		Mortgage or loan less than	
conditions	25	$10,000	17

The now-classic Holmes-Rahe Scale of Life Change Events showing the original Life Change Units (LCU) as determined by a representative group of Seattle adults. A reference value of 50 units was arbitrarily assigned to marriage, and each subject was then asked to assign proportional values to others.

[From J. P. Henry & P. M. Stephens. (1977). *Stress, health, and the social environment. A sociobiologic approach to medicine,* p. 9. New York: Springer-Verlag.]

The larger society beyond the marital scene has been studied by Harburg and his associates (see Gentry et al., 1982). They focused on evaluating neighborhoods as high or low stress. The distinction was based on the extent to which their subjects were or were not exposed to risks of psychological or physical abuse in their neighborhoods. The Harburg data showed that the extent to which social environment was likely to lead to a greater number of anger-provoking situations and also evoke a greater tendency to inhibit an anger response—presumably from fear of consequences—paralleled chances that the subject's blood pressure would be elevated. A critical point in their most recent work (Gentry et al., 1982) was that the subject's habitual anger-coping method (trait) was more important than his or her situational specific anger response (state). The habitual anger-coping method and the tendency to suppress anger or express low levels of anger were important determinants of eventual high blood pressure.

From the socioecological point of view, Harburg's data on the number of arrests in the precinct, the amount of arbitrary harassment by local authorities, the quality of housing, and other sources of emotional arousal proved to be important. These facts provide a model for defining psychosocial risks for disease. Moreover, the socioeconomic status and social instability of the group may be the underlying reason for the high incidence of high blood pressure.

Thus the number of emotional episodes is related to the social state of the subject. The aging person in an institution experiences a set of conflicting stimuli that differ sharply from those experienced by an aging person living at home with an extended family. The extent to which the emotions aroused by various social interactions can be freely admitted and expressed appears, to Harburg and others, to be of great importance in determining susceptibility to disease.

Failure to Express Emotion: Alexithymia and Disease

The failure to express emotion, for which the term alexithymia has been coined, is attracting interest (Lesser, 1981) because it carries with it a vulnerability to the so-called psychosomatic diseases. It is possible that the underlying mechanism is a persisting neuroendocrine arousal despite the individual's failure to consciously perceive and respond to, and hence suffer from, the negative effects of an emotional response. The absence of proper communication with the emotional systems may be the cause of the individual's inadequate sensitivity to others and use of immature patterns of defense.

A great step in defining the defect in alexithymia was made when Hoppe and Bogen (1977) in a unique series of observations demonstrated that 12 patients commissurotomized for epilepsy were alexithymic. Reviewing the evidence from these split-brain patients, Hoppe (1977) concluded that patients with severe psychosomatic disturbance may suffer from a functional commissurotomy. He considered that it was the elimination of the left-right hemispheric interaction that led to the observed quantitative and qualitative impoverishment of dreams, fantasies, and symbolizations of split-brain patients. Lesser (1981) points out that this neurophysiological explanation of the alexithymia concept is theoretical and speculative. However, he also recognizes the heuristic value of the concept of a deficiency in interhemispheric information transfer. The author suspects that this theory will eventually be supported by convincing evidence and that Hoppe and Bogen's remarkable observations of commissurotomized victims of epilepsy are merely forerunners of more solid studies yet to come.

Insofar as persons in their middle to late adult years suffer from coronary heart disease, hypertension, or chronic arthritis, they are likely to be alexithymic, i.e., to suffer from difficulties in perceiving and expressing emotion and relating to others. Victims of an impoverished fantasy life with a resultant utilitarian way of thinking, they suffer from a tendency to use action to avoid conflicting stressful situations. They are unable to express emotion and have difficulty in finding appropriate words to describe their feelings (Lesser, 1981). It is increasingly suspected that such inadequate contact with the emotional mechanisms of the limbic system is a major predisposing factor in psychosomatic illness. In some way, by suppressing awareness of anger, victims lose the normal mechanisms of mature control and make themselves vulnerable to excessive arousal of the sympathetic adrenal-medullary system. Perhaps by also suppressing anxiety and helplessness, they become vulnerable to sustained adrenal-cortical activation and immunosuppression with vulnerability to arteriosclerotic and autoimmune disorders.

One purpose of this chapter is to present the various patterns of emotional response that accompany the perception of challenge or threat to status or to pleasant social support. The theme of behavioral medicine as expressed in many reports (Henry & Stephens, 1977; Weiss et al., 1981) is that repeated arousals of the neuroendocrine system eventually lead to disease. It is now realized that not only minor inconveniences, such as hay fever, tension headaches, or colds develop, but also chronic diseases that take the lives of both 50- and 60-year-olds who would otherwise live an extra 15 to 20 productive years. Not only does this lessen national competence and productivity, but the progressive slow deterioration of health at this relatively early age imposes an extra burden of care on the family, preventing even devoted members from giving the support they would wish. Extending the mean longevity of human beings into their 80s when time and resources to care for the ailing are more available to the family does not demand a major breakthrough in understanding the aging process per se. Rather the problem demands an imaginative, resourceful response to the socioecological stress problem.

Control of Chronic Cardiovascular Disease by Controlling Social Stress

The consequences of social interaction between disturbed personalities is shown by a study by D'Atri, Fitzgerald, Kasl, and Ostfeld (1981) which demonstrates the relationship between change in mode of housing, lifestyle, and blood pressure in persons who have experienced sufficient difficulty with society to be incarcerated. Over 500 male prisoners were observed, and the authors made an analogy between the social interaction of the men behind bars and the stressful social interaction of psychosocially inept, formerly isolated mice in population cages described by Henry and Stephens (1977). D'Atri's group found a significant increase in the systolic blood pressure of men who were transferred from single occupancy cells to dormitories. Those who were retransferred to cells experienced a decline in blood pressure, but the men who remained in the single cells had little change. The authors suggest that loss of privacy and personal control may be critical factors. Increases in threatening interactions between the men may have resulted in corresponding states of vigilance and arousal.

The extraordinary difference between the blood pressure of persons living in societies with a subsistence economy and those in societies with a money economy, including modern industrialized societies, has been reviewed recently by Waldron, Nowotarski, Freimer, Henry, Post, and Witten (1982) (Figure 2-3). Blood pressure was higher and blood pressure increase with age was greater in groups which had greater involvement in a money economy, more economic competition, more contact with persons of different cultures or beliefs, and more unfulfilled aspirations for return to traditional values and beliefs.

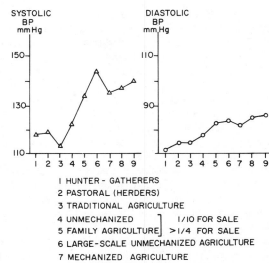

FIGURE 2-3.
Average systolic blood pressure for 50- to 60-year-old men in societies with different economies. (See Waldron et al., 1982, for more details regarding types of economy and correlation coefficients.)

1 HUNTER - GATHERERS
2 PASTORAL (HERDERS)
3 TRADITIONAL AGRICULTURE
4 UNMECHANIZED   ⎤ 1/10 FOR SALE
5 FAMILY AGRICULTURE⎦ >1/4 FOR SALE
6 LARGE-SCALE UNMECHANIZED AGRICULTURE
7 MECHANIZED AGRICULTURE
8 INDUSTRY/TRADE - SMALL TOWN
9 URBAN INDUSTRIAL

They concluded that cross-cultural variation in blood pressure is due to multiple factors, an important one being psychosocial stress due to cultural disruption, including disruption of cooperative relationships and traditional cultural patterns which frequently occurs during economic modernization. Another factor considered was the very low-salt diet of many primitive communities. However, if the veteran hypertensiologist Pickering (1980) is correct in his most recent assessment of the role of salt in hypertension, this agent cannot carry the responsibility. If so, much of the burden of responsibility for this crippling disorder must fall on the socioecological issue.

The role of behavioral factors also seems to be important in coronary heart disease, an especially devastating source of premature death and disability for persons in their 50s and 60s. Friedman and Thoresen's new work further supports the growing evidence (Friedman, Thoresen, Gill, Ulmer, Thompson, Powell, Price, Elek, Rabin, Breall, Piaget, Dixon, Bourg, Levy, & Tasto, 1982; Taylor, Miller, & DeBusk, 1983, in press; Thoresen, Friedman, Gill, & Ulmer, 1982). In their continuing work, Friedman and Thoresen reviewed their first few years of attempting to decrease recurrent myocardial infarcts by changing the lifestyles of patients. Their statistically significant study contrasts large numbers of 50- to 60-year-old patients divided into subgroups of 10. Patients in the first experimental group were exposed to 1½ hours of instruction on how to control the classic cardiovascular risk factors, such as smoking, cholesterol, and blood pressure. Skilled cardiologists presented lectures and instructed participants, for example, advising diets containing low fat and low salt and extolling the value of exercise. Patients in the second experimental group met each week for 90 minutes; they focused on modifying their lifestyle along the lines proposed by Friedman and Rosenman (1974) in their famous book, *Type A Behavior and Your Heart.* Currently the new approach of modifying lifestyle seems about twice as effective as the classic cardiologic approach.

The Friedman-Thoresen advice includes no smoking, low caffeine, and stress-coping education in an attempt to match inner resources to outside demands. In their view, a person is in trouble when demands exceed resources. At home, these demands can be spouse, friends, children, or those arising from owning a home or property. At work the demands can include those of supervisors, of meeting deadlines, and of distress from interpersonal relationships with co-workers. In the community the demands can be problems with neighbors, irritations like waiting in lines, and so on (unpublished data).

Patients were encouraged to review their ties with intimate others and to seriously evaluate how these ties were being nurtured. They were asked to review their stability and closeness to their children and were encouraged to have something to love, including, if possible, an affectionate pet (Bustad, 1980; Holden, 1981; Lynch, 1977). Patients were trained to avoid hurry, especially in driving, always keeping the speed below 55 miles per hour; to avoid irritating lineups, perhaps by spending a little more money; to reduce stimulants like alcohol, caffeine, and nicotine; to relax regularly in a quiet place with adequate space; to listen actively to others, carefully appreciating what they have to say; to express love and affection; to love self, being less self-critical, and to accept the beauty of being average in most things.

These approaches have a sound basis in human biobehavioral patterning for the 50- to 60-year-old men vulnerable to coronary or hypertensive heart disease. They fit in with the growing understanding that the critical stress mechanism in hypertensives is connected with suppressed anger. Not only does Harburg's group bear witness to this (Gentry et al., 1982; Harburg, Julius, McGinn, McLeod, & Hoobler, 1964), but independent studies, such as McClelland's (1979), also accept the role of suppression of emotion in hypertension. The critical psychosocial stress factor in coronary heart disease, even more than the well-known ones of competitiveness and time urgency, is a hard-driving irritable hostility with impatience. Not only do Rosenman, Brand, Jenkins, Friedman, Straus, and Wurm (1975) comment on this in the Western Collaborative Group Study, but later Marmot and Syme (1976) note the contrasting social cohesion and group loyalty of the low-coronary, hard-working, competitive Japanese. They compared the Japanese people's social characteristics with the American patients' anger-out hostility and individualistic denigration of others. This is also reported by Williams, Haney, Lee, Kong, Blumenthal, and Whalen (1980) in their recent paper focusing on hostility as the critical behavioral factor in coronary heart disease. Perhaps the consequence of the combination of being hard driving and hostile in a closely knit society is that one becomes disliked, and that, as a result, it becomes progressively more difficult to achieve the goals that depend on the cooperation of others. The result of this progressive loss of control, despite the individual's great effort to achieve, is depression which becomes a demonstrable symptom of his coronary disease, as noted by Troxler, Sprague, Albanese, Fuchs, and Thompson (1977). Thus a lack of skill in human relationships (probably due to defective childhood bonding) has led to persistent alienation and hostility.

Persons vulnerable to neoplasm represent a further group whose behavior expresses a somewhat different pattern of neuroendocrine response, which also leads to disease. They have a certain incapacity to express emotion and to relate to others, and their loneliness and isolation, rather than their hostility, leads to their perception of loss of control (Morris, Greer, Pettingale, & Watson, 1981; Thomas & Duszynski, 1974). These persons are more depressed than hostile.

PATTERNS OF NEUROENDOCRINE RESPONSE

Territoriality and Attachment

Two major instinctual mechanisms have been considered basic by those students of animal behavior known as ethologists. The name of Konrad Lorenz is associated with the instinct for territoriality and the fight-flight response to maintain control over resources; that of John Bowlby is associated with attachment behavior which induces the necessary bonding to hold a social system together (Henry & Stephens, 1977). These basic instincts motivate mammals and are of critical importance to primates and human beings. Aggression by dominant animals assures social order within the group and is necessary for the defense of territory from outside threat (Henry & Stephens, 1977). The mechanism of attachment behavior is skillfully presented by Bowlby in his three treatises dealing with this behavioral cement that unites a group by bonding its members to one another (Henry & Stephens, 1977). In humans, more newly evolved, adult male-female attachment bonds develop which are as permanent as the older mammalian bond of mother to young. This male-female bonding ensures the unique cohesion of human society and brings the male into full partnership in the task of feeding and raising the young. Bonding also helps in feeding and caring for the aged, thus preserving their store of memory useful to the group (Lovejoy, 1981).

These master instincts of territoriality and attachment or bonding are behavioral patterns by which members of a society are integrated into a viable team of males and females, dominants and subordinates, old and young, working together to present a united front to environmental challenge. The health of such a society is dependent on having its members effectively act out the behaviors demanded by their roles on the team. Life changes and deficiencies in socialization, and hence bonding, can result in strains on the adaptive mechanisms. Difficulty in meeting threat with limited resources of time, energy, and skill lead to emotional arousal. In sustained socioecological deficiency, this emotional arousal can persist so long and be so severe that pathophysiological changes occur. Already, two important patterns of neuroendocrine response have been identified; one involves activation of the adrenal medulla and the other, activation of the cortex. The fight-flight response was first studied by Cannon (1929) and was later described by Mason (1968b) as the sympathetic adrenal-medullary response. The other stress response is that demonstrated so extensively by Selye and attributed by Mason (1968a) to the pituitary adrenal-cortical axis. It is associated with the loss of control and depression. Many papers detail the different behaviors and physiological changes involved. Those of Obrist (1981) are reviewed in his book *Cardiovascular Psychophysiology: A Perspective.* Stock, Schlör, Heidt, and Buss (1978) have performed highly relevant experiments contrasting responses coming from the stimulation of different areas of the amygdala in the conscious cat.

The Physiological Patterns of Anger, Fear, and Depression

The contrasting behavior and neuroendocrine accompaniments of emotion associated with major psychosocially activated patterns of response are presented in Figures 2-4, 2-5, and 2-6.

Figures 2-4 and 2-5 contrast the response to a situation perceived as threatening with one perceived as socially supportive. An arrow at the top of both figures represents the subject's psychosocial perceptions. These perceptions involve the left and the right parietal and the frontal associational neocortex, regions that have been called the sociocultural brain (Henry & Stephens, 1977). These regions in the two hemispheres interact with the subcortical limbic system structures. In a threatening situation, there is activation of frontal amygdalar pathways, and feelings of anger or fear or a mixture of both will ensue. An alternative response, perhaps with origins in the dorsal right frontal cortex, as opposed to its ventral aspects, may run in the rich connections to the hippocampal regions. Here the response can relate to cognitive mapping not only of the physical space but also of the hierarchic space that determines the social status to which primates are so sensitive (Henry & Stephens, 1977). The subject with strong hippocampal arousal may be responding to a perceived mismatch between old stored patterns and the present situation. Such activation could occur when lost and detached from the intimate others to whom the subject is bonded, for instance, as in a mother-infant relationship when the two are accidentally separated.

Pursuing the implications of Figure 2-4, the fear or anger responses to perceived threat involve arousal of the amygdalar value-assigning systems (Rolls, 1975). If the primary outcome is a perception that the challenge can be mastered, a series of behaviors ensue which involve the attempt to master the threat by fight, effort, and persistence. Subjectively the feeling will be anger. The ensuing activation of the right or left or of both amygdalar central nuclear systems and the associated hypothalamic controls of the autonomic system result in release of norepinephrine. There is a sharp rise in blood pressure and pulse rate with vasoconstriction (Stock et al., 1978). Together with this, impulses run in the β sympathetic pathway to the renin-producing juxtaglomerular apparatus in the kidney, also to the adrenal medulla where the amount of tyrosine hydroxylase, the norepinephrine-synthesizing enzyme, begins to increase (Henry & Stephens, 1977). At the same time, impulses to the vascular smooth muscle initiate both increased sensitivity to angiotensin (Webb, Johnson, Vander, & Henry, 1983) and hypertrophy so that if this anger response pattern persists for days, vascular walls will begin thickening structurally (Folkow, 1978). This will eventually lead to Folkow's structural autoregulation with a greater increase in resistance for a given stimulus; the thicker walls take up more space and thereby encroach on the lumen of the vessel raising blood pressure (Folkow, 1978). There are other changes, and one factor accompanying the successful norepinephrine fight response will be an increase in the gonadotropic luteinizing hormone (LH) activity with the release of testosterone (Rose, Bernstein, & Gordon, 1975).

By contrast, should the feeling of fear predominate, the response will involve basal amygdalar activation with a different neurohormonal pattern in which epinephrine predominates. Pulse and blood pressure do not rise so dramatically (Stock

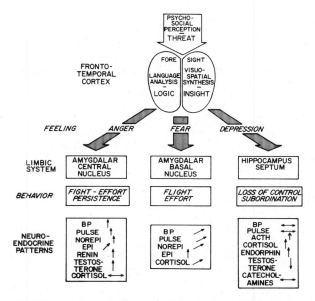

FIGURE 2-4. Psychosocial stimulation by the external environment can result in a perception of challenge by the sociocultural analyzers of the frontotemporal cortices. Ventral frontoamygdalar pathways arouse the central nucleus if anger is involved, the basal nucleus if fear is involved, and dorsal frontoactivity pathways arouse the hippocampus septum if depression is involved. In contrast to the fight-flight response of the amygdala, the hippocampus has a depressive response characterized by helplessness and loss of control. The ensuing neuroendocrine patterns differentiate between three responses: norepinephrine (anger), epinephrine (fear), and cortisol (depression).

et al., 1978), in part because cholinergic activation of the muscle vascular bed involves a regional decrease in resistance. The overall response of the anxious animal is one of sudden, intense explosion of effort directed toward flight along with greatly increased cardiac output. Increased glucose and other metabolic changes prepare the animal for the demands of rapid and often prolonged escape from threat (Folkow & Neil, 1971).

During evolution, the grafting together of the adrenal medulla and the cortex in the mammal represents a combination of separate nervous and hormonal response capabilities whose significance in terms of reaction to challenge differ (Axelrod & Weinshilboum, 1972). The biosynthesis of norepinephrine is dependent on neural activity, and tyrosine hydroxylase, the enzyme involved, is controlled by the sympathetic nerves. The methylation of norepinephrine is controlled by the important adrenocorticotropic hormone (ACTH) produced by the pituitary gland (Ganong, 1971). The production of this hormone in response to challenge depends on hippocampal activation of the pituitary system (Henry & Meehan, 1981).

With ACTH a new reaction has been added, which is independent of the fight or flight response, but is intimately related to the complex social context in which higher animals live. The ACTH-corticosterone-endorphin mechanism is aroused when, instead of fight or flight, the animal elects to submit to the situation. The behavioral consequence of ACTH activation is depression, loss of effort, and inhibition of previous behavioral patterns (De Wied, van Delft, Gispen, Weijnen, & van Wimersma Greidanus, 1972). When animals are fighting, ACTH activation influences the loser to submit and accept a role that does not conflict with that of the winner. High ACTH is accompanied by a rise in adrenal-cortical secretions; a striking effect is that they create euphoria, countering the depression associated with ACTH. At the same time, closely related endorphins which act like morphine are released. The defeated animal literally "feels no pain" as the result of the combined endogenous opiate and corticosterone activity (Miczek, Thompson, & Shuster, 1982).

The additional effects of corticoids act not only on the metabolism of glucose and blood volume but also on T and B cells. The humoral immune response constitutes a chapter in the rapidly growing discipline of psychoimmunology. It has important repercussions in autoimmune diseases and defense against the spread of cancer (Visintainer, Volpicelli, & Seligman, 1982). The newly evolved pattern of response to defeat involving the adrenal cortex has only a limited direct effect on the cardiovascular system. Defeat activates the related parasympathetic vagal response. The ensuing release of antidiuretic hormone, slowing of heart beat, and relaxation of muscular vessels can lead to syncope. Fainting in response to threat is a short-term, immediate, noncatecholamine response which avoids fight or flight and relies on feigning death to survive the immediate crisis (Henry & Meehan, 1971). The hippocampus, anterior hypothalamus, pituitary, and adrenal cortex take part in the rest of the response to loss of control involving hormonal changes directed at relearning appropriate patterns of response, inhibition of activity, and mobilization of metabolic resources dealing with loss of blood and pain of wounds. This facilitates withdrawal by the animal, opening avenues of escape and thus ultimate survival.

The Physiological Patterns of Relaxation and Elation

The patterns of response to threat were considered. Figure 2-5 takes up the opposite perception: response to social support. Here the frontotemporal sociocultural cortex releases impulses activating feelings of relaxation as opposed to the catecholamine-driven effort. The typical behavior of the relaxed animal is to groom and be groomed (Kling, Deutsch, & Steklis, 1977) or, in the female, to nurse. In humans certain types of friendly or polite conversations probably represent grooming. Patel's current work on meditation and relaxation shows it will reduce blood pressure and pulse rate with an accompanying reduction of sympathetic outflow and plasma renin (Patel, Marmot, & Terry, 1981). The extent of these changes is dependent on the degree of involvement of the subject, and as Luborsky et al. (1982) have recently shown, relaxation therapy is less effective than drugs, but it does work. They comment that impatient, hard-driving persons with Type A personalities profit most from the quite simple relaxation techniques.

The role of elation in the perception of social support as opposed to loss of control and depression has received little quantitative study. Animals exposed to

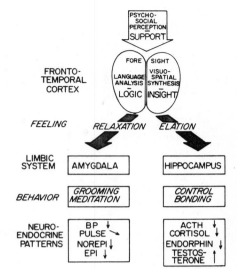

FIGURE 2-5.
Amygdalar and hippocampal responses to psychosocial perception of support, solidarity, and bonding lead to a feeling of relaxation: the amygdala is involved. Grooming behavior and decreased arousal of the sympathetic adrenal-medullary system lead to a fall in blood pressure, catecholamines, and renin. With elation, limerence, and bonding, there is hippocampal arousal, and cortisol and endorphins decrease. Testosterone may increase.

restraint stress appear to reduce corticosterone levels as the result of rewarding adjunctive activities. Dantzer and Mormede (1981) have shown that tethered swine that are allowed to pull on leather thongs will have reduced plasma corticosterone. Bourne's (1970) study of troops in dangerous combat in Vietnam showed a remarkable reduction of corticoids when there was bonding between the men. One example was between helicopter medics and the downed pilots they rescued. The same observation may explain the low corticoids reported for a successful flight crew orbiting in space (Henry & Stephens, 1977). Sachar, Fishman, and Mason (1965) have reported a reduction of corticoids during pleasant hypnotic trances.

Mazur (1976) in reviewing evidence for the luteinizing hormone or gonadotropic axis, including his own ingenious studies contrasting the winners of tennis matches (affecting ego) with winners of an event such as a lottery (not affecting ego), concludes that testosterone is elevated when the individual perceives his or her status as having improved. Others have shown increased persistence in the chicken or rat when testosterone is elevated (Archer, 1972).

As yet the evidence is not strong, nevertheless during elation and social support there is probably a reduction of the adrenocorticotropic hormone and its accompanying assuaging endorphin effects (MacLennan, Drugan, Hyson, Maier, Madden, & Barchas, 1982). The lowered endorphins are accompanied by a rise of testosterone in the male, and prolactin, estrogen, and progesterone in the female.

Relating the Sympathetic and the Adrenal-Cortical Emotional Axes

Figure 2-6, developed in collaboration with Dr. John P. Meehan, summarizes these neuroendocrine observations, adds some quantitative data, and relates behavioral data to certain common clinical conditions. We have used general levels of plasma catecholamines as recorded in the standing subject by de Champlain, Cousineau, Lapointe, Lavallée, Nadeau, and Denis (1981) and blood pressure as

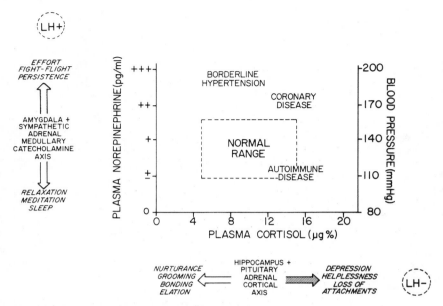

FIGURE 2-6. With arousal the amygdalar, sympathetic adrenal-medullary axis is responsible for the fight-flight effort and persistence. With social support, grooming behavior, and meditation, there is decreased arousal of this axis. The pituitary adrenal-cortical axis elicits helplessness and depression when activated. States of elation, solidarity, and bonding lead to reduction of cortisol. Blood pressure and plasma catecholamines are increased in borderline hypertension, but only marginally increased in coronary heart disease. Cortisol is significantly increased in depression and to some degree in active coronary heart disease, which also shows a mild increase in catecholamines. Autoimmune responses may be impaired in states of arousal of the adrenal-cortical axis. Lutenizing hormone (LH+) and testosterone increase with the fight-flight effort and decrease with depression.

observed by the clinician Julius (1982). The ordinate of the graph serves as a measure of activation of the amygdalar, sympathetic adrenal-medullary axis. The response ranges from low values during relaxation, grooming, and meditation through a normal of 300–400 pg/ml, i.e., + norepinephrine or 100–140 mm Hg, systolic blood pressure, to effort, persistence, and fight-flight arousal at catecholamine levels in excess of 400 pg/ml, i.e., ++ norepinephrine or systolic blood pressure in excess of 150 mm Hg.

On the abscissa, plotting plasma cortisol levels for both normal and depressed patients permits correlation of a different range of behavior and emotion with the fight-flight sympathetic axis. Starting with depression, helplessness, and loss of attachment at higher values of 12–20 μg% (Sachar et al., 1965), a normal range of 8–20 μg% intervenes, followed by values of less than 8 μg% for elation, solidarity, and bonding.

The normal range is defined as the area in the middle of the diagram where activation of the adrenal-medullary and the adrenal-cortical axes is not commonly exceeded for prolonged periods. In conditions such as borderline hypertension, it is known that the disorder of regulation applies primarily to the fight-flight or catecholamine axis. For those conditions such as autoimmune disease or resistance to neoplasms, areas that are receiving increasing research attention from medical behaviorists, the adrenal-cortical axis comes increasingly under suspicion (Riley, Fitzmaurice, & Spackman, 1981).

Persons with coronary heart disease respond to challenge with an increase of catecholamines and corticoids. The former has been demonstrated by Dembroski (1981) and by Glass (1977) in experiments in which the subject is confronted and challenged by a confederate. The blood pressure of persons with coronary heart disease is commonly at the upper border of normal; indeed, during the challenge of major surgery, it often rises to an extent not found in other persons with different medical histories. The important work of Troxler et al. (1977) points to increased corticoids in persons with active coronary heart disease. This increase is characteristic of depression and is compatible with the difficulty a person with a Type A personality has with hostility, which when taken together with a lack of emotional awareness (i.e., alexithymia) makes it difficult to enjoy supportive relations with others, including the spouse. Thus in coronary heart disease, and no doubt in other conditions, there is arousal of both the sympathetic and the pituitary adrenal-cortical systems. If Glass (1977) is correct, these states of arousal of the two systems alternate with some overlap as the individual swings from attempts to control, to a perception that control may be lost, and thence to depression.

BEHAVIORAL ACCOMPANIMENTS OF NEUROENDOCRINE PATTERNS

Power and Status: Mutuality and Attachment

The foregoing evidence that specific patterns of neuroendocrine response are matched to certain behaviors is now reaching a point of conviction. Power and status, respectively, have been attributed to primary analytic dimensions of interaction in social relationships by the social scientist Kemper (1978). Such social power has been ably studied by McClelland for decades. Under the guise of achievement, it represents the capacity to attain goals and control others by manipulation of aversive and rewarding stimuli (McClelland, Floor, Davidson, & Saron, 1980). Bakan (1966) describes agency as a self-protective, self-assertive, self-expressive activity. These characteristics fit with the ethologists' "defense of status and territory." The individual is responding with arousal of the fight-flight pattern as described in the discussion of Type A behavior. This is the sympathetic adrenal-medullary catecholamine axis: the ordinate of Figure 2-6.

By contrast there is an axis that concerns mutuality, interdependence, and joint welfare. Kemper (1978) speaks of granting status without regard for territorial prerogatives. In this relationship the other person is admired, has prestige, and enjoys affection and devotion. This selfsame bonding or attachment behavior has been presented as love between parent and child by Bowlby (1979), has been described in adults as limerence by Tennov (1979), and has been described as newly evolved bonding between the sexes by Lovejoy (1981).

Bonding or attachment is founded on mutuality, interdependence, and joint welfare and is the basis of solidarity in a group. Kemper defines love as a relationship in which one gives high-status recognition to another, as in mother-infant bonding. Depression or dejection is the behavior accompanying the neuroendocrine condition which follows perception of insufficient status, that is, denial of benefits, of respect, approval, and love. Depression or dejection corresponds to pituitary adrenal-cortical activation; the opposite extreme is elation of social success. Thus, in brief, we have described the role of the hippocampus in control of the elation-dejection response axis and the role of the amygdalar nuclei in the contrasting behavior of control of territory in response to value judgments (Henry & Meehan, 1981; Rolls, 1975).

The recent work of Lundberg and Frankenhaeuser (1980) with human subjects supports the concept that effort without distress involves release of catecholamines and that release of cortisol is signaled by the subject's distress and perception of a threat of loss of mastery of the task at hand. Ely and Henry's (1978) work with dominant and subordinate mice, von Holst, Fuchs, and Stöhr's (1983) with tree shrews, and Sassenrath's (1983) with primates came to similar conclusions. Catecholamine synthesis is increased in the controlling animal and, contrastingly, plasma corticoid levels rise in those undergoing subordination (Henry & Stephens, 1977). Hucklebridge, Gamal-el-Din, and Brain (1981) came to the conclusion that there are basic differences between the physiology of defeat and subordination and aggressive victory. The former involves activation of a hippocampal septal mechanism leading to adrenocorticotropic hormone release, and the latter is associated with adrenal stimulation by neural factors and an increase in adrenal norepinephrine and adrenal content of the synthetic enzyme tyrosine hydroxylase.

In his book, *Cardiovascular Psychophysiology*, Obrist (1981) reviews the cardiovascular evidence, including his own studies, and concludes that subjects successfully avoiding shock have an anticipatory, accelerated heart rate corresponding to catecholamine response, but those unable to avoid shock develop a slower heart rate and remain helpless, which suggests parasympathetic vagal activation and depression. Miller (1980) comes to similar conclusions when discussing work based on Weiss's technique for inflicting equally strong, avoidable and unavoidable shock to yoked animals.

McClelland's Achievement and the Type A Personality

The inescapable conclusion is that neuroendocrine responses differ according to the emotional perception of the subject. McClelland's work with achievement or the power axis led him to study behavioral patterns related to high blood pressure. He perceives persons scoring high on power as more argumentative and more competitive in games. They accumulate more prestigious symbols and act to enhance their impact on others. In many respects, he considers them like persons with Type A behavior. They are assertive and hard driving, but inhibited in the direct expression of aggression (Bowlby, 1979). In a recent paper McClelland et al. (1980) cited the work of Harburg's group (Gentry et al., 1982) who found that suppressed anger increases blood pressure through activation of the sympathetic nervous system and that plasma norepinephrine also rises. If anger is a regularly experienced trait but cannot be expressed openly, blood pressure response is greater than if aggression can be expressed. The consensus by these two groups is that by some mechanism the internal restraints individuals place on their assertive urges lead to the high blood pressure response.

In studies of coronary heart disease, Williams et al. (1980) have found that the profile of the classic Type A personality shows high levels of hostility; but another factor, depression, adds to the patient's pathophysiological burdens (Henry, 1983). Medalie and Goldbourt's (1976) data shows that Israeli civil service workers who were anxious but perceived their wives as supportive had half the rate of coronary heart disease (expressed as angina) as those who did not perceive their wives as supportive. But awareness is often limited by alexithymia; and in coronary heart disease, there is also evidence of inhibition and denial, that is, arousal along both the power axis (catecholamine) and the affectual axis (corticoid) as shown in Figure 2-6.

Psychological Correlates of Cancer

Finally in their study of patterns of expression of anger and their psychological correlates in women with breast cancer, Morris et al. (1981) reconfirmed their earlier observation that younger women with breast cancer suppress anger. Despite this control over their expression of emotion, women with as yet undiagnosed breast cancer are apparently more stressed by the impending diagnostic biopsy than women with clinically indistinguishable benign tumors. The authors see the patients' general suppression of emotion as an expression of a culture that promotes concealment of feelings and maintenance of imperturbable composure under the most trying circumstances.

Changes of Male and Female Patterns with Aging

By the time we reach the later stages of life, most of our marital and family relationships have been deeply entrenched for many years, and such bonding is very difficult to break without devastating emotional consequences. Yet changes in lifestyle are forced upon us by retirement from work, and we lose our intimate relationships with our friends. This can be impoverishing, especially if an individual's relationships were confined to those made at work, as men's so often are. Because of their restricted social skills these retirees can be at a disadvantage in the task of reintegrating their lives.

If Gutmann (1977) is correct, the aging man's developmental need to withdraw from his excessive early and midlife masculinization and overly zealous concentration on the power fight-flight axis is matched by the aging woman's need to withdraw from her strong tendency toward feminization and parenting (attachment behavior). If she stayed at home caring for the family full time, she may have failed to familiarize herself with the agentic attitude of business and other institutions. The two sexes have major tasks of reorientation that are made more difficult by a culture-backed alexithymic failure to perceive emotion. The result is that psychological defense mechanisms remain immature. The growing evidence that alexithymia is related to chronic disease has been reviewed by Lesser (1981). The consequences of this condition in terms of lack of social skills and concern are that the alexithymic person lacks the quality of supporting emotional relationships that Vaillant's group (Andrews et al., 1978) cites as the principal determinant of effective crisis support. They speak of social support "melting away in the face of neurotic behavior." Apparently the problem of managing stress from the viewpoint of preventing chronic disorders, such as arteriosclerosis, hypertension, and disturbances of the immune response, is bound up with the reeducation of these responses. As Stevens (1981) points out in his recent monograph on archetypes, it is related to what Jung called *individuation*: the union of instinct and feeling with logic and insight, and the effective functional union of the left and right hemispheres with the limbic system.

SUMMING UP

Certain styles of behavior are appropriate at different stages in the lives of men and women (Levinson, Darrow, Klein, Levinson, & McKee, 1978). In early manhood, the young husband and father may show outstanding energy, ambition, and agentic coping. He may be assertive and independent, aggressive and persistent, and is encouraged to be so. As Brazelton, Tronick, Adamson, Als, and Wise (1975) point out, to succeed in the care of her infant the young mother is under pressure to display skills in attachment behavior and bonding. The mother had best be sensitive to the nuances of her relationship, sensing the baby's affective expressions of its various needs. The demand on her for this nurturant posture will become less acute and change with the maturation of the family (Hoyenga & Hoyenga, 1979; Walster & Walster, 1978). By the time she is 50, a woman's estrogen and progesterone drop with menopause, yet there is beginning evidence that women who work outside the home, in managerial positions, for example, have increased testosterone (Purifoy & Koopmans, 1979). This hormone is also higher in active homosexual females (Gartrell, Loriaux, & Chase, 1977). In both cases, the agentic axis (Figure 2-6) may be emphasized by the social situation. At the same time, if Gutmann (1977) is correct, the now aging man will have shifted toward nurturance and will be more interested in personal relationships, as the mentor of his children and students.

Some investigators have regarded these changes as shifting from the masculine agentic axis toward feminine relatedness and vice versa (Bakan, 1966; Gutmann, 1977). They occur at different stages of life and their timing is important and appropriate for human biology. If marriage takes place between the years of 20 and 25, children will normally be born by the age of 30. Recent work suggests that women frequently develop a longing for parenting (Davitz, 1981); also, the dangers of deferring pregnancy too long are now well understood. So it is adaptive for women to have a tendency to ignore the immediate demands of a career and bear children at an appropriate biological age before becoming "ancient" thirtyish primaparae. Thus by their 30s most couples have children in kindergarten, and by the time they have reached 50 or 60, these children will be able to fend for themselves in a complex society.

It can be argued that the differentiation of gender roles in the nuclear family is most important during the early years of marriage when children are young and are developing their own gender roles, using their parents as models. Later, after children have left home, the social need is for a more androgynous pattern: women get jobs, men lose physical endurance, and both sexes gain wisdom, knowledge, and experience from the individuation of maturity.

In a primitive society, growing children have usually been exposed not only to parents, but also to peers and grandparents, so they develop a perception of the continuity of life and a knowledge from observing intimate others of what to expect in progressing from youth to maturity to old age. In our society the only child has no peers at home, and the busy 45-year-old parents of a teenager will often barely tolerate the presence of their own parents, now 70 years old, in their small living quarters. Indeed, by the time the aging children retire, their now elderly parents will be in their 80s.

The normal pattern of aging appears to be the rectangular one toward which the survival curves are showing a trend (Figure 2-1). The factor most responsible for the chronic diseases that so often prevent 60-year-olds from surviving into their 80s may well be their patterns of emotional response to psychosocial stimulation. Chronic arousal of the sympathetic adrenal-medullary system or the pituitary adrenal-cortical system or both lead directly to hypertension and to coronary artery disease and possibly to autoimmune disease and cancer (Figure 2-6).

Biological constraints dictate 25 to 30 years for human beings to mature. This puts parents into their 50s to 60s before their children are fully independent. Hypertension, coronary heart disease, and arthritis are chronic disorders of this age group, and its victims are a burden to the younger generation. To be active and healthy into our 80s, closer to the limits of our normal life span, would not only greatly increase the skilled productivity of our society, but would also give the succeeding generation time to assist, protect, and nurse failing elders during their later years. Recent advances in behavioral medicine and epidemiology will help resolve the dilemma. Although it is often unperceived and denied, the chronically aroused neuroendocrine system leads to pathophysiological changes and premature failure. Suppressed anger relates to high blood pressure; and anxiety and helplessness, to disordered immune responses and atherosclerosis. An avenue for controlling these conditions opens up in the better management of socioecology, sex differences, and psychosocial stress.

REFERENCES

ANDREWS, G., TENNANT, C., HEWSON, D. M., & VAILLANT, G. E. (1978). Life event stress, social support, coping style, and risk of psychological impairment. *The Journal of Nervous and Mental Disease, 166*(5), 307–316.

ARCHER, J. (1977). Testosterone and persistence in mice. *Animal Behavior, 25,* 479–488.

AXELROD, J., & WEINSHILBOUM, R. (1972). Catecholamines. *New England Journal of Medicine, 287,* 237–242.

BAKAN, D. (1966). Agency and communion in human sexuality. In *The duality of human existence: An essay on psychology and religion* (Chap. 4, pp. 102–153). Skokie, IL: Rand McNally.

BERKMAN, L. F., & SYME, S. L. (1979). Social networks, host resistance, and mortality: A nine-year follow-up of Alameda County residents. *American Journal of Epidemiology, 190*(2), 186–204.

BERKSON, J. (1962). Mortality and marital status. Reflections on the derivation of etiology from statistics. *American Journal of Public Health, 52*(8), 1318–1329.

BOURNE, P. G. (1970). *Men, stress and Vietnam.* Boston: Little, Brown.

BOWLBY, J. (1979). *The making and breaking of affectional bonds.* London: Tavistock Publications.

BRAZELTON, T. B., TRONICK, E., ADAMSON, L., ALS, H., & WISE, S. (1975). Early mother-infant reciprocity. In R. Porter & M. O'Connor (Eds.), *Parent-infant interaction. Ciba Foundation Symposium 33* (pp. 137–154). Amsterdam: Associated Scientific Publishers.

BUSTAD, L. K. (1980, April). The veterinarian and animal-facilitated therapy (0401E General Lacroix Lecture). *Proceedings of the 47th Annual Meeting of the American Animal Hospital Association.* Los Angeles: April 19–25, 1980.

CANNON, W. B. (1929). *Bodily changes in pain, hunger, fear and rage: An account of recent researches into the function of emotional excitement* (2d. ed.). New York: D. Appleton & Co.

DANTZER, R., & MORMEDE, P. (1981). Pituitary-adrenal consequences of adjunctive activities in pigs. *Hormones and Behavior, 15,* 386–395.

D'ATRI, D. A., FITZGERALD, E. F., KASL, S. V., & OSTFELD, A. M. (1981). Crowding in prison: The relationship between changes in housing mode and blood pressure. *Psychosomatic Medicine, 43*(2), 95–105.

DAVITZ, L. L. (1981, November). Baby hunger. *McCall's,* pp. 10, 12–13.

DE CHAMPLAIN, J., COUSINEAU, D., LAPOINTE, L., LAVALLÉE, M., NADEAU, R., & DENIS, G. (1981). Sympathetic abnormalities in human hypertension. *Clinical and Experimental Hypertension, 3*(3), 417–438.

DEMBROSKI, T. M. (1981). Environmentally induced cardiovascular response in Type A and B individuals. In S. M. Weiss, J. A. Herd, & B. H. Fox (Eds.), Perspectives on behavioral medicine. *Proceedings of the Academy of Behavioral Medicine Research Conference, Snowbird, Utah, June 3–6, 1979* (pp. 321–328). New York: Academic Press.

DE WIED, D., VAN DELFT, A.M.L., GISPEN, W. H., WEIJNEN, J.A.W.M., & VAN WIMERSMA GREIDANUS, T.J.B. (1972). The role of pituitary-adrenal system hormones in active avoidance conditioning. In S. Levine (Ed.), *Hormones and behavior* (pp. 135–171). New York: Academic Press.

EAKER, E. D., HAYNES, S. G., & FEINLEIB, M. (1983). Spouse behavior and coronary heart disease in men: Prospective results from the Framingham study II. *American Journal of Epidemiology, 118,* 23–41.

ELY, D. L., & HENRY, J. P. (1978). Neuroendocrine response patterns in dominant and subordinate mice. *Hormones and Behavior, 10,* 156–169.

FOLKOW, B. (1978). Cardiovascular structural adaptation: Its role in the initiation and maintenance of primary hypertension (The Fourth Volhard Lecture). *Clinical Science and Molecular Medicine, 55,* 3–22.

FOLKOW, B., & NEIL, E. (1971). *Circulation.* New York: Oxford University Press.

FRIEDMAN, M., & ROSENMAN, R. H. (1974). *Type A behavior and your heart.* New York: Knopf.

FRIEDMAN, M., THORESEN, C. E., GILL, J. J., ULMER, D., THOMPSON, L., POWELL, L., PRICE, V., ELEK, S. R., RABIN, D. D., BREALL, W. S., PIAGET, G., DIXON, T., BOURG, E., LEVY, R. A., & TASTO, D. L. (1982). Feasibility of altering Type A behavior pattern after myocardial infarction. Recurrent coronary prevention project study: Methods, baseline results and preliminary findings. *Circulation, 66*(1), 83–92.

FRIES, J. F., & CRAPO, L. M. (1981). *Vitality and aging: Implications of the rectangular curve.* San Francisco: W. H. Freeman and Company.

GANONG, W. F. (1971). *Review of medical physiology* (5th ed.). Los Altos, CA: Lange Medical Publications.

GARTRELL, N. K., LORIAUX, D. L., & CHASE, T. N. (1977). Plasma testos-

terone in homosexual and heterosexual women. *American Journal of Psychiatry, 134*(10), 1117-1119.
GENTRY, W. D., CHESNEY, A. P., GARY, H. E., JR., HALL, R. P., & HARBURG, E. (1982). Habitual anger-coping styles: I. Effect on mean blood pressure and risk for essential hypertension. *Psychosomatic Medicine, 44*(2), 195-202.
GLASS, D. C. (1977). *Behavior patterns, stress, and coronary disease* (Complex Human Behavior Series). Hillsdale, NJ: Lawrence Erlbaum Associates, Publishers.
GUTMANN, D. (1977). The cross-cultural perspective: Notes toward a comparative psychology of aging. In J. E. Birren, K. Warner Schaie, J. Botwinick, S. Chown, & C. Eisdorfer (Eds.), *Handbook of the psychology of aging (The Handbooks of Aging)* (Chap. 14, pp. 302-326). New York: Van Nostrand Reinhold.
HACKETT, T. P., CASSEM, N. H., & WISHNIE, H. A. (1968). The coronary-care unit. An appraisal of its psychologic hazards. *New England Journal of Medicine, 279*, 1365-1370.
HARBURG, E., JULIUS, S., McGINN, N. F., McLEOD, J., & HOOBLER, S. W. (1964). Personality traits and behavioral patterns associated with systolic blood pressure levels in college males. *Journal of Chronic Diseases, 17*, 405-414.
HAYNES, S. G., EAKER, E. D., & FEINLEIB, M. (1983). Spouse behavior and coronary heart disease in men: Prospective results from the Framingham heart study I. *American Journal of Epidemiology, 118*, 1-22.
HAYNES, S. G., & FEINLEIB, M. (1980). Women, work and coronary heart disease: Prospective findings from the Framingham heart study. *American Journal of Public Health, 70*(2), 133-141.
HELSING, K. J., SZKLO, M., & COMSTOCK, G. W. (1981). Factors associated with mortality after widowhood. *American Journal of Public Health, 71*, 802-809.
HENRY, J. P. (1982). The relation of social to biological processes in disease. *Social Science and Medicine, 16*(4), 369-380.
HENRY, J. P. (1983). Coronary heart disease and arousal of the adrenal cortical axis. In T. M. Dembrowski, T. Schmidt, & G. Blümchen (Eds.), *Biobehavioral basis of coronary prone behavior.* Basel, Switzerland: S. Karger A.G.
HENRY, J. P., & MEEHAN, J. P. (1971). *The circulation: An integrative physiologic study.* Chicago: Year Book Medical Publishers, Inc.
HENRY, J. P., & MEEHAN, J. P. (1981). Psychosocial stimuli, physiological specificity, and cardiovascular disease. In H. Weiner, M. A. Hofer, & A. J. Stunkard (Eds.), *Brain, behavior, and bodily disease* (Chap. 16, pp. 305-333). New York: Raven Press.
HENRY, J. P., & STEPHENS, P. M. (1977). *Stress, health, and the social environment. A sociobiologic approach to medicine.* New York: Springer-Verlag.
HOLDEN, C. (1981). Human-animal relationship under scrutiny. Veterinarians, psychologists, and others believe time is ripe for a new interdisciplinary field. *Science, 214*, 418-420.
HOPPE, K. D. (1977). Split brains and psychoanalysis. *Psychoanalytic Quarterly, 46*, 220-244.
HOPPE, K. D., & BOGEN, J. E. (1977). Alexithymia in twelve commissurotomized patients. *Psychotherapy and Psychosomatics, 28*, 148-155.
HORNUNG, C. A., McCULLOUGH, B. C., & SUGIMOTO, T. (1981). Status relationships in marriage: Risk factors in spouse abuse. *Journal of Marriage and the Family, 43*, 675-692.
HOYENGA, K. B., & HOYENGA, K. T. (1979). *The question of sex differences: Psychological, cultural, and biological issues.* Boston: Little, Brown.

HUCKLEBRIDGE, F. R., GAMAL-EL-DIN, L., & BRAIN, P. F. (1981). Social status and the adrenal medulla in the house mouse (*Mus musculus, L.*). *Behavioral and Neural Biology, 33,* 345–363.

JACOBSON, P. H. (1964). Cohort survival for generations since 1840. *Milbank Memorial Fund Quarterly, 42,* 36–53.

JULIUS, S. (1982). Borderline hypertension. In H. R. Brunner & H. Gavras (Eds.), *Clinical hypertension and hypotension* (Chap. 14, pp. 313–325). New York: Marcel Dekker, Inc.

KEMPER, T. D. (1978). *A social interactional theory of emotions.* New York: John Wiley.

KLING, A., DEUTSCH, S., & STEKLIS, H. D. (1977). Radiotelemetered electrical activity from amygdala during social behavior in monkey (abstract). *Society for Neuroscience Abstracts, 3,* 200.

LESSER, I. M. (1981). A review of the alexithymia concept. *Psychosomatic Medicine, 43*(6), 531–543.

LEVINSON, D. J., DARROW, C. N., KLEIN, E. B., LEVINSON, M. H., & McKEE, B. (1978). *The seasons of a man's life.* New York: Ballantine.

LOVEJOY, C. O. (1981). The origin of man. *Science, 211*(4480), 341–350.

LUBORSKY, L., CRITS-CRISTOPH, P., BRADY, J. P., KRON, R. E., WEISS, T., COHEN, M., & LEVY, L. (1982). Behavioral versus pharmacological treatments for essential hypertension—a needed comparison. *Psychosomatic Medicine, 44*(2), 203–213.

LUNDBERG, U., & FRANKENHAEUSER, M. (1980). Pituitary-adrenal and sympathetic-adrenal correlates of distress and effort. *Journal of Psychosomatic Research, 24,* 125–130.

LYNCH, J. J. (1977). Bridging the gap: Lessons from the laboratory. In *The broken heart: The medical consequences of loneliness* (Chap. 6, pp. 156–180). New York: Basic Books.

MacLENNAN, A. J., DRUGAN, R. C., HYSON, R. L., MAIER, S. F., MADDEN, J., IV, & BARCHAS, J. D. (1982). Corticosterone: A critical factor in an opioid form of stress-induced analgesia. *Science, 215,* 1530–1532.

MARMOT, M. G., & SYME, S. L. (1976). Acculturation and coronary heart disease in Japanese-Americans. *American Journal of Epidemiology, 104,* 225–247.

MASON, J. W. (1968a). A review of psychoendocrine research on the pituitary-adrenal cortical system. *Psychosomatic Medicine, 30,* 576–607.

MASON, J. W. (1968b). A review of psychoendocrine research on the sympathetic-adrenal medullary system. *Psychosomatic Medicine, 30,* 631–653.

MAZUR, A. (1976). Effects of testosterone on status in primate groups. *Folia Primatologica (Basel), 26,* 214–226.

McCLELLAND, D. C. (1979). Inhibited power motivation and high blood pressure in men. *Journal of Abnormal Psychology, 88*(2), 182–190.

McCLELLAND, D. C., FLOOR, E., DAVIDSON, R. J., & SARON, C. (1980). Stressed power motivation, sympathetic activation, immune function, and illness. *Journal of Human Stress, 6,* 11–19.

MEDALIE, J. H., & GOLDBOURT, U. (1976). Angina pectoris among 10,000 men. II. Psychosocial and other risk factors as evidenced by a multivariate analysis of a five-year incidence study. *American Journal of Medicine, 60,* 910–921.

MICZEK, K. A., THOMPSON, M. L., & SHUSTER, L. (1982). Opioid-like analgesia in defeated mice. *Science, 215,* 1520–1522.

MILLER, N. E. (1980). Effects of learning on physical symptoms produced by psychological stress. In H. Selye (Ed.), *Selye's guide to stress research* (Vol. 1, Chap. 7, pp. 131–167). New York: Van Nostrand Reinhold.

MORRIS, T., GREER, S., PETTINGALE, K. W., & WATSON, M. (1981). Patterns of expression of anger and their psychological correlates in women with breast cancer. *Journal of Psychosomatic Research, 25*(2), 111-117.

OBRIST, P. A. (1981). *Cardiovascular psychophysiology: A perspective.* New York: Plenum.

PATEL, C., MARMOT, M. G., & TERRY, D. J. (1981). Controlled trial of biofeedback-aided behavioural methods in reducing mild hypertension. *British Medical Journal, 282,* 2005-2008.

PICKERING, G. (1980). Position paper: Dietary sodium and human hypertension. *Cardiovascular Reviews and Reports, 1,* 13-17.

PURIFOY, F. E., & KOOPMANS, L. H. (1979). Androstenedione, testosterone, and free testosterone concentration in women of various occupations. *Social Biology, 26,* 179-188.

RAY, J. J., & BOZEK, R. (1980). Directing the A-B personality type. *British Journal of Medical Psychology, 53,* 181-186.

RILEY, V., FITZMAURICE, M. A., & SPACKMAN, D. H. (1981). Animal models in biobehavioral research: Effects of anxiety stress on immunocompetence and neoplasia. In S. M. Weiss, J. A. Herd, & B. H. Fox (Eds.), *Perspectives on behavioral medicine: Proceedings fo the Academy of Behavioral Medicine Research Conference, Snowbird, Utah, June 3-6, 1979* (pp. 371-400). New York: Academic Press.

ROLLS, E. T. (1975). *The brain and reward.* New York: Pergamon Press.

ROSE, R. M., BERNSTEIN, I. S., & GORDON, T. P. (1975). Consequences of social conflict on plasma testosterone levels in rhesus monkeys. *Psychosomatic Medicine, 37,* 50-61.

ROSENMAN, R. H., BRAND, R. J., JENKINS, C. D., FRIEDMAN, M., STRAUS, R., & WURM, M. (1975). Coronary heart disease in the Western Collaborative Group Study. Final follow-up experiences of 8½ years. *Journal of the American Medical Association, 233*(8), 872-877.

SACHAR, E. J., FISHMAN, J. R., & MASON, J. W. (1965). Influence of the hypnotic trance on plasma 17-hydroxycorticosteroid concentration. *Psychosomatic Medicine, 27,* 330-341.

SASSENRATH, E. N. (1983). Studies in adaptability: Experiential, environmental, and pharmacological influences. In H. D. Steklis & A. Kling (Eds.), *Hormones, drugs, and social behavior in primates.* New York: Spectrum Publications, Inc.

STERN, M. J., & PASCALE, L. (1979). Psychosocial adaptation post-myocardial infarction: The spouse's dilemma. *Journal of Psychosomatic Research, 23,* 83-87.

STEVENS, A. (1981). *Archetypes.* New York: Morrow.

STOCK, G., SCHLÖR, K. H., HEIDT, H., & BUSS, J. (1978). Psychomotor behaviour and cardiovascular patterns during stimulation of the amygdala. *Pfluegers Archiv; European Journal of Physiology, 376,* 177-184.

TAYLOR, C. B., MILLER, N. H., & DeBUSK, R. (1983). Studies of intervention techniques for groups with increased cardiovascular risk factors: Post myocardial infarction, post surgery, highly stressed groups. *Journal of the South Carolina Medical Association, 79,* 604-610.

TENNOV, D. (1979). *Love and limerence.* Briarcliff Manor, NY: Stein & Day.

THOMAS, C. B., & DUSZYNSKI, K. R. (1974). Closeness to parents and the family constellation in a prospective study of five disease states: Suicide, mental illness, malignant tumor, hypertension and coronary heart disease. *Johns Hopkins Medical Journal, 134,* 251-270.

THORESEN, C. E., FRIEDMAN, M., GILL, J. K., & ULMER, D. K. (1982). The recurrent coronary prevention project. Some preliminary findings. *Acta Medica Scandinavica 660*, (Suppl.), 172–192.

TROXLER, R. G., SPRAGUE, E. A., ALBANESE, R. A., FUCHS, R., & THOMPSON, A. J. (1977). The association of elevated plasma cortisol and early atherosclerosis as demonstrated by coronary angiography. *Atherosclerosis, 26*, 151–162.

VISINTAINER, M. A., VOLPICELLI, J. R., & SELIGMAN, M.E.P. (1982). Tumor rejection in rats after inescapable or escapable shock. *Science, 216*, 437–439.

von HOLST, D., FUCHS, E., & STÖHR, W. (1983). Physiological changes in male *Tupaia belangeri* under different types of social stress. In T. M. Dembrowski, T. Schmidt, & G. Blümchen (Eds.), *Biobehavioral basis of coronary prone behavior*. Basel, Switzerland: S. Karger A.G.

WALDRON, I., NOWOTARSKI, M., FREIMER, M., HENRY, J. P., POST, N., & WITTEN, C. (1982). Cross-cultural variation in blood pressure. A quantitative analysis of the relationships of blood pressure to cultural characteristics, salt consumption, and body weight. *Social Science and Medicine, 16*(4), 419–430.

WALSTER, E., & WALSTER, G. W. (1978). *A new look at love*. Reading, MA: Addison-Wesley.

WEBB, R. C., JOHNSON, J. C., VANDER, A. J., & HENRY, J. P. (1983). Increased vascular sensitivity to angiotensin II in psychosocial hypertensive mice. *Hypertension, 5*(I), 165–169.

WEINER, H. (1977). *Psychobiology and human disease*. New York: Elsevier North-Holland, Inc.

WEISS, S. M., HERD, J. A., & FOX, B. H. (Eds.). (1981). Perspectives on behavioral medicine. *Proceedings of the Academy of Behavioral Medicine Research Conference, Snowbird, Utah, June 3-6, 1979*. New York: Academic Press.

WILLIAMS, R. B., JR., HANEY, T. L., LEE, K. L., KONG, Y.-H., BLUMENTHAL, J. A., & WHALEN, R. E. (1980). Type A behavior, hostility, and coronary atherosclerosis. *Psychosomatic Medicine, 42*, 539–558.

3

TOWARD A HOLISTIC MODEL OF HEALTH, BEHAVIOR, AND AGING

Gary T. Reker

The last two decades have witnessed a tremendous increase in the study of aging. Research efforts of the 1960s attempted to answer the question, What is successful of optimal aging? Recently, research has shifted toward the identification of conditions under which aging is satisfying or debilitating; the kind and quality of coping strategies used by the elderly; and the resources available to the elderly (George & Bearon, 1980). Relatively little emphasis has been given to the development of theoretical models to guide research, particularly in the field of health-behavior relationships.

The lag in model development is due, in part, to the failure of social scientists, especially psychologists, to contribute to the body of knowledge on health, behavior, and aging. In an archival cross-disciplinary survey of the research literature on the relationship between life circumstances and physical illness, Hull (1977) observed that relative to other disciplines, the contribution of psychologists seems to have declined steadily in the early 1970s. In a review of research reports published in the *Journal of Gerontology*, Abrahams, Hoyer, Elias, and Bradigan (1975)

The preparation of this chapter was supported by a Leave Fellowship (No. 451-81-2093) awarded to the author by the Social Sciences and Humanities Research Council of Canada. The author wishes to thank Drs. Raymond Steinberg and Paul T. P. Wong and the anonymous reviewers for their valuable comments and critical review of earlier drafts of this chapter.

found a decline over a 10-year period from 1963 to 1974 in the percentage of studies concerned with health-related issues. Fortunately, the decline has reversed itself in the past five or six years (Larson, 1978; Matarazzo, 1980, 1982; Pelletier, 1977).

The traditional medical model of health care, based on the diagnosis of a disease, the repair of injury and the treatment of symptoms, has been the predominant force in the alleviation of health-related problems. However, while the medical model has virtually eradicated infectious diseases as a leading cause of death in the early twentieth century, it has not been effective in extending the potential life span of adults. Data provided by the U.S. Public Health Service (1974) show that although there has been a dramatic increase in average life expectancy at birth, from 47.3 years in 1900 to 70.7 years in 1970, the average life expectancy at age 65 has increased only slightly from 11.9 years in 1900 to 15.2 in 1970. The infectious diseases have been replaced by stress-related psychological and physiological disorders described as the afflictions of modern civilization; namely, cardiovascular disorders, cancer, arthritis, and respiratory diseases (Pelletier, 1977; Ryan & Travis, 1981). More importantly, these diseases afflict mainly older people. In order to prolong the life expectancy of adults at 65, it is necessary to find the means to alleviate or prevent these lifestyle-related killers.

Among the limitations of the medical model in dealing with modern health problems, apart from the rapidly increasing costs and an overburdened health care system (Matarazzo, 1982; Pelletier, 1977; Ryan & Travis, 1981), is the failure of the model to give recognition to lifestyle as an exceedingly important determinant of health and well-being. The Canadian government has begun to acknowledge the shortcomings of the medical model and has announced its intention to give equal emphasis to human biology, the environment, and lifestyle in promoting the health status of Canadians (LaLonde, 1974). This renewed emphasis undoubtedly will not only add years to our life but life to our years.

The reconceptualization of health by the World Health Organization as a positive state of physical and emotional well-being and the absence of disease, psychopathology, and disabilities has broadened the concept of health considerably. Subjective or perceived health has become an important indicator and the focus of research has shifted towards factors that prevent illness and promote physical and mental well-being, culminating in wellness and growth models of health (Antonovsky, 1979; Ardell, 1977; Bloomfield & Kory, 1978; Ryan & Travis, 1981). In the wellness model, health is a continuum, anchored by premature death and high levels of well-being. A high level of wellness is achieved when an individual is physically active, mentally alert, and emotionally satisfied. A complete description of overall well-being should also take into account the mind/body interaction orientation toward health and the holistic approach to the prevention of stress disorders (Matarazzo, 1980; Pelletier, 1977). Thus, high-level wellness is achieved when physical, mental, and affective states interact harmoniously, leading to psychosomatic well-being.

For the purpose of this chapter, health is viewed as a multidimensional construct defined as a state of positive physical, mental, and psychosomatic well-being and the absence of disease, psychopathology, and disabilities. Physical well-being includes mobility, general activity level, physical stamina, ability to perform self-maintenance activity, and the absence of disease and physical disabilities. Mental well-being is conceptualized more broadly and includes mental functioning (e.g., mental alertness, intact memory), subjective or perceived well-being (e.g., happiness, high morale, life satisfaction), and the absence of psychopathology (e.g., depression). Psychosomatic well-being is indicated by the absence of psychosomatic complaints (e.g., insomnia, appetite loss).

Physical, mental, and psychosomatic health comprise both the objective conditions and the subjective perceptions of well-being. Thus health or well-being can be assessed objectively through illness inventories and observational rating scales and subjectively through self-rated health inventories. There is now a growing body of evidence that one's perceptions or beliefs are more importantly related to reported well-being than objective conditions. In the area of health, there is some evidence that self-rated health is a strong predictor of mortality (Singer, Garfinkel, Cohen, & Srole, 1976) even when objective health status is controlled (Mossey & Shapiro, 1982).

There is no question that health, whether objectively or subjectively assessed, is a major life concern of elderly people. Health problems have been identified by elderly respondents as potential threats to independent living (Louis Harris & Associates, 1975). Survey research has revealed significantly higher incidence rates of chronic diseases among the elderly compared to younger persons (U.S. Public Health Service, 1972), and that the elderly take longer to recover from acute illnesses (U.S. Public Health Service, 1971).

Given the matrix of factors involved in the aging process, there is a growing need for a multidisciplinary approach to health-related problems. A theoretical prerequisite for such an approach is a model which effectively integrates the physiological, psychological, and sociological factors in the genesis of disease and in the maintenance of health.

The purpose of this chapter is to describe an integrated, holistic model of health and stress-related diseases; to relate empirical findings from animal and human studies to various aspects of the model; to propose effective intervention strategies for the alleviation of illness and the maintenance of physical and mental health; and to provide directives for future research. The mosaic model is presented as a heuristic device for integrating existing research from allied fields and suggesting areas for future multidisciplinary exploration and application.

THE MOSAIC MODEL

The mosaic model describes a multifactorial approach to health-behavior relationships. Its scope is arbitrarily limited to a description of major pathways; many additional sources of influence are possible and could be added to the model. The mosaic model takes into account the physiological hardware that a person is equipped with from birth, the psychological software of cognition, emotion, and motivation, and the cultural and social contexts in which organisms develop. Focus is on the reciprocal relationship between the physiological hardware and the psychological software. It is anticipated that a mixed model with simultaneous emphasis on physiological and psychological orientations and their interaction will be a better predictor of health outcomes. The mosaic model is conceptualized as a feedback-loop system that tends to be static and self-regulatory. However, a disrup-

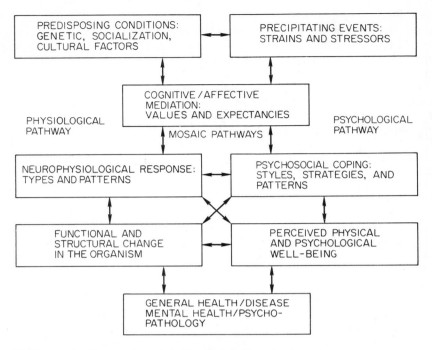

FIGURE 3-1. The mosaic model of health-behavior relationships.

tion can be amplified or dampened through its effects on other components of the system. Questions of causation are not relevant since what is cause and what is effect is arbitrary, depending on where one enters the system. Once a precipitating event has occurred, the entire system is affected. Thus, outcomes cannot be predicted well from knowledge of the precipitating events. Processes within the system must be identified and understood in order to gain considerable explanatory power. For a lucid presentation of the system theory approach to health, see Schwartz (1980).

In the mosaic model, optimal aging is viewed as the promotion of psychological and physical well-being and the avoidance of disease and psychopathology. While conceptual and intervention models of health-behavior relationships (Cobb, 1974; Garrity, Somes, & Marx, 1978; Guze, Matarazzo, & Saslow, 1953; Henry & Stephens, 1977; Kagan & Levi, 1974; Moos, 1981; Rahe, 1974; Schwartz, 1980) have been offered, few have specifically addressed the important role of cognitive/ affective variables as mediators of potentially stressful life events and *positive* physical and mental health. The mosaic model of health-behavior relationships, presented in Figure 3-1, is proposed as an integrated approach toward meeting this need.

Predisposing Conditions

The model begins at the level of predisposing conditions. These are of a general and pervasive nature and represent broad antecedent circumstances. Predisposing conditions set the range of vulnerability of the organism to subsequent precipitating events. Genetic (e.g., temperament and physical make-up), cultural (e.g., ethnic group), and socialization (e.g., past experiences, social status) factors constitute three categories of predisposing conditions. An individual's susceptibility to illness or disease at the time stress is operating is determined by the interaction of constitutional factors, both genetic and acquired, and life experiences.

The arrow leading from predisposing conditions to precipitating events signifies that predisposing conditions determine to some degree those events which will be considered potentially stressful and those which will not. For example, in a study of the effects of experience and ethnicity on ratings of life events as stressors, Rosenberg and Dohrenwend (1975) found that Asian, black, or Hispanic college students gave significantly lower stress ratings to several life events compared to non-Hispanic Caucasians. Experience with life events was unrelated to stress ratings. The ethnic background of the individual was the determining factor. In our research, we found Chinese elderly to rate health problems (arthritis and rheumatism) and problems of aging as significantly more serious (i.e., stressful) compared to a group of Caucasian elderly (Wong & Reker, 1982). The number of problems, however, did not differentiate the two groups. Myers, Lindenthal, and Pepper (1974) and Larson (1978) reported that socioeconomic status was correlated to some degree with levels of life change. Higher levels of life change were experienced by individuals from lower socioeconomic backgrounds, leaving them more vulnerable to the negative effects of life situations.

As an example of the influence of socialization factors, Pelletier (1977) described a study by Wolff of the closely knit Italian community of Roseto, Pennsylvania. The Rosetans adhered to their values, provided mutual supportiveness, socialized freely, and invested their wealth back into their community. A 1962 study of the Rosetans showed that, despite high intake of animal fat and widespread obesity, the incidence of death from myocardial infarction was less than half that of the surrounding area; coronary artery disease was also reduced. Furthermore, when Rosetans who had moved to New York or New Jersey were followed up, it was found that the rate of death by myocardial infarction and coronary heart disease increased significantly. Thus, the close-knit life style buffered the Rosetans against potentially stressful precipitating events.

Marmot and Syme (1976) cite evidence that the traditional Japanese culture with emphasis on community strength, group cohesion, and social stability may be stress-reducing, thereby protecting the Japanese from heart disease.

Predisposing conditions also influence the nature of cognitive/affective mediation. Cultural expectations and traditions may affect people's views of themselves and their health (Shanas, et al., 1968). For example, in his study of suicide among the Danish and Norwegian cultures, Farber (1967) found Danes to view life less optimistically, to live in the present, to become more depressed, and to be unable to delay gratification. In another study of the reporting of illness symptoms among Irish and Italians, Zola (1966) found cultural beliefs and value systems to influence the type of psychosocial coping patterns used by the patients. The Italians used the ego mechanism of dramatization, while the Irish made use of symptom denial. In a recent study in collaboration with Professor Paul T. P. Wong, we found that the Chinese elderly are more inclined to use the palliative mode of coping while their Caucasian counterparts are more apt to employ the instrumental mode (Wong & Reker, 1982). Thus, cultural factors play a role in the type of cognitive/affective mediation that a person from that culture may employ. For a more comprehensive examination of the effects of cultural beliefs about health and aging on the health of older people, see Newquist, Chapter 6, in this volume.

Precipitating Events

Precipitating events are specific antecedent circumstances which are either current (acute) or ongoing (chronic) and variable in terms of impact. Precipitating events may originate from within the individual, brought on either by physical alteration in body composition, hair loss, etc., or by the individuals themselves through nutritional habits, exercise, sexual difficulties, changes in sleeping habits, marital conflicts, etc. The effect of exercise, sexual adjustment, nutrition, and sleep patterns on the subsequent physical and mental health of the elderly has been amply demonstrated (Corby & Solnick, 1980; DeVries & Adams, 1972; Prinz, 1977; Sherwood, 1977; Watson, 1982; Wiswell, 1980). A detailed treatise of the findings, however, is beyond the scope of this chapter.

Precipitating events may also originate from outside the individual. Such events constitute the objective conditions of life including physical and environmental events (e.g., air pollution, loss of significant others, economic situation, income level, place of residence, etc.). It may be useful to refer to internally generated events as *strains* and to externally imposed events as *stressors*.

All precipitating events are potentially stressful and may be characterized by a number of objective attributes including affective valence, ambiguity, magnitude, chronicity, and multiplicity. However, it is the perception of the attributes, not the attributes *per se*, to which the organism responds. Thus, stress is psychological in nature. Consistent with Lazarus (1966), stress is defined as any demand, either externally imposed or internally generated, which taxes the psychosocial coping resources and the neurophysiological system of the organism, following cognitive/affective mediation. The phrase *potentially stressful* is important because it indicates that a particular precipitating event may not be a source of stress for every individual and may vary for the same individual from one time to another. Given the ubiquitous nature of stressors, it is their management which contributes to individual differences in response to stressful situations (Selye, 1974). Furthermore, potential stressors are not all negative; positive or pleasurable events can also be perceived as stressful (Holmes & Rahe, 1967; Selye, 1974). Holmes and Rahe (1967) have made the assumption that it is the accumulation of life event *changes* over a short period of time that appears to be critical in terms of illness outcome. However, recent findings have raised questions regarding the validity of combining desirable and undesirable events in measures of life stress. When the effects of positive and negative events are assessed independently, only negative events are related systematically to mental health indices of aggression, paranoia, suicidal tendencies, depression, trait and state anxiety, neuroticism, social nonconformity, external locus of control, and increased somatic preoccupation (Johnson & Sarason, 1978; Mueller, Edwards, & Yarvis, 1977; Vinokur & Selzer, 1975).

Precipitating events can influence the nature of the predisposing conditions. For example, relocation of the elderly from the community to an institutional environment may have an effect on the quality and the quantity of subsequent socialization experiences and these in turn will influence the nature of cognitive/affective mediation.

Cognitive/Affective Mediation

Cognitive/affective mediation is the central concept in the mosaic model. Cognition is defined as the perception of stimuli ranging from the lowest level of sensation to conscious awareness. At the level of sensing, an organism can experience affect without necessarily involving higher mental processes. At the level of the neocortex, however, such affect is interpreted or appraised as a particular feeling state, its meaning determined by the environmental context.

Since perception can occur at several levels, the dual term cognitive/affective mediation is preferred. Cognitive/affective mediators are a set of psychological variables that mediate between precipitating events and subsequent neurophysiological response types/patterns and psychological coping styles/patterns. Cognitive appraisal of precipitating events as controllable and/or predictable; the projection of positive expectations, feelings and goal-directed striving into the future (personal optimism); and the cognitive assessment of life as meaningful and purposeful (meaningfulness) constitute examples of mediators.

The importance of cognitive/affective mediation in coping with potentially stressful events has been eloquently expounded in the writings and research of Lazarus and his associates (Lazarus, 1966, 1980; Lazarus, Averill, & Opton, 1974). Recent studies by endocrinologist Mason and his collaborators (Mason et al., 1976) and by Weiss, Glazer, Pohorecky, Bailey, and Schneider (1979) have emphasized the importance of cognitive mediation in stress research. Lazarus et al. (1974) have emphasized the mediating cognitive processes of primary and secondary appraisal and reappraisal. Primary appraisal is the perception that some event will be either harmful, beneficial, or irrelevant to the individual. Secondary appraisal refers to the perception of coping alternatives available to the individual. Reappraisal refers to change in the original perception as a response to changing internal and external conditions.

Mason et al. (1976) investigated the effects of physical stressors including exercise, fasting, heat, and cold on the neuroendocrine response patterns of monkeys and humans. When Mason carefully controlled for psychological factors such as novelty, uncertainty, and threat, he found that, contrary to the General Adaptation Syndrome of Selye (1956), each physical stressor produced its own unique hormonal response profile. More importantly, there was no elevation of 17-hydroxycorticosteroid, a response highly sensitive to psychological threat, to any of the physical stressors except for the cold condition. Thus, it is the perception and interpretation of events as threatening or challenging, not the physical stressor *per se*, that leads to specific neuroendorcine response patterns. Along similar lines, the work of Weiss et al. (1979) showed that perceived control over a physical stressor influenced the level of brain norepinephrine in rats. Rats who could not escape or avoid shock had the lowest levels of norepinephrine compared to yoked rats who could control their environment.

Cognitive/affective mediators aid in the perception, interpretation, and anticipation of precipitating events. Mediators operate to minimize or maximize stressors and to facilitate or hinder optimal coping. Effective mediators promote the use of adaptive psychosocial coping styles/patterns and neurophysiological homeostasis. In order to understand psychosocial coping and neurophysiological changes, it is important to examine the nature of the cognitive/affective mediation process and its influence on the organism. Recently, Krantz (1980) has documented the importance of cognitive processes, particularly control and predictability, in the recovery from heart attacks.

Cognitive/affective mediators can also become potentially stressful precipitating events. For example, an overly optimistic perspective can add to the demands for higher rates of achievement and goal attainment that may tax the organism's coping capabilities beyond normal limits. Predisposing conditions can be similarly influenced. Individuals with high levels of optimism or strong personal belief systems may seek environments in which such values or ideals are continually validated. Thus, cognitive/affective mediators can influence the nature of the socialization experiences, which in turn will influence the precipitating events and subsequent cognitive/affective mediation.

THE MOSAIC PATHWAYS

The psychological (dark arrows), the physiological (light arrows), and the psychophysiological pathways (dark/light arrows) of the mosaic model describe three primary influences in health-behavior relationships. Their mutual interactions form a network of interrelationships, hence the term *mosaic*.

The Psychological Pathway

Psychosocial coping styles/patterns. Psychosocial coping styles/patterns consist of a wide range of responses that assist the organism to adapt to potentially stressful situations (Coelho, Hamburg, & Adams, 1974). Lazarus et al. (1974) have classified the coping responses into two classes: palliative and instrumental. Palliative coping refers to attempts to make oneself feel better without attempting to change the situation; instrumental coping refers to attempts at solving the problem directly through appropriate action (including inaction, if such is deemed appropriate). Recently, Wong and Reker (1982) found it fruitful to classify instrumental coping into two distinct coping styles: internal instrumental and external instrumental. The former is aimed at solving the problem by one's own effort; the latter is based on dependence or the seeking of help from others to solve the problem. A coping style is a preferred mode of dealing with potential stressors; a coping pattern consists of several interrelated ways of dealing with a demanding situation. Coping styles and patterns can be either palliative, instrumental, or both.

Internal-external locus of control is an example of a coping style; challenge, flight, and resource utilization are examples of instrumental coping behaviors; strategies of denial and rationalization are examples of palliative coping; the Type A personality (Friedman & Rosenman, 1974) is an example of a specific behavioral coping pattern. The instrumental coping behavior which I have termed resource utilization is characterized by: (1) seeking of relevant information; (2) requesting reassurance and emotional support; (3) setting concrete limited goals; and (4) learning specific action-oriented procedures.

There is a feedback loop from the psychosocial coping styles/patterns to the cognitive/affective mediators. In this loop, if a particular coping strategy is perceived to be adaptive, it will receive validation and will be invoked under similar conditions in the future. If it is perceived to be maladaptive, it is invalidated and alternative strategies may be tried.

Psychosocial coping strategies influence the organism's perception of psychological and physical well-being.

Perceived psychological and physical well-being. Perceived psychological well-being is defined as the presence of positive affect such as happiness, contentment, peace, joy, and the absence of negative affect such as fear, anxiety, or depression. Perceived physical well-being is defined as the presence of physical health, vigor, and vitality and the absence of physical ailments or discomforts.

A number of studies have investigated the influence of psychosocial coping strategies on perceived psychological and physical well-being. One of the most heavily researched coping styles is the locus of control construct. Locus of control refers to one's perception of events as either under one's control (internal) or beyond one's control (external). Lefcourt (1976) has reviewed the large body of research on locus of control and Strickland (1978) has documented the relation between locus of control and health-related behavior (e.g., precautionary health practices and reactions to physical disorders, etc.). There is now a growing body of literature linking locus of control in the elderly to physical and psychological well-being, mental alertness, physical health, and a reduction in the mortality rate (Iso, 1980; Kuypers, 1972; Langer & Rodin, 1976; Mancini, 1980; Schulz, 1980). For a more comprehensive review of this literature, see Shupe, Chapter 8, this volume.

Recently, Wong and Sproule (1984) have proposed the concept of dual control or shared responsibility. Rotter's construct of internal versus external locus of control views the two loci as two opposite poles of the same continuum; thus, internal and external control are inversely related. The construct of dual control, on the other hand, means that internal and external locus of control are two independent dimensions; thus, in some conditions, internal and external control may be positively correlated. This dual dimensional view of locus of control is particularly relevant to the elderly population; in a study just completed in collaboration with Professor Paul T. P. Wong, we have obtained evidence that the elderly, especially those who are 70 years and over, preferred shared control in most of life's situations rather than internal control. Currently, we are testing the hypothesis that belief in shared control is more adaptive for the elderly than belief in internal control.

Palliative coping strategies have also been shown to influence perceived psychological and physical well-being in the elderly. The expectation that stressful events such as chronic economic and/or health problems are unchangeable has been related to low scores in life satisfaction (Thomae, 1981). Belief in life after death was found to be a very strong predictor of personal well-being and life satisfaction (Steinitz, 1980). McCrae (1981) found faith to be an effective coping mechanism for the elderly. In one of the earlier studies of palliative coping, McMahon and Rhudick (1964) found that nondepressed elderly reminisced more than depressed elderly did. Apparently, reminiscing about the "good old days" makes one feel good about oneself.

Perceived well-being can have a reciprocal influence on the kind and quality of psychosocial coping strategies that are invoked. For example, a high degree of well-being may invoke a mastery coping strategy (Caplan, 1981), whereas a low degree of well-being might invoke a series of maladaptive, nonfunctional coping strategies (as might be seen in an individual following the death of a loved one).

A high degree of perceived psychological and physical well-being can lead to positive general and mental health; a low degree of perceived well-being can lead to disease or psychopathology.

The Physiological Pathway

Neurophysiological response types/patterns. Neurophysiological response types/patterns are physiological reactions of the organism to the cognitively mediated precipitating events. The type (e.g., neuroendocrine versus immunological system) as well as the pattern of response within each system (e.g., neuroendocrine system: catecholamine versus corticosterone) will depend on how the organism perceives, interprets, and anticipates the potentially stressful event. A hopeful, optimistic interpretation of a specific precipitating event will eventuate in a different neurophysiological response type/pattern compared to an interpretation of hopelessness or helplessness. Schmale (1972) suggests that a person who responds to life with hopelessness, depression, and submission may trigger a biological response pattern that encourages an already present disease potential leading to functional and structural change in the organism. It is the attitude toward the disease, not the magnitude of the disease (e.g., infectious disease versus cancer), that is critical (see Reker and Wong, Chapter 7, this volume, for a further discussion of this issue).

Henry (1979) has pointed out how different neuroendocrine response patterns are triggered depending on how the organism perceives a potentially stressful event. If the organism perceives the event as a challenge to control, then the fight-flight defense response is aroused and the hormonal pattern emphasizes the catecholamines of the sympathetic adrenal-medullary system. If, on the other hand, the organism perceives loss of control, then the conservation-withdrawal response is aroused and the corticoids of the pituitary adrenal-cortical system gain dominance (see Henry, Chapter 2, this volume).

The results of a study of university students conducted by Lundberg and Frankenhaeuser (1980) strongly suggest that the perception of controllability/predictability can suppress the secretion of cortisol, whereas the perception of a task as distressing and effort-demanding can elevate cortisol excretion. Thus the *same* neurophysiological system can either elevate or suppress hormonal output depending on how the environment is perceived.

There is a feedback loop from the neurophysiological response types/patterns to the cognitive/affective mediators. In this loop, a particular neurophysiological response may undergo cognitive appraisal. Pelletier (1977) describes the tendency for individuals to regard perfectly normal reactions such as high hydrochloric acid levels (severe indigestion) or chronic diarrhea as abnormal and consequently as a sign of disease. This cognitively mediated misinterpretation produces a new state of alarm—the dread of disease—which in and of itself can become a secondary stressor. The neurophysiological response may also alter the ability of the organism to mediate effectively. For example, chronically elevated blood pressure can result in changes in the cognitive functioning of the individual (Eisdorfer & Wilkie, 1977).

Functional and structural change in the organism. Neurophysiological response types/patterns will lead to functional and structural changes in the organism.

Continuous override of neuroendocrine feedback controls can lead to negative changes which become evident in the form of somatic alterations and subsequent pathology (Henry, 1981). Homeostasis, on the other hand, can lead to positive change (vigor of body and mind) which will be evident in the form of somatic and mental health.

Functional and structural change can also influence the neurophysiological systems. This is in the form of a feedback loop that attempts to restore homeostatic conditions. Huntington's chorea and Parkinson's disease may be two examples of functional and structural changes in the organism that influence neurophysiological response types/patterns.

The Psychophysiological Pathway

Psychosocial coping and the neurophysiological response. Psychosocial coping styles/patterns influence the neurophysiological response types/patterns, as is evident in the association between Type A behavior pattern and coronary atherosclerosis (Williams et al., 1980). Friedman and Rosenman (1974) found that Type A behavior pattern individuals, prior to their illness, exhibit every blood fat and hormone abnormality that the majority of coronary patients exhibited. Thus, the behavior pattern precedes and may contribute to neurophysiological change. For thorough reviews of this literature, see Jenkins (1971, 1976). (For an up-to-date treatise on aspects of the subject see Henry, Chapter 2, and Heckenmueller, Chapter 5, this volume.)

In a study of the effects of palliative coping strategies used by women awaiting surgery for breast cancer, Katz, Weiner, Gallagher, and Hellman (1970) found that those who coped by either intellectualization, prayer, or denial showed little corticosteroid increase; however, those who coped ineffectively (distress and anxiety) had a high secretion of cortisol.

In a review of the stress literature involving humans and animals, Henry (1979) reported that increasingly high levels of catecholamines (adrenalin and noradrenalin) triggered a flight or fight response; whereas high levels of corticosterone triggered submissive coping patterns. Henry and Stephens (1977) have proposed a model of the neuroendocrine response/psychosocial coping relationship. According to their model, the sympathetic-adrenal system is activated when the organism's control of the environment is challenged, while the pituitary-adrenal system is associated with loss of control and the conservation-withdrawal response.

Lundberg and Frankenhaeuser (1980) cite evidence that relate indices of pituitary-adrenal and sympathetic-adrenal activity to psychosocial coping patterns in male and female university students. Consistent with the model of Henry and Stephens (1977), they found the two neuroendocrine systems to respond selectively to different psychosocial conditions. Pituitary-adrenal activation (cortisol excretion) was shown to be associated with feelings of distress; the sympathetic-adrenal activation (adrenalin excretion) with feelings of alertness and action proneness.

Perceived well-being and change in the organism. The influence of perceived psychological and physical well-being on functional and structural change in the organism is evident in studies of self-rated health (physical well-being) and postillness adjustment. Heart surgery patients with higher levels of perceived physical well-being reportedly recovered faster (Brown & Rawlinson, 1975). Myocardial infarction patients with good perceived health showed higher levels of morale and faster return to gainful employment (Garrity, 1973). Singer, Garfinkel, Cohen, and Srole (1976) found self-assessment of health to be the stronger predictor of longevity. Schmale (1972) found that "giving up" psychologically in the presence of a disease (low perceived physical well-being) had a negative effect on the organism, leading to further physical deterioration. Simonton and Simonton (1975) observed that cancer patients who had undergone spontaneous remissions had also revisualized themselves as being in good health and had maintained such a positive image of themselves. In a systematic follow-up evaluation, patients with positive attitudes had good responses while patients with negative attitudes had poor responses to comparable cancer treatment.

Psychosocial coping and change in the organism. Psychosocial coping strategies exert an influence affecting functional and structural changes in the organism. If one can view the amount of physical exertion in an occupation as a form of coping behavior, then the work of Brackenridge (1979) on the relation between physical exertion and age at onset of Huntington's chorea serves as a suitable example. In this study, low and high levels of physical exertion were more potent precipitants of illness than intermediate levels. The age of onset of Huntington's chorea (functional and structural change) can be suppressed by as much as nine years under moderate levels of physical exertion.

Cohen and Lazarus (1973) report a study of how surgical patients coped with the threat of surgery and how this influenced postsurgical recovery. They interviewed patients the night before surgery to determine how they actually coped with the threat. They found that patients coping by avoidance-denial (repression) had a shorter hospital stay, fewer minor complications, and showed less distress compared to those who coped by vigilance (sensitization).

Perceived well-being and the neurophysiological response. The most significant pathway, from the point of view of a wellness concept, is the relation between perceived well-being and the neurophysiological system. It is also the least explored. Much of the animal and human research evidence has focussed on low levels of perceived well-being. For example, Henry (1979, 1981) and Henry and Stephens (1977) have summarized some of the evidence that links depression, distress, and helplessness with activation of the pituitary adrenal-cortical axis leading to increased cortical secretion. They labelled this state of the organism *dejection.*

In a study of suicidal patients described as being in psychic distress (feelings of worthlessness, attitudes of hopelessness), Bunney and Fawcett (1967) found significant elevation of 17-hydroxycorticosteroid (17-OHCS) in males and females compared to controls. The authors point out that the patient is not suicidal because of 17-OHCS levels; rather, the quality and magnitude of perceived distress is so great that it is reflected in biochemical changes in the body.

Evidence of the effect of high levels of perceived well-being on the neurophysiological system is scanty. Henry (1981) referred to the contrast pole of the pituitary adrenal cortical axis as *elation*, a state characterized by a sense of security, loss of ego boundaries, transcendent consciousness, and bliss. In this state, the pituitary adrenal-cortical axis is depressed and cortisol is decreased. The euphoric state appears to be due to the release of serotonin which activates high-voltage waves in the hippocampal septal system (Mandell, 1980).

In a rather interesting study of American combat troops in Vietnam, Bourne (1970) found that men with high morale and high motivation showed a *drop* in 17-OHCS levels. This finding is even more impressive considering their highly threatening environment. This study suggests that high levels of perceived well-being can modulate the intensity of the neuroendocrine response.

Perhaps the most significant breakthrough in understanding the link between perceived well-being and the neurophysiological system lies with the role of the endorphins, the natural brain chemicals whose effects are similar to morphine. Endorphins have been shown to modulate painful sensations, social behaviors, social emotions, and to ameliorate negative affect (Amir, Brown, & Amit, 1980; Bolles & Fanselow, 1982). Endorphins may be released naturally during moments of great joy and exhilaration, resulting in heightened psychological and physical well-being (see Heckenmueller, Chapter 5, this volume, for a fuller discussion of the role of endorphins and social behavior).

INTERVENTION FOR OPTIMAL AGING

An attempt has been made to describe and develop a model to facilitate the integration of existing research evidence pertaining to sources of variance in health-behavior relationships. In terms of practical intervention, the mosaic model is more concerned with psychosocial prescriptions for the prevention of illness and the promotion of health than with the remediation of pathological conditions. In that sense, it is a growth, not a deficit, model of health. Implicit in the model is the positive mental attitude of "older and growing" as opposed to the more negative view of "growing old." It is a model geared toward the treatment of psychosclerosis, better known as "hardening of the attitudes."

Practical application for optimal aging involves intervention at various choice points in the model. The type and quality of possible interventions at the level of precipitating events, cognitive/affective mediation, psychosocial coping, and the psychophysiological pathways will be presented and described briefly in this section.

Intervention at the level of precipitating events. The mosaic model places greater emphasis on the perception of events than on the events *per se.* Nevertheless, stressors possess a number of attributes or objective characteristics including ambiguity, affective valence, severity, chronicity, and multiplicity. Since a change in the objective attributes will lead to a change in the perception of those attributes, intervention at the level of precipitating events can be most effective by changing some or all of the objective attributes.

For example, the impact of a stressor has been shown to be a function of its ambiguity or unpredictability. In a review of relocation stress among institutionalized elderly, Schulz and Brenner (1977) reported that the stress level is reduced to the extent that the individual can predict and exercise some control over the relocation. Furthermore, when elaborate preparations for relocation are implemented, the negative effects are reduced (Zweig & Csank, 1975). Programs or procedures designed to reduce ambiguity or unpredictability in stressors will help reduce their negative consequences (Schulz, 1980).

It is also possible to decrease the number and duration of dissatisfying life events through environmental restructuring. This can be achieved in several ways including physical removal from the stressful environment, establishing personal priorities, and exercising effective time management so that a higher percentage of the time is spent in worthwhile activities.

Intervention at the level of cognitive/affective mediation.   Since the perception of events is a crucial intervening activity in the mosaic model, intervention at the level of cognitive/affective mediation will have an overriding influence on subsequent physiological response patterns and psychosocial coping styles. Possible intervention strategies include cognitive restructuring; mobilization of individual volition; alteration of values and attitudes; and lifestyle reevaluation and modification. Cognitive restructuring can take several forms: (1) cognitive redefinition; (2) cognitive problem-solving; and (3) emotional reconditioning. Cognitive redefinition involves changing the individual's perception of what constitutes a threat. Cognitive problem-solving strategies such as means-ends thinking (Spivack, Platt, & Shure, 1976) can expose the individual to a variety of alternative ways of construing events. Through affective reconditioning, the emotional impact of a stressor can be reduced by shifting the individual to the cognitive end of the cognitive/ affective continuum.

An individual's perceived sense of efficacy and control over his or her life and health is an important mediating factor. Both Selye (1974) and Pelletier (1977) have stressed the importance of mobilizing the individual's volition as a way of preventing and alleviating psychosomatic disorders. A sense of one's own volition can be fostered by embracing positive future expectations, finding meaning and purpose in life, and having a strong will to live.

It is also possible to alter values and attitudes and to induce a cognitive/affective reevaluation of lifestyles with the expectation that these will lead to significant behavioral shifts. Two promising techniques of lifestyle reevaluation are life review therapy (Butler, 1974) and guided autobiography (Birren & Hateley, 1981; Reedy & Birren, 1980).

Life review therapy includes taking an extensive autobiography from the older person and from other members of the family. The process of taking the individual back to former places and events evokes crucial memories and emotional responses. Life review therapy often results in reconciliation of family relationships, deeper understanding of life, and resolution of internal conflicts (Butler, 1974).

Guided autobiography is a structured, systematic approach to life review. It includes information exchange through lectures on human development; writing on selected autobiographical themes (e.g., personal history, family history); and the concept of developmental exchange or the process of small group discussion of the written autobiographies (Birren & Hateley, 1981).

Life review therapy and guided autobiography share a number of therapeutic components that have been shown to be effective in maintaining physical and mental health in the elderly. These are: (1) the opportunity to reminisce about the past; (2) the re-creation of social supports through reconciliation of family members; and

(3) the opportunity to place the past into time perspective that gives meaning and purpose to existence. Reedy and Birren (1980) cite evidence that guided autobiography facilitates the life review and results in greater self-acceptance, lower anxiety and tension, a greater sense of energy and vigor, a more positive view of others, and greater social connectedness. These positive indicators resemble the characteristics of personal optimism, commitment to life, and meaningfulness—the central mediators of the mosaic model.

Intervention at the level of psychosocial coping. Lazarus (1980) has identified two functions of psychosocial coping: instrumental or problem-solving and palliative or the regulation of emotional distress. Often, though not always, each coping mode supports the other. Effective copers use a combination of direct action and palliative coping strategies in dealing with stressful life situations.

Training in palliative and instrumental coping can alleviate illness and promote wellness. The adaptive value of reminiscence in alleviating depression, maintaining self-esteem, reinforcing personal identity, and reducing anxiety in the elderly have been well documented (Lieberman & Falk, 1971; McMahon & Rhudick, 1964; Pincus, 1970). The use of constructive procrastination, a strategy of "wait and see" and quiet reflection, may also have potential in reducing the negative effects of undesirable stressors. The technique of role playing in which problems can be rehearsed and solved under simulated conditions would appear to be a potentially useful approach to enhance the effectiveness of instrumental coping.

Perhaps the most promising techniques in which palliative and instrumental coping are mutually supportive involves the mobilization of the individual's personal resources to achieve high levels of psychological and physical well-being. This is the wellness concept of health. Implicit in the wellness concept is the assertion that the individual has the responsibility and the power to take control of his or her health.

The wellness concept is an approach that extends the medical treatment model beyond the alleviation of illness to a state of positive health through awareness, education, and growth (Ardell, 1977; Ryan & Travis, 1981). Ryan and Travis (1981) believe that high-level wellness is achieved through an assessment of self-responsibility, taking care of the physical self, using the mind constructively, channeling stressors positively, expressing emotions effectively, becoming creatively involved with others, and staying in touch with the environment. Through a program of exercises, idea exchanges, and personal challenges, the individual in a group environment is guided to marshal personal coping resources in four main areas: (1) stress control; (2) self-responsibility; (3) nutrition; and (4) physical fitness.

Since the focus is on the individual and on self-maintenance, the wellness concept has the potential for promoting higher levels of perceived psychological and physical well-being. Its effectiveness as a health enhancer will need to be demonstrated in future investigations.

Intervention at the level of psychophysiological pathways. Effective intervention at the psychophysiological pathways requires strategies that link the psychological with the physiological. One reciprocal pathway involving mental operations and physiological functions is the bridge between cognitive/affective mediators and the neurophysiological response types/patterns. Three promising intervention strategies appropriate at this level are meditation training, autogenic training, and visualization (Pelletier, 1977).

Meditation is an experiential exercise involving the individual's attentional mechanism. The goal of meditation is to gain mastery over attention. Meditation produces a pattern of response resulting in inhibition of the sympathetic nervous system. There is a slowing of breath and heart rate, lowering of blood pressure, decrease in oxygen consumption, decrease in skin conductivity, and the appearance of characteristic brain-wave patterns (Pelletier, 1977).

Autogenic training is a deep relaxation technique designed to induce simultaneous states of physiological and mental relaxation. The technique is similar to hypnosis and when practiced correctly and regularly, achieves an integrated low arousal state of mind and body. The relaxed state, however, is a passive physical one.

Visualization is an extension of autogenic training involving the holding of images in the mind for examination and exploration. This technique has been demonstrated to induce an increase in alpha rhythms in the brain as well as to deepen a hypnotic state (Pelletier, 1977).

Through meditation training, autogenic training, and visualization, the individual can learn to exercise direct control over the neurophysiological response and thereby prevent or alleviate the effects of stressors.

Intervention at the level of psychophysiological pathways can also involve the link between psychosocial coping styles/patterns and the neurophysiological response. The goal is to make the individual fully aware of how his or her current coping strategies are affecting the physiological system. The most promising technique to achieve this goal is biofeedback training.

Biofeedback training is an attempt to attain a state of relaxed internal awareness of the neurophysiological systems and how they are affected by external demands. It is based on three basic principles: (1) neurophysiological functions can be measured, amplified, and fed back to the individual through any one of the senses; (2) neurophysiological change is accompanied by mental/emotional change and vice-versa; and (3) autonomic functions can be brought under conscious control in an atmosphere of deep relaxation, provided that the individual obtains information about those functions (Pelletier, 1977). Unlike the meditative and deep relaxation techniques which induce a general relaxation response, biofeedback training can directly influence a particular organ system. For example, the high blood pressure of a hypertensive individual may not necessarily drop under meditative or deep relaxation strategies. With biofeedback, however, the specific physiological function can be isolated, monitored, and managed through instantaneous feedback.

Not only are these techniques useful in alleviating illness, they have their greatest value in the maintenance of health and well-being. The application of general relaxation methods such as meditation, autogenic training, and visualization in combination with the regulation of specific neurophysiological systems through biofeedback training captures the essence of the holistic treatment model. For a comprehensive review of the efficacy of these interventions as applied to hypertension, see Taylor (1980).

Most, if not all, of the intervention approaches discussed have focussed on resources that can be utilized effectively by the individual. We need to marshal the individual resources for collective application so that many more people in society can benefit from more effective coping strategies. Social networks, social support systems, and social institutions can provide the necessary vehicle. A discussion of how this might be accomplished, however, is beyond the scope of this chapter.

FUTURE PROSPECTS AND DIRECTIVES

A useful model should be able to incorporate much of the existing research literature, generate predictive statements, and provide a guide for future exploration. The usefulness of the mosaic model will depend on how well the cognitive/affective mediation concept can explain the complex network of psychosocial and physiological interrelationships between precipitating events and health outcomes.

The effects of precipitating events on health outcomes are measurable through the assessment of cognitive/affective mediators, observation of behavior, physiological measurement, and self-report data. Many retrospective and prospective studies have related dissatisfying life stressors to illness outcomes (Rabkin & Struening, 1976; Rahe, 1974; Rahe & Lind, 1971; Sales & House, 1971; Theorell & Rahe, 1971; Wyler, Masuda, & Holmes, 1971) and poor mental health (Dohrenwend & Dohrenwend, 1974; Paykel, 1974; Paykel et al., 1969; Vinokur & Selzer, 1975). The life stressors in these studies, however, rarely account for more than 10 percent of the variance in the dependent measures (Johnson & Sarason, 1978). Apart from method and measurement problems, the lack of attention to variables which mediate the effects of stressors may be the most important contributing factor accounting for the low correlation. Furthermore, while these studies demonstrate that stressful life events contribute to illness outcomes, it is also possible that illness-prone individuals have a lower tolerance to stressors and consequently different subjective experiences of stressors. Such *retrospective contamination* raises questions related to meaningful interpretation of stress data (Brown, 1972).

In most of the previously cited studies, the objective conditions of the stressors are confounded by the subjective perception of those events. One way of dealing with this problem is to measure objectively the level of stress represented by various precipitating events and to study the relationship between such events and health outcomes, independent of the individual's subjective experience. Conversely, one would measure the subjective experience of life and study the relationship between such events and health outcomes, independent of the objective conditions. In this way, the relative contribution of objective conditions and subjective experiences to health outcomes can be meaningfully examined.

A study (Reker, 1982) is currently underway to investigate the differential effects of objective conditions and subjective perception of desirable and undesirable events on health outcomes in the elderly. Subjects (65+ years) will be asked to rate recent life events on the 57-item Life Experience Survey (LES) developed by Sarason, Johnson, and Siegel (1978). The LES is similar to the 42-item Schedule of Recent Experiences (SRE; Holmes & Rahe, 1967) in that 34 items are common to both scales. The scales differ, however, in at least two important respects. First, the life change unit scores of the SRE represent mean adjustment ratings while the life change scores of the LES represent individualized ratings of desirability (positive and negative) and impact. Second, the SRE makes no distinction between desirable and undesirable events while the LES does. It is possible to apply group-derived values of the SRE to the common items on the LES and obtain a measure of the objective conditions of life. The individually derived scores of the LES can be used to measure the subjective perception of the same life events.

In addition to the LES, outcome measures of physical and psychological well-being (Reker & Wong, in press), self-rated physical health symptoms, and an objective assessment of physical health as rated by a physician will be obtained. Through analysis-of-variance and partial correlational techniques, it will be possible to assess the relative contribution of desirable and undesirable objective conditions and subjective experiences to health outcomes. Consistent with the cognitive/affective mediation concept of the mosaic model and based on previous findings (Fengler & Jensen, 1981; Keith & Dobson, 1977), it is predicted that the subjective experiences of undesirable life events will be more predictive of health outcomes than will the undesirable objective conditions of life. Support for the prediction should help to clarify the determinants of health problems.

Since not all health problems are preceded by identifiable stressors and since many individuals under stress do not become ill, life stress research must begin to specify *what* events influence *what* health problems under *what* conditions and by *what* mechanisms (Mechanic, 1974). Highly relevant to this line of inquiry is the important role of variables which moderate the effects of life stressors. To the extent that individuals are differentially affected by life events, the identification of such moderator variables should result in increased predictability of specific health outcomes. The available evidence points to social supports (see Heckenmueller, Chapter 5, this volume; Cobb, 1976; Silver & Wortman, 1981); perceived control (see Shupe, Chapter 8, this volume; Lefcourt, Martin, & Ebers, 1981); personality factors (Garrity, Somes, & Marx, 1977; Kobasa, 1979); stimulation seeking and level of arousability (Johnson & Sarason, 1979) as potentially important moderator variables. Two additional cognitive/affective mediators that have not received sufficient attention are personal optimism and meaningfulness. Consistent with predictions based on the mosaic model, personal optimism and meaningfulness should account for an increased proportion of the variance in health outcomes (see Reker & Wong, Chapter 7, this volume, for a fuller discussion of personal optimism).

Of equal importance are studies designed to investigate how the neurophysiological systems influence and are influenced by the moderator variables, psychosocial coping styles/patterns, and perceived well-being. One line of inquiry should be directed toward establishing whether negative and positive life events lead to different neuroendocrine response profiles as might be predicted based on the work of Mason et al. (1976) and Weiss et al. (1979). While more is known of the impact of negative life changes on the organism, very little research relates positive life events to neurophysiological responses. Much more work needs to be done in this important preventive health area.

Along similar lines, several investigators have attempted to establish a link between the cognitively mediated construct of hopelessness and suppression of the vital immune responses leading to cancer (Goldfarb, Driesen, & Cole, 1967; Pelletier, 1977; Simonton, Matthews-Simonton, & Creighton, 1978). However, many of these studies are retrospective and open to varying interpretations. Although some promising results have emerged, more systematic investigations of the links between psychosocial factors and the immunological system are needed (see Reker & Wong, Chapter 7, this volume).

A full understanding of the mediating mechanisms that reduce illness and promote wellness will require retrospective and prospective investigations both within the same individuals across a wide variety of occasions or over time and across individuals of different ages. Within the mosaic model, the ultimate goal is to identify the bidirectional influence of life stressors on health outcomes and to assess their predictive power.

Innovative research designs and methodologies are required to pinpoint the multiple paths of influence. Lazarus (1980) has argued strongly for a balance between inter-individual and intra-individual perspectives in research and proposes that more use be made of ipsative-normative research designs. New methodologies that appear to be promising are path analysis (Werts & Linn, 1970), causal analysis (Heise, 1975), cross-lagged panel correlation (Kenny, 1975), and linear structural relations (LISREL) methodology (Joreskog & Sorbom, 1979). All are methods of decomposing and interpreting linear relationships among a set of variables and testing a limited set of causal hypotheses. A full description of these methods is beyond the scope of this chapter. For an assessment of the potential of cross-lagged correlation, see Clegg, Jackson, and Wall (1977); for an application of cross-lags to life stress research, see Vossel and Froehlich (1979); and for an application of causal analysis to job stress and essential hypertension, see Weyer and Hodapp (1979). The LISREL methodology is particularly relevant to the mosaic model because of its ability to handle latent factors, multiple indicators, measurement error, reciprocal causation, and multiple population comparisons (Joreskog & Sorbom, 1979). For a nontechnical presentation and application of LISREL to studies of aging, see Campbell and Mutran (1982).

We are on the brink of exciting new breakthroughs in medical and biological technologies and preventive health care. The time has come for a new interdisciplinary perspective that places equal emphasis on behavioral medicine and behavioral health (Matararazzo, 1980, 1982). The bottom line of all of our efforts is the extension of life through the prevention of disease and the promotion of wellness.

REFERENCES

ABRAHAMS, J. P., HOYER, W. J., ELIAS, M. F., & BRADIGAN, B. (1975). Gerontological research in psychology published in the Journal of Gerontology 1963-1974: Perspectives and progress. *Journal of Gerontology, 30,* 668-673.

AMIR, S., BROWN, Z. W., & AMIT, Z. (1980). The role of endorphins in stress: Evidence and speculations. *Neuroscience and Biobehavioral Reviews, 4,* 77-86.

ANTONOVSKY, A. (1979). *Health, stress, and coping.* San Francisco: Jossey-Bass.

ARDELL, D. D. (1977). *High-level wellness: An alternative to doctors, drugs, and disease.* Emmaus, PA: Rodale Press.

BIRREN, J. E., & HATELEY, B. J. (1981). Psychological development through autobiography (Course outline). University of Southern California, Los Angeles, Andrus Gerontology Centre, Summer Institute for Study in Gerontology.

BLOOMFIELD, H. H., & KORY, R. B. (1978). *The holistic way to health and happiness.* New York: Simon & Schuster.

BOLLES, R. C., & FANSELOW, M. S. (1982). Endorphins and behavior. *Annual Review of Psychology, 33,* 87-101.

BOURNE, P. G. (1970). *Men, stress, and Vietnam.* Boston: Little, Brown.

BRACKENRIDGE, C. J. (1979). Relation of occupational stress to the age at onset of Huntington's disease. *Acta Neurologica Scandinavica, 60*, 272–276.

BROWN, G. W. (1972). Life-events and psychiatric illness: Some thoughts on methodology and causality. *Journal of Psychosomatic Research, 16*, 311–320.

BROWN, J. S., & RAWLINSON, M. (1975). Relinquishing the sick role following open-heart surgery. *Journal of Health and Social Behavior, 16*, 12–27.

BUNNEY, W. E., & FAWCETT, J. A. (1967). 17-Hydrocorticosteroid excretion prior to severe suicidal behavior. In N. L. Farberow (Ed.), *Proceedings of the Fourth International Conference for Suicide Prevention* (pp. 128–139). Los Angeles: University Park Press.

BUTLER, R. N. (1974). Successful aging and the role of the life review. *Journal of the American Geriatrics Society, 22*, 529–535.

CAMPBELL, R. T., & MUTRAN, E. (1982). Analyzing panel data in studies of aging: Applications of the LISREL model. *Research on Aging, 4*, 3–41.

CAPLAN, G. (1981). Mastery of stress: Psychosocial aspects. *The American Journal of Psychiatry, 138*, 413–420.

CLEGG, C. W., JACKSON, P. R., & WALL, T. D. (1977). The potential of cross-lagged correlation analysis in field research. *Journal of Occupational Psychology, 50*, 177–196.

COBB, S. (1974). A model for life events and their consequences. In B. S. Dohrenwend & B. P. Dohrenwend (Eds.), *Stressful life events: Their nature and effects* (pp. 151–156). New York: John Wiley.

COBB, S. (1976). Social support as a moderator of life stress. *Psychosomatic Medicine, 38*, 300–314.

COELHO, G. V., HAMBURG, D. A., & ADAMS, J. E. (1974). *Coping and adaptation.* New York: Basic Books.

COHEN, F., & LAZARUS, R. S. (1973). Active coping processes, coping dispositions, and recovery from surgery. *Psychosomatic Medicine, 35*, 375–389.

CORBY, N., & SOLNICK, R. L. (1980). Psychosocial and physiological influences on sexuality in the older adult. In J. E. Birren & R. B. Sloane (Eds.), *Handbook of mental health and aging* (pp. 893–921). Englewood Cliffs, NJ: Prentice-Hall.

DeVRIES, H. A., & ADAMS, G. M. (1972). Electromyographic comparison of single doses of exercise and meprobamate as to effects on muscular relaxation. *American Journal of Physical Medicine, 51*, 130–141.

DOHRENWEND, B. S., & DOHRENWEND, B. P. (1974). Overview and prospects for research on stressful life events. In B. S. Dohrenwend & B. P. Dohrenwend (Eds.), *Stressful life events: Their nature and effects* (pp. 313–331). New York: John Wiley.

EISDORFER, C., & WILKIE, F. (1977). Stress, disease and behavior. In J. E. Birren & K. W. Schaie (Eds.), *Handbook of the psychology of aging* (pp. 251–275). New York: Van Nostrand Reinhold.

FARBER, M. L. (1967). Suicide and hope: A theoretical analysis. In N. L. Farberow (Ed.), *Proceedings of the Fourth International Conference for Suicide Prevention* (pp. 297–306). Los Angeles: University Park Press.

FENGLER, A. P., & JENSEN, L. (1981). Perceived and objective conditions as predictors of life satisfaction of urban and non-urban elderly. *Journal of Gerontology, 36*, 750–752.

FRIEDMAN, M., & ROSENMAN, R. H. (1974). *Type A behavior and your heart.* New York: Knopf.

GARRITY, T. F. (1973). Social involvement and activeness as predictors of morale six months after first myocardial infarction. *Social Science and Medicine, 7*, 199–207.

GARRITY, T. F., SOMES, G. W., & MARX, M. B. (1977). Personality factors in resistance to illness after recent life changes. *Journal of Psychosomatic Research, 21,* 23–32.

GARRITY, T. F., SOMES, G. W., & MARX, M. B. (1978). Factors influencing self-assessment of health. *Social Science and Medicine, 12,* 77–81.

GEORGE, L. K., & BEARON, L. B. (1980). *Quality of life in older persons: Meaning and measurement.* New York: Human Sciences.

GOLDFARB, O., DRIESEN, J., & COLE, D. (1967). Psychophysiologic aspects of malignancy. *American Journal of Psychiatry, 123,* 1545–1551.

GUZE, S. B., MATARAZZO, J. D., & SASLOW, G. (1953). A formulation of principles of comprehensive medicine with special reference to learning theory. *Journal of Clinical Psychology, 9,* 127–136.

HEISE, D. R. (1975). *Causal analysis.* New York: John Wiley.

HENRY, J. P. (1979, September). *Present concept of stress theory.* Paper presented at the Second International Symposium on Catecholamines and Stress, Czechoslovakia.

HENRY, J. P. (1981). *The relation of social to biological processes in disease.* Unpublished manuscript, University of Southern California, School of Medicine, Los Angeles.

HENRY, J. P., & STEPHENS, P. M. (1977). *Stress, health and the social environment: A sociobiologic approach to medicine.* New York: Springer-Verlag.

HOLMES, T. H., & RAHE, R. H. (1967). The social readjustment rating scale. *Journal of Psychosomatic Research, 11,* 213–218.

HULL, D. (1977). Life circumstances and physical illness: A cross disciplinary survey of research content and method for the decade 1965–1975. *Journal of Psychosomatic Research, 21,* 115–139.

ISO, A. S. E. (1980). Perceived control and responsibility as mediators of the effects of therapeutic recreation on the institutionalized aged. *Therapeutic Recreation Journal, 14,* 36–43.

JENKINS, C. D. (1971). Psychologic and social precursors of coronary disease. *New England Journal of Medicine, 284,* 244–255, 307–317.

JENKINS, C. D. (1976). Recent evidence supporting psychologic and social risk factors for coronary disease. *New England Journal of Medicine, 294,* 987–994, 1033–1038.

JOHNSON, J. H., & SARASON, I. G. (1978). Recent developments in research on life stress (Technical Report SCS-LS-006). Arlington, VA: Office of Naval Research.

JOHNSON, J. H., & SARASON, I. G. (1979). Moderator variables in life stress research. In I. G. Sarason & C. D. Spielberger (Eds.), *Stress and anxiety* (Vol. 6, pp. 151–164). Washington, DC: Hemisphere.

JORESKOG, K. G., & SORBOM, D. (1979). *Advances in factor analysis and structural equation models.* Cambridge, MA: ABT Books.

KAGAN, A. R., & LEVI, L. (1974). Health and environment-psychosocial stimuli: A review. *Social Science and Medicine, 8,* 225–241.

KATZ, J. L., WEINER, H., GALLAGHER, T. F., & HELLMAN, L. (1970). Stress, distress, and ego defenses: Psychoendocrine response to impending breast tumor biopsy. *Archives of General Psychiatry, 23,* 131–142.

KEITH, P., & DOBSON, C. (1977). Change, perceived change, and life satisfaction. *Gerontologist, 17* (Part I), 81.

KENNY, D. A. (1975). Cross-lagged panel correlation: A test for spuriousness. *Psychological Bulletin, 82,* 887–903.

KOBASA, S. C. (1979). Stressful life events, personality and health: An inquiry into hardiness. *Journal of Personality and Social Psychology, 37,* 1–11.

KRANTZ, D. S. (1980). Cognitive processes and recovery from heart attack: A review and theoretical analysis. *Journal of Human Stress, 6,* 27-38.

KUYPERS, J. A. (1972). The internal-external locus of control and ego functioning correlates in the elderly. *The Gerontologist 2,* 168-173.

LALONDE, M. (1974). *A new perspective on the health of Canadians.* Ottawa, Ontario: Ministry of National Health and Welfare.

LANGER, E. J., & RODIN, J. (1976). The effect of choice and enhanced personal responsibility for the aged. A field experiment in an institutional setting. *Journal of Personality and Social Psychology, 34,* 191-198.

LARSON, R. (1978). Thirty years of research on the subjective well-being of older Americans. *Journal of Gerontology, 33,* 109-125.

LAZARUS, R. (1966). *Psychological stress and the coping process.* New York: McGraw-Hill.

LAZARUS, R. (1980). The stress and coping paradigm. In L. A. Bond & J. C. Rosen (Eds.), *Competence and coping during adulthood.* Hanover, CT: University Press of New England.

LAZARUS, R. S., AVERILL, J. R., & OPTON, E. M. (1974). The psychology of coping: Issues of research and assessment. In G. V. Coelho, D. A. Hamburg, & J. E. Adams (Eds.), *Coping and adaptation* (pp. 249-315). New York: Basic Books.

LEFCOURT, H. M. (1976). *Locus of control: Current trends in theory and research.* Hillsdale, NJ: Erlbaum-Wiley.

LEFCOURT, H. M., MARTIN, R. A., & EBERS, K. (1981). Coping with stress: A model for clinical psychology. *Academic Psychological Bulletin, 3,* 355-364.

LIEBERMAN, M. A., & FALK, M. (1971). The remembered past as a source of data for research on the life cycle. *Human Development, 14,* 132-141.

LOUIS HARRIS AND ASSOCIATES. (1975). *The myth and reality of aging in America.* Washington, DC: National Council on Aging.

LUNDBERG, U., & FRANKENHAEUSER, M. (1980). Pituitary-adrenal and sympathetic-adrenal correlates of distress and effort. *Journal of Psychosomatic Research, 24,* 125-130.

MANCINI, J. A. (1980). Effects of health and income on control orientation and life satisfaction among aged public housing residents. *International Journal of Aging and Human Development, 12,* 215-220.

MANDELL, A. J. (1980). Toward a psychobiology of transcendence: God in the brain. In J. M. Davidson & R. J. Davidson (Eds.), *The psychobiology of consciousness* (pp. 379-464). New York: Plenum.

MARMOT, M. G., & SYME, S. L. (1976). Acculturation and coronary heart disease in Japanese-Americans. *American Journal of Epidemiology, 104,* 225-247.

MASON, J. W., MAHER, J. T., HARTLEY, L. H., MOUGEY, E. H., PERLOW, M. J., & JONES, L. G. (1976). Selectivity of corticosteroid and catecholamine responses to various natural stimuli. In G. Serban (Ed.), *Psychopathology of human adaptation* (pp. 147-171). New York: Plenum.

MATARAZZO, J. D. (1980). Behavioral health and behavioral medicine: Frontiers for a new health psychology. *American Psychologist, 35* (9), 807-817.

MATARAZZO, J. D. (1982). Behavioral health's challenge to academic, scientific, and professional psychology. *American Psychologist, 37* (1), 1-14.

McCRAE, R. R. (1981). *Age differences in the use of coping mechanisms.* Paper presented at the 34th Annual Meeting of the Gerontological Society of America, Toronto, Ontario, Canada.

McMAHON, A., & RHUDICK, P. (1964). Reminiscing: Adaptational significance in the aged. *Archives of General Psychiatry, 10,* 292-298.

MECHANIC, D. (1974). Discussion of research programs on relations between stressful life events and episodes of physical illness. In B. S. Dohrenwend & B. P. Dohrenwend (Eds.), *Stressful life events: Their nature and effects* (pp. 87–97). New York: John Wiley.

MOOS, R. H. (1981). *Creating healthy human context: Environmental and individual strategies.* Paper presented at the Annual Meeting of the American Psychological Association, Los Angeles.

MOSSEY, J. M., & SHAPIRO, E. (1982). Self-rated health: A predictor of mortality among the elderly. *American Journal of Public Health, 72,* 800–808.

MUELLER, D. P., EDWARDS, D. W., & YARVIS, R. M. (1977). Stressful life events and psychiatric symptomatology: Change as undesirability. *Journal of Health and Social Behavior, 18,* 307–317.

MYERS, J. K., LINDENTHAL, J. J., & PEPPER, M. P. (1974). Social class, life events, and psychiatric symptoms: A longitudinal study. In B. S. Dohrenwend & B. P. Dohrenwend (Eds.), *Stressful life events: Their nature and effects* (pp. 191–205). New York: John Wiley.

PAYKEL, E. S. (1974). Life stress and psychiatric disorder: Applications of the clinical approach. In B. S. Dohrenwend & B. P. Dohrenwend (Eds.), *Stressful life events: Their nature and effects* (pp. 135–149). New York: John Wiley.

PAYKEL, E. S., MYERS, J. K., DIENELT, M. N., KLERMAN, G. L., LINDENTHAL, J. J., & PEPPER, M. P. (1969). Life events and depression: A controlled study. *Archives of General Psychiatry, 21,* 753–760.

PELLETIER, K. R. (1977). *Mind as healer, mind as slayer.* New York: Dell Pub. Co., Inc.

PINCUS, A. (1970, July). Reminiscence on aging and its implication for social work practice. *Social Work,* 47–53.

PRINZ, P. N. (1977). Sleep patterns in the healthy aged: Relationship with intellectual function. *Journal of Gerontology, 32,* 179–186.

RABKIN, J. G., & STRUENING, E. L. (1976). Life events, stress, and illness. *Science, 194,* 1013–1020.

RAHE, R. H. (1974). The pathway between subjects' recent life changes and their near-future illness reports: Representative results and methodological issues. In B. S. Dohrenwend & B. P. Dohrenwend (Eds.), *Stressful life events: Their nature and effects* (pp. 73–86). New York: John Wiley.

RAHE, R. H., & LIND, E. (1971). Psychosocial factors and sudden cardiac death: A pilot study. *Journal of Psychosomatic Research, 15,* 19–24.

REEDY, M. N., & BIRREN, J. E. (1980, September). *Life review through guided autobiography.* Poster presentation at the Annual Meeting of the American Psychological Association, Montreal.

REKER, G. T. (1982). *The differential effects of objective conditions and subjective experiences of desirable and undesirable life events on health outcomes in the elderly.* Unpublished manuscript. Trent University, Peterborough, Ontario.

REKER, G.T., & WONG, P.T.P. (in press). Psychological and physical well-being in the elderly: The Perceived Well-Being Scale (PWB). *Canadian Journal on Aging.*

ROSENBERG, E. T., & DOHRENWEND, B. S. (1975). Effects of experiences and ethnicity on ratings of life events as stressors. *Journal of Health and Social Behavior, 16,* 127-129.

RYAN, R. S., & TRAVIS, J. W. (1981). *The wellness workbook.* Berkeley, CA: Ten Speed Press.

SALES, S. M., & HOUSE, J. S. (1971). Job dissatisfaction as a possible risk factor in coronary heart disease. *Journal of Chronic Disabilities, 23,* 861–873.

SARASON, I. G., JOHNSON, J. H., & SIEGEL, J. M. (1978). Assessing the impact of life changes: Development of the Life Experiences Survey. *Journal of Counselling and Clinical Psychology, 46* (6), 932–946.

SCHMALE, A. H. (1972). Giving up as a final common pathway to changes in health. *Advances in Psychosomatic Medicine, 8,* 18–28.

SCHULZ, R. (1980). Aging and control. In J. Garber & M. E. P. Seligman (Eds.), *Human helplessness: Theory and applications* (pp. 261–277). New York: Academic Press.

SCHULZ, R., & BRENNER, G. (1977). Relocation of the aged: A review and theoretical analysis. *Journal of Gerontology, 32,* 323–333.

SCHWARTZ, G. E. (1980, Winter). Behavioral medicine and systems theory: A new synthesis. *National Forum,* 25–30.

SELYE, H. (1956). *The stress of life.* New York: McGraw-Hill.

SELYE, H. (1974). *Stress without distress.* New York: Signet.

SHANAS, E., TOWNSEND, P., WEDDERBURN, D., FRIIS, H., MILHOJ, P., & STEHOUWER, J. (1968). The psychology of health. In E. Shanas (Ed.), *Old people in three industrial societies* (pp. 18–70). New York: Atherton Press.

SHERWOOD, S. (1977). Sociological factors in nutrition for the elderly. In R. A. Kalish (Ed.), *The later years: Social applications of gerontology* (pp. 186–189). Monterey, CA: Brooks/Cole.

SILVER, R. I., & WORTMAN, C. B. (1981). Coping with undesirable life events. In J. Garber & M.E.P. Seligman (Eds.), *Human helplessness: Theory and application* (pp. 274–340). New York: Academic Press.

SIMONTON, O. C., MATTHEWS-SIMONTON, S., & CREIGHTON, J. L. (1978). *Getting well again.* New York: Bantam.

SIMONTON, O. C., & SIMONTON, S. (1975). Belief systems and management of the emotional aspects of malignancy. *Journal of Transpersonal Psychology, 7* (1), 29–48.

SINGER, E., GARFINKEL, R., COHEN, S. W., & SROLE, L. (1976). Mortality and mental health: Evidence from the Midtown Manhattan restudy. *Social Science and Medicine, 10,* 517–525.

SPIVACK, G., PLATT, J. J., & SHURE, M. B. (1976). *Problem-solving approach to adjustment* (1st ed.). San Francisco: Jossey-Bass.

STEINITZ, L. Y. (1980) Religiosity, well-being, and weltanschauung among the elderly. *Journal for the Scientific Study of Religion, 19,* 60–67.

STRICKLAND, B. L. (1978). Internal-external expectancies and health-related behavior. *Journal of Consulting and Clinical Psychology, 46,* 1192–1211.

TAYLOR, C. B. (1980). Behavioral approaches to hypertension. In J. M. Ferguson & C. B. Taylor (Eds.), *The comprehensive handbook of behavioral medicine* (Vol. 1, pp. 55–88). New York: SP Medical and Scientific Books.

THEORELL, T., & RAHE, R. H. (1971). Psychosocial factors and myocardial infarction. I: An inpatient study in Sweden. *Journal of Psychosomatic Research, 15,* 25–31.

THOMAE, H. (1981). Expected unchangeability of life stress in old age: A contribution to a cognitive theory of aging. *Human Development, 24,* 229–239.

U.S. PUBLIC HEALTH SERVICE. (1972). *Limitation of activity due to chronic conditions.* Washington, DC: Government Printing Office.

U.S. PUBLIC HEALTH SERVICE. NATIONAL CENTER FOR HEALTH STATISTICS. (1971). *Health in the later years of life.* Washington, DC: Government Printing Office.

U.S. PUBLIC HEALTH SERVICE. NATIONAL CENTER FOR HEALTH STATIS-

TICS. (1974). *Vital statistics of the United States: Vol. II. Mortality.* Washington, DC: Government Printing Office.

VINOKUR, A., & SELZER, M. L. (1975). Desirable versus undesirable life events: Their relationship to stress and mental distress. *Journal of Personality and Social Psychology, 32,* 329–337.

VOSSEL, G., & FROEHLICH, W. D. (1979). Life stress, job tension and subjective reports of task performance effectiveness: A cross-lagged correlational analysis. In I. G. Sarason & C. D. Spielberger (Eds.), *Stress and anxiety* (Vol. 6, pp. 199–211). Washington, DC: Hemisphere.

WATSON, W. H. (1982). *Aging and social behavior: An introduction to social gerontology* (pp. 267–280). Monterey, CA: Wadsworth Health Sciences.

WEISS, J. M., GLAZER, H. I., POHORECKY, L. A., BAILEY, W. H., & SCHNEIDER, L. H. (1979). Coping behavior and stress-induced behavioral depression: Studies of the role of brain catecholamines. In R. A. Depue (Ed.), *The psychobiology of the depressive disorders* (pp. 125–160). New York: Academic Press.

WERTS, C. E., & LINN, R. L. (1970). Path analysis: Psychological examples. *Psychological Bulletin, 74,* 193–212.

WEYER, G., & HODAPP, V. (1979). Job stress and essential hypertension. In I. G. Sarason & C. D. Spielberger (Eds.), *Stress and anxiety* (Vol. 6, pp. 151–164). Washington, DC: Hemisphere.

WILLIAMS, R. B., HANEY, T. L., LEE, K. L., KONG, T.-H., BLUMENTHAL, J. A., & WHALEN, R. E. (1980). Type A behavior, hostility and coronary atherosclerosis. *Psychosomatic Medicine, 42,* 539–549.

WISWELL, R. A. (1980). Relaxation, exercise and aging. In J. E. Birren & R. B. Sloane (Eds.), *Handbook of mental health and aging* (pp. 943–958). Englewood Cliffs, NJ: Prentice-Hall.

WONG, P.T.P., & REKER, G. T. (1982, November). *Coping strategies and wellbeing in Caucasian and Chinese elderly.* Paper presented at the 11th Annual Meeting of the Canadian Association on Gerontology, Winnipeg, Manitoba.

WONG, P.T.P., & SPROULE, C. F. (1984). An attribution analysis of locus of control and the Trent Attribution Profile. In H. M. Lefcourt (Ed.), *Research with the locus of control construct* (Vol. 3, 309–360). New York: Academic Press.

WYLER, A. R., MASUDA, M., & HOLMES, T. H. (1971). Magnitude of life events and seriousness of illness. *Psychosomatic Medicine, 33,* 115–122.

ZOLA, I. K. (1966). Culture and symptoms: An analysis of patients' presenting complaints. *American Sociological Review, 31*(5), 615–630.

ZWEIG, J. P., & CSANK, J. Z. (1975). Effects of relocation on chronically ill geriatric patients of a medical unit: Mortality rates. *Journal of the American Geriatrics Society, 23,* 132–136.

4

AFFECTIONAL BONDING AND THE ELDERLY BEREAVED

Joan B. Stoddard and James P. Henry

Although it had been known for some time that widowers incur a higher mortality rate than married men (Parkes, 1972), the first large-scale study of that phenomenon was published by Young, Benjamin, and Wallis in 1963. They reported that during the first six months after bereavement a group of elderly widowers showed a forty percent higher mortality rate than married men of the same age. Rees and Lutkin (1967) found that widows and widowers had a twelve percent higher mortality rate than married persons; however, while later investigations were able to provide further evidence for the effect of widowerhood on men, the findings with regard to women were inconclusive (Helsing, Szklo, & Comstock, 1981; Parkes, Benjamin, & Fitzgerald, 1969; Mellstrom, Nilsson, Oden, Rundgren, & Svanborg, 1981; Stroebe, Stroebe, Gerber, & Gerber, 1981; Ward, 1976).

The present chapter is intended to explore the question of the sex differential in the effect of widowhood on the elderly. An analogy will be drawn to another sex differential which, it will be suggested, may be related to the first—namely, the greater tendency of women to make and maintain confidant, or close, intimate friendships with persons other than their spouses (Komarovsky, 1962; Lowenthal & Haven, 1968; Powers & Bultena, 1976).

Specifically, the purpose of this chapter will be to discuss the effect of spousal bereavement on the elderly in terms of the loss of an affectional bond.

Affectional bonds have been defined by Bowlby (1979) as occurring when two people feel strongly drawn to each other; when an introspective feeling of positive emotion exists between two people; and when the two feel anxiety, grief, and depression following separation.

A further criterion is also being employed in the use of the term *affectional bond* in this chapter. Weiss (1973) proposed a theoretical dichotomization among personal relationships for his discussion of the phenomenon of loneliness. While there may be many levels of intensity among relationships, Weiss suggested that an arbitrary division could be made between those that are characterized by a high degree of emotional intensity, e.g., Bowlby's affectional bond (1979), and those that exist on a more casual, or social level. For example, a marital relationship might represent an affectional bond depending upon the quality of the relationship existing between the two partners. A person with several siblings might have an affectionally bonded relationship with one or more of them and casual relationships with the others; or he or she may have an affectionally bonded relationship to a close friend, to a parent, or to a child, and feel less close to his or her siblings. In brief, the existence of an affectional bond is determined solely by the strength of positive feeling two people have for each other, and not arbitrarily by social, legal, or blood relationships (Barrett, 1981; Beckman, 1981; Wentowski, 1981).

Other relationships or friendships that do not meet the criteria of affectional bonds form an important part of one's social network, but the distinction between the two areas must be observed. A loss of an affectional bond cannot be compensated for by a large social network unless one of the relationships in that network undergoes a qualitative change (Barrett, 1981; Weiss, 1973). A person with a larger social network has a greater chance of having more affectionally bonded relationships, e.g., confidants (Lowenthal & Haven, 1968), but the fact that the social network provides a potential source from which such relationships are recruited does not imply equality between the two groups. According to Weiss's theory, both kinds of relationships are necessary to the happiness of the individual; however, it will be argued here that it is the affectional bond which is crucial to an individual's mental and physical health because of the more intense emotional involvement of the individual in the relationship (Beckman, 1981).

Finally, one more thing should be said in regard to the proposal for the use of affectional bonds as a research variable (as will be recommended in this chapter). In the social sciences one can only propose solutions to problems in the terms in which the research was designed. For example, if a piece of research shows that married men have a lower mortality rate from heart disease than widowers, the only recommendation which could be made on the basis of that data would be to do more research to establish a causal connection between marriage and longevity, and then encourage all widowers to remarry (e.g., Helsing, Szklo, & Comstock, 1981). Moreover, if no effect was found for bereavement among women, the problems of widows would, by the protocol for reporting and discussing results, be denied further comment by the investigators. On the other hand, if one were to consider the possibility that women are more likely than men to have an affectionally bonded relationship with a person other than their spouse—i.e., a confidant (Bell, 1981; Komarovsky, 1962; Lowenthal & Haven, 1968)—one could then ask if there was a difference in the survivorship of widows who maintained such a confidant relationship and those who did not. Thereafter that data could be related to the survivorship of widowers and a general suggestion might be made in favor of encouraging widowers to establish new affectional bonds, including, but not limited to, marriage as a means of coping with the stress of their bereavement.

MARITAL STATUS AS A VARIABLE

The use of marital status as an independent variable has a long history in socio-logical and psychological literature. Because population statistics included such information as marital status, religion, and number of children, sociologists were able to compare specific segments of the population using these parameters in order to formulate theories about the effect of social group membership on the behavior and well-being of individuals. For example, as a result of his statistical research, Durkheim (1897/1951) theorized that marriage conferred on individuals a *coeffi-cient of preservation* from suicide. By that he meant that while marriage would not prevent suicide, a man who was married was statistically less likely to commit suicide than one who was not.

Such methods may allow certain observations to be made on a global level, but they are unsatisfactory for finer analyses of the mechanisms involved in human emotional responses. Use of marital status as a descriptive variable divides the entire population into four categories (never married, married, formerly married but pres-ently divorced, and formerly married but presently widowed). These categories can be considered as mutually exclusive only within the limited time in which a particu-lar piece of research is carried out.

Marital status is a temporary condition, and is more accurately considered as a series of stages through which people move during their lifetimes. Married per-sons consist of those who were formerly single, widowed, or divorced. Those who are widowed or divorced were formerly married, and before that they were single. Those who are single may later choose to marry.

As to their feelings of life satisfaction, or their morale, it should be recog-nized that all marriages are not necessarily happy (Bohannon, 1970; Campbell, 1975). Presently, divorces equal between one-third and one-half the number of marriages in the United States (U.S. Bureau of Census, 1981). Many divorced per-sons, and widowed persons as well, may feel that their present status is one of relief or independence. By the same token, divorce may, particularly for an unwillingly divorced partner, be more traumatic and grievous than the experience of widow-hood since it involves not only the loss of an affectional bond, but also rejection by the former spouse (Bohannon, 1970). Single persons may be entirely satisfied with their lifestyle, or they may be living with a lover so that they are single only in a legal sense.

Considering the many possible emotional states subsumed under the four marital statuses, one may make two assumptions about the use of marital status as a research variable: (1) an underlying mechanism, congruent to some extent with marital status, is influencing sociological and psychological research results; and (2) that mechanism is sufficiently robust so that it can exert its influence on research results despite the heterogeneity of the relationships within each of the marital statuses.

These assumptions may be tested in the following manner: (1) it must be shown that under certain conditions marital status does not of itself produce the expected effect of increasing longevity; (2) that factors other than marital status can exert the same kind of influence on physiological health and well-being as that commonly attributed to marriage; and (3) that within one marital status (i.e., married persons) this factor can differentiate among people by condition of health.

Five studies have been selected from the social science and medical science literature as examples of the kinds of research that would support the assumptions stated above.

1. Helsing et al. (1981) found that widowers incurred a higher risk of death from heart disease than did married men. However, it was also noted that those widowers who remarried regained the same lower level of risk from heart disease as they had shown prior to their bereavement. This would seem to indicate that the higher risk of heart disease among the widowers who did not remarry was due to the uncompensated loss of an affectionally bonded relationship, rather than to the fact of their being widowed.

2. In 1958 a longitudinal study was begun in the towns of Chapel Hill and Carboro, North Carolina, to test the efficacy of various predictors of longevity (Stone in Palmore & Stone, 1973). Over 900 people 60 years of age or older were interviewed, and information was gathered on their sociological and psychological characteristics. In 1971 Palmore and Stone did a follow-up study to determine which of these data best predicted longevity. The researchers were able to contact or determine the fate of 864 of the original participants in the study. On the basis of their evaluation of the data, they reported that marital status was not a predictor of longevity for either sex. The fact that such a large number of the original sample could be accounted for after 13 years gives some indication of the stability of the population and their social network. It is very likely that the regional tendency toward maintaining close, multigenerational ties with one's family and lifelong friends was part of the pattern of life for the inhabitants of these towns (Scott, 1970). Since, in this study marital status did not differentially affect longevity, one might surmise that some other factor, perhaps proximity to friends and relatives, or the existence of affectional bonds with one or more of those people, acted as a uniform mechanism to promote longevity among persons regardless of their marital status.

3. In a study of suicides among elderly widowed persons, Bock and Webber (1972) found that those who had relatives living nearby or who belonged to one or more organizations were less likely to commit suicide than were widowed persons possessing neither of these social attachments. An individual who had both characteristics (i.e., relatives living nearby and organizational ties) was least likely to commit suicide. These data support the early findings of Durkheim that other social ties could supply coefficients of preservation similar in effect to marriage.

Bock and Webber did not try to evaluate the quality of the ties in assessing their effects in preventing suicide. However two additional studies point out the importance of considering this facet of relationships in social research.

4. Lowenthal and Haven (1968) investigated the effect of intimacy and confidant relationships on the morale and feeling of life satisfaction among the elderly. They found, as expected, that among the married persons, there were a higher percentage who were satisfied with their lives compared to the percentage of satisfied persons among the widowed. However, when the married group was compared with

the widowed, the results clarified the aspect of marriage that contributed to feelings of life satisfaction. They found that widowed persons with confidants were more likely to report higher degrees of life satisfaction than were married persons who did not name a confidant. The significance of this result can be seen in the fact that persons interviewed were allowed to name anyone, including their spouse, as a confidant. They were asked simply, "Is there anyone in particular you confide in, or talk to about yourself or your problems?" (p. 22). A married person who did not name his or her spouse in response to that question was admitting that there was a lack of communication or closeness in his or her marriage. Failure of an individual to name any confidant indicated a void in that level of affectionally bonded relationships. Lowenthal and Haven reported that morale and life satisfaction were more closely related, not to marital status, but rather to the presence or absence of a confidant relationship, either between the person and his or her spouse, or between the person and some other significant person in his or her life.

5. A final example sums up the argument in favor of the use of affectional bonds as a research variable in preference to marital status in studies concerned with subjective well-being and/or bereavement. Medalie and Goldbourt (1976) conducted a study of the incidence of angina pectoris among 10,000 male Israeli civil servants. They found that even in the presence of psychological and physiological high-risk factors, the incidence of angina pectoris was substantially lower among those men who described their wives as loving and supportive. This result indicates that some of the physiological advantages ascribed to marriage may depend upon the existence of an affectional bond between the spouses rather than on the fact of their being married.

Taken together these studies provide a strong indication that some of the psychological and physiological benefits ascribed to marriage may be due to its congruency with an affectional bond. Since in our culture marriage is entered into voluntarily by two persons, acting independently of their family interests, it can be presumed that at the time of their marriage, the two persons believe that an affectional bond exists between them (Gadlin, 1977). Persons who are not married may have affectional bonds with their parents, siblings, other relatives, friends, or lovers; but married persons represent a self-selected group who, by being married, indicate that they are more likely than people in the other three marital status groups to have such a bond with at least one other person. It is for this reason that marital statuses are biased as groupings; it is also for this reason that researchers may have mistaken the effects of affectional bonds for the benefits customarily ascribed to marriage.

It is proposed, therefore, that a more precise focus for research would be to study the effects of affectional bonds rather than marital status. It will be shown below that affectional bonds exist between mothers and infants of the primate species, and that attenuated bonds also exist among adult apes. This generality of behavior among the primates suggests that the tendency to form bonds is genetically determined. Research has shown that separation of mother and infant monkeys produces physiological effects, which further suggests that the beneficial and stressful mechanism commonly attributed to the married or widowed states are, at a somatic level, the result of the existence or the loss of an affectionally bonded relationship.

GENETIC INFLUENCES ON ADULT
AFFECTIONAL BONDING

Affectional bonding can be shown to be the result of a combination of genetic and learned cultural influences. A genetic predisposition to form bonds may be assumed to exist in infants as evidenced by their attachment-eliciting behavior observed immediately after birth (Bowlby, 1957; Lorenz, 1966). This basic bonding behavior is shared across primate species and is vital to the survival of the infants of each species.

Affectional bonding among adults is not under as strong a genetic imperative as is infant bonding. Among apes there are two species that pair-bond, one in which the adult male is solitary except during periods of female estrus, and two which form friendly, aggregate troops. Of the latter, chimpanzees also show a strong tendency to bond among their uterine kin (Galdikas-Brindamour, 1975; Schaller, 1963; van Lawick-Goodall, 1971; Wilson, 1980). The fact that adults of each species of ape form different social patterns suggests that an impulse to bond may exist among adult apes but that the expression of the impulse is species specific.

Among humans there is a great variety of adult bonds including pair-bonding of males and females, patrilineal, matrilineal, and ambilateral bonding, and intimate- and close friend-bonding. These relationships may be formed under a cultural aegis specifying the person or persons to whom one is expected to bond, the bond or bonds given preference within a society, and the breadth and intensity of bonded relationships considered desirable (Averill, 1968; Bohannon, 1965). A further indication of the genetically determined need for affectional bonds may be indicated by the use, in many cultures, of isolation or exile from the group as the ultimate punishment, short of death, imposed by a society on offending members (Bohannon, 1965).

LONELINESS AND GRIEF:
THE PAIN OF BEING UNBONDED

People have been said to die of grief resulting from the death of a spouse (Helsing et al., 1981; Mellstrom et al., 1981; Young et al., 1963), the death of a parent, a child, a close relative or close friend, or even the death of a pet (Averill, 1968; Parkes, 1972; Rees & Lutkin, 1967). The connection of the bereaved person's death to the fact of bereavement itself can be attested to by the proximity of the two events (Parkes, 1972).

Grief is, to some extent, culturally controlled in that the preferred choice among affectionally bonded relationships is determined by the culture in which they exist. Additionally, a bereaved person is expected to display an appropriate degree of grief, and its absence is considered to be somewhat pathological, or even pathogenic—e.g., repressed grief (Averill, 1968).

Because of our cultural conventions we often fail to accept the type of mourning due to a divorce that is accepted in cases of bereavement (Bohannon, 1970). However, divorce is the legal end to a relationship, the traumatic effects of which also depend on the individual's feeling of relief, or of loss and abandonment

(Goode, 1956); an unwilling partner to a divorce may grieve for months or years (Bart, 1971).

In short, grief is characteristically a response to a loss of an affectional bond whether through death, divorce or any intervening situation that results in separation (Averill, 1968; Rosenblatt, Walsh, & Jackson, 1976).

Loneliness, on the other hand, is a feeling that one lacks or has been deprived of the company of a specific person or group of persons (Weiss, 1973). Loneliness may be incurred by an event which also causes grief (e.g., death of a spouse), but the two emotions can also be experienced independently of each other.

While not all people who are alone are unhappy, for example, lifelong isolates (Lowenthal, 1964), most lonely people report being unhappy because they are alone (Hunt, 1966). Lonely people generally have lower levels of perceived health and lower morale than persons who do not complain of loneliness (Berg, Mellstrom, Persson, & Svanborg, 1981).

The pain involved in grief and loneliness has caused some theorists to speculate on the evolutionary utility of those emotions and their value as adjuncts to the bonding process. Averill (1968) has suggested that, from the sociobiological point of view, a positive motivation for forming a group might reasonably be assumed during periods of stress, e.g., to gain protection from predators, access to food, or access to sexual partners (Wilson, 1980). However, an additional mechanism would be required to maintain the group cohesion during periods of relative safety or satiation. Operational conditioning does not provide such a mechanism since any animal who wandered off and encountered a predator would be unlikely to be able to return to the group alive and profit from the experience by remaining in the group in the future. Moreover, even if such a sequence of events could be imagined, such a learning process would affect only one animal at a time; learned behavior is not transmitted from generation to generation except when the second animal can observe a whole sequence of behaviors and outcomes (Kawamura cited in Wilson, 1980). What might supply an evolutionary justification for the continued existence of the emotions of grief and loneliness would be a paradigm involving aversive conditioning. The unpleasant feeling experienced by a young animal in brief separations from its mother could be later generalized to feelings of anxiety and discomfort when it was separated from the aggregate social group (Averill, 1968; Eibl-Eibesfeldt, 1974). The animal would then feel discomfort when it was separated from the group, and relief (i.e., reinforcement) when it returned. The animals most sensitive to these feelings would be motivated to stay with the group regardless of their temporary feelings of need or satiety, and they would therefore have a better chance of survival.

Bowlby (1961) has theorized that the inherited pattern of response to separation is experienced in three stages: (1) anxiety, disbelief, and searching for the lost one; then (2) depression, withdrawal, and despair; and finally (3) acceptance and recovery. These stages have been modeled with monkeys in laboratories, and there is some evidence that physiological changes take place as the monkeys experience separation.

During the period when the infants and their mothers are first separated, the behaviors reported in the infant monkey separation studies are calling and agitated motion, followed later by depression (e.g., Gunnar, Gonzalez, & Levine, 1980). Reite, Short, Kaufman, Stynes, and Pauley (1978) implanted telemetry equipment in infant monkeys to record their physiological responses attendant to the separation experience. They found that there was an initial agitated response on the first day of separation marked by increased heart rate. Twenty-four hours following separation, the infants settled into depression marked by the physiological signs of decreased heart rate and lowered body temperature. After approximately four days of separation, the heart rate and body temperature returned to baseline levels. Reite et al. proposed that this sequence of responses corresponded to the stages in Bowlby's theory (i.e., agitated searching for the mother, depression, and finally recovery from grief).

THE LIMBIC SYSTEM'S RESPONSE TO EMOTIONAL AROUSAL

Cannon (1929) and Funkenstein (1955) have shown that the adrenal-medullary system produces responses which correlate with the behaviors of fear (flight) or of anger (fight). These behaviors seem to be associated with two separate hormones, noradrenalin (norepinephrine) and adrenalin (epinephrine) respectively, and both represent an aroused condition compatible with the first phase of the separation response.

The pituitary-adrenal system produces adrenocorticotropin (ACTH) which induces release of corticosterone. It is believed that corticosterone or plasma cortisol is present concurrently with behaviors identified as depression. In separation studies using mothers and infant monkeys it has been found that cortisol is greatly elevated during the second phase of the separation response, corresponding to the behavior described as conservation and withdrawal (Levine, Coe, Smotherman, & Kaplan, 1978; Coe, Mendoza, Smotherman, & Levine, 1978).

Studies of the relative levels of hormones produced by the adrenal-medullary system and the pituitary-adrenal systems show that the two systems are independent of each other (Russo, Kapp, Holmquist, & Musty, 1976; Van Loon, Scapagnini, Moberg, & Ganong, 1971).

Indeed, their independence suggests that an alternating inhibitory relationship may exist between them. For example, two rats, caged together and given electric shock, will fight with each other. Their experience of arousal is accompanied by lower levels of ACTH than is observed in the rats who are alone when they are shocked (Conner, Vernikos-Danellis, & Levine, 1971).

Kvetnansky and Mikulaj (1970) found that hormone levels in the blood of rats exposed to 40 consecutive daily two-hour periods of stress changed from a high level of corticosterone after the first period to a high level of noradrenalin and lower level of corticosterone after the fortieth two-hour period. This could indicate an initial condition of depression and helplessness, followed by a gradual recovery of the fight-flight response as the animal began to be familiar with the routine.

These two studies provide evidence that the arousal hormones associated with anger can show negative variation with the hormones associated with depression. In the first experiment the shock incited the rats to fight (a noradrenalin-associated or noradrenalin-induced behavior). This was accompanied by a decrease in ACTH (Conner et al., 1971). The other study shows that a depressive reaction (corticosterone) can be dissipated, and that as familiarity with the situation increases, anger and rage can replace helplessness (Kvetnansky & Mikulaj, 1970).

In generalizing these results to humans, we are no longer bound to the premise that the regulation of these physiological functions are solely under the influence of somatic mechanisms.

> We have moved from a view of endocrine systems as controlled largely by humoral self-regulatory mechanisms to the view that a wide range of psychologic influences can profoundly affect humoral balance in both a short- and a long-term basis . . . The superimposition of such complex and idiosyncratic psychological factors as emotions, defense styles and neurotic processes on virtually all bodily functions via the neuroendocrine machine deserves prime suspicion in our search for fallibility or proneness to disease . . . psychoendocrine approaches now provide us with new leverage in getting at the bodily mechanisms that play a mediating role between psychosocial input and diseased peripheral tissues. (Mason, 1975, pp. 14–15)

Applied to the case of death from grief, we must first note that heart disease and heart attacks occur more often among persons who are depressed (Appels, 1979; Thomas, Ross, & Duszynski, 1975) and then look again at the studies that show that hormones involved with depression vary independently from those related to anger or arousal (Conner et al., 1971; Kvetnansky & Mikulaj, 1970). Studies show that people who express anger during bereavement are less likely to incur increased mortality rates in bereavement. For example, Parkes (1972) has observed that American men tend to show little anger during bereavement, while American widows are able to express anger freely against the hospital, the doctor, importunate persons who intrude on their feelings of grief, or against the deceased for having left or abandoned them; as noted above, Helsing et al. (1981) reported that American widowers have a significantly higher mortality rate than do married men, while American widows do not have a significantly higher mortality rate than married women. It is also interesting to note in this context that in Sweden, where there is a strong social tradition for men and women to conceal their feelings (including anger) in all circumstances (Hendin, 1964), the mortality rates of both widowers and widows are higher than those of their married peers (Mellstrom et al., 1981).

FRIENDSHIP AND AFFECTIONAL BONDS

One of the difficulties encountered by investigators attempting to measure the effects of friendship or affectionally bonded relationships is the limitation imposed on them by our language (Farb, 1973). We have in English only a few words to define various levels of friendship (e.g., confidant, companion, ally, acquaintance) and only one word to express the three Greek words (*eros, agape,* and *philos*) for love. Furthermore, there is no general agreement among English speakers on the exact qualities of relationships designated by specific words. Because of this, sociologists and psychologists find themselves doing research, the results of which are difficult to compare because they have no common and exact definitions of relationships (e.g., friend or confidant) on which they or their subjects can agree.

For example, dictionary definitions of the word *friend* can range from those that imply close attachment, to the broadest applications such as when it is used as a salutation in a political speech. However, in a recent survey one of the most frequent responses (89 percent) to the question of how one defined a friend was that such a person was someone in whom one could confide (Parlee, 1979). This definition has been used in a number of studies as the operational definition not of a friend, but rather of a *confidant* to denote someone with whom one has a close, personal relationship that includes sharing one's intimate thoughts and feelings, and who is also (1) someone other than a spouse (Komarovsky, 1962; Powers & Bultena, 1976); (2) someone who may or may not be a spouse (Lowenthal & Haven, 1968); and (3) someone (with special emphasis on her husband or boyfriend) with whom the [female] subject lives or whom she sees frequently (Brown & Harris, 1978). It should be noted that the latter study included only female subjects.

These data indicate a need for some means of analyzing relationships in terms other than those in colloquial usage. As mentioned above, the conceptualization by Weiss (1973) of a dichotomy of relationships (i.e., the social network of friends, and the affectionally bonded level of relationships with a spouse, or close friend or relative) provides a useful method for such research.

Weiss points out that a person with many friends and family connections might be inconsolable if they were to lose the person who represented their only close, or intimate relationship. Such reactions have been explored on an empirical basis primarily in connection with the death of a spouse (e.g., Mellstrom et al., 1981) but there is anecdotal evidence for similar reactions in the case of the death of a twin or a sibling with whom a person had a particularly close, lifelong relationship (Scheinfeld, 1967).

Weiss' conceptualization of the two types of relationships can be used in analyzing the effects of bereavement on elderly men and women. It can be shown that men more often tend to form a time-limited social network of friends—friends at school, friends at work, and friends with whom they engage in some form of sport, e.g., golf or tennis (Fein, 1977). However, in general, men are not encouraged to find their major source of emotional satisfaction in these associations (Blau, 1981). It is commonly expected that as a man moves up the ladder professionally, relocates due to the demands of his occupation, or retires, these friendships will no longer be kept up. An exception to this pattern of friendship is found in certain blue-collar or ethnic communities where having "buddies" with whom one spends much of one's time is accepted as a social norm for men (Bott, 1957; Komarovsky, 1962; Rubin, 1976). In addition to the social distance men are expected to place between themselves and their friends, they are also expected to become independent of their parents and siblings early in their lives. While a certain amount of attachment to his family is acceptable, keeping too close ties to his family may pose a threat to the future stability of his marriage (Komarovsky, 1950; Rubin, 1976). In our society men are expected to derive their emotional satisfaction from their marriage (Brain, 1977; Gadlin, 1977) and once married they generally rely upon their wives to manage their social and family contacts for them (Berardo, 1970;

Sweetser, 1966). Given these social prescriptions, it is not surprising to find that men are less likely than women to have a confidant apart from their spouses (Komarovsky, 1962; Powers & Bultena, 1976) or that they are more likely than women to name their spouses as their confidant (Lowenthal & Haven, 1968).

Furthermore, if men lose a close friend or a confidant, they are less likely than women to form a new affectional bond with another person (Powers & Bultena, 1976).

Women form their social support network under different social imperatives than do men. They are allowed and expected to maintain their social networks in the service of first their natal family, and then their conjugal family. As a consequence, after marriage, women maintain closer ties with their own familes than their husbands do (Komarovsky, 1950, 1962; Sweetser, 1966; Willmott & Young, 1960). Women are more likely to keep up lifelong friendships that endure even when they or their friends move away (Weiss, 1973). When women lose a friend or a confidant, most will try to replace that person (Powers & Bultena, 1976). Women are the designated caretakers of the family, as daughters, daughters-in-law, sisters, spouses and mothers (Brody, 1981; Willmott & Young, 1960). They are the ones who coordinate the helping behavior within the family network. They often engage in church or community service activities that bring them into contact with others with whom they share interests and goals. As noted above, people who have a large circle of friends and acquaintances are more likely to have one or more affectionally bonded relationships.

Using Weiss' concept as a framework by which to analyze the results of bereavement, one can postulate that men have less resiliency supplied by other emotional attachments (i.e., fewer men have confidants) to help them overcome the grief caused by the death of a spouse. By not developing close friendships and affectional bonds with more than one person, they are, as widowers, totally bereft of anyone who could offer them meaningful comfort (Cobb, 1979). Perhaps the real meaning of the improvement of life expectancy among widowers who remarry is that the damage or alienation resulting from the combined loss of one's spouse and one's confidant is compensated for by the establishment of a bond of similar quality with a new spouse.

Women, on the other hand, are more likely to have confidants to whom to turn when they are bereaved—people to whom they can talk about their grief and from whom they can derive comfort (Komarovsky, 1962; Lowenthal & Haven, 1968; Powers & Bultena, 1976). Studies have shown that the support of one's friends is an important factor in recovering from such a loss (Lopata, 1973).

There are undoubtedly many reasons for the difference in life expectancy incurred by widows and widowers due to bereavement (e.g., the difference in longevity between men and women in general, or perhaps the difference in cultural permission granted to men and women to display anger during bereavement). However given the genetic basis for bonding, and the evidence of a physiological reaction to loss or separation, it is possible to speculate that a physiological stress results from the psychological emotional trauma connected with the loss of an affectional bond; further, since it appears that the ill effects of such an occurrence can be mitigated by having or acquiring another similar bond, and since women are generally acknowledged as having more close relationships than men, the survivorship differential between male and female widowed persons may be due in part to the differential between the sexes in making and maintaining affectional bonds.

NEW APPROACHES TO THE PROMOTION
OF BONDING AMONG THE ELDERLY

It is impossible for everyone in this country over the age of 65 to marry. In this age bracket there is a majority of women; over the age of 65 the ratio of females to males is 142:100 (U.S. Bureau of the Census, Supplementary Report, 1981). The other side of the coin is that many people who are unmarried may want to stay that way. Some may have established satisfactory living arrangements with a sibling, relative, or friend. Others may be discouraged from marrying by children who believe that remarriage of a senior citizen is inappropriate, or who may wonder what the effect of that marriage would be in terms of responsibilities or legal claims on their parent's estate (McKain, 1972; Treas & VanHilst, 1976).

For elderly people, then, the question of marriage is somewhat academic. In 1970, 60,000 senior citizens got married (Treas & VanHilst, 1976). This figure represents only 0.7 percent of all of the persons over 65 who were unmarried in that year (U.S. Bureau of the Census, 1970).

It is therefore necessary when considering programs aimed at enhancing the mental and physical well-being of the elderly, to consider other sources of emotional and social support in addition, or as alternatives to marriage. In order to deal with the situation effectively, the individual's needs should be analyzed with reference to the two kinds of bonds that Weiss has defined—the emotional bonds and the social network bonds.

The social network bonds are the easiest to acquire or to enlarge. Older persons should be encouraged to join social or special interest groups, or service clubs in their community. These organizations offer the advantage of bringing together people with similar interests who are also oriented toward sharing those interests with others. New members are welcomed as participants in ongoing club activities, in the course of which they can make friends with other members (Menninger, 1942). Another area in which encouragement may be needed is in reestablishing friendships. Studies have shown that the most valued of the friendships older people have are those they maintain with friends who have moved away, or from whom they have moved (Cohen & Rajkowski, 1982). These friendships often carry associations of long-shared memories and affection (Wentowski, 1981).

Loneliness caused by the lack of an emotional, or a personal bond is more difficult to remedy. The norms of our society encourage young people to get married and to look forward to a lifetime in which their social and emotional needs will be fulfilled within their conjugal family unit (Blau, 1981; Komarovsky, 1950). For the eleven million unmarried persons over the age of 65, no such norms apply, nor is there any alternative pattern provided as a part of our culture for forming emotional bonds (Treas & VanHilst, 1976).

The Brown and Harris (1978), Komarovsky (1962), and Lowenthal and Haven (1968) studies show that having a confidant or close friend can help to maintain one's morale and avoid depression. However, apart from having one's spouse as one's confidant, such relationships usually develop serendipitously (Brain,

1977). The social network contacts cannot, per se, supply this needed level of social support; however, as the Lowenthal and Haven (1968) and the Blau (1981) studies have pointed out, people with more social roles and social contacts are more likely to acquire confidants.

There is, therefore, a need to teach people how to develop social friendships and acquaintanceships into relationships that can both enrich their lives and provide comfort and insulation from the stressful experiences of life (Brain, 1977; Cobb, 1979).

The recent development of therapy groups has shown that very strong bonds can be formed between people which do not necessarily involve relatedness or sexual attraction. The gradual stripping away of personal defenses which occurs in these groups causes intense feelings of uneasiness and fear of rejection. This is followed by relief resulting from the recognition of similarity between oneself and others, and a warm feeling of pleasure at the acceptance of oneself by the group (Menninger, 1942). "Once this mutual understanding and identification takes place, friendship merges into love . . . Love can be fostered by talking together . . ." (pp. 273-274).

Samuel Johnson said of friendship that people had to work at acquiring friends all their lives or they would come to the end of their lives alone. The same could be said of bonds. In our society where the emphasis is on bonds with one's own conjugal family, in which each member is encouraged to go in whatever direction his or her interest may lead, people who rely solely on this source of bonding are literally putting all their eggs in one basket.

The progressively narrowing circle of one's family due to aging and death in the older generation, and to losses of work-related friendships after retirement, can result in an elderly couple's becoming overly reliant on each other as the source of both emotional and social support. In that situation the loss of one's spouse could be devastating to the surviving partner (Payne, 1975; Thompson & Streib, 1961). Encouragement to establish adequate social and emotional ties over one's lifetime, as well as understanding by friends and professionals of the complex social support needs of the elderly bereaved, can improve these persons' chances of avoiding the hazards ascribed to bereavement, and of leading a fuller and happier life.

SUMMARY

Interest in the increase in mortality rates attributed to the effects of bereavement on widowers was addressed in terms of a human need for and effects of the presence or absence of emotional relationships or affectional bonds. Such bonds often exist between a married couple; however close affectional bonds may also exist between parent and child, siblings, friends, relatives, or lovers. Since women are traditionally expected in our society to play the role of the principal caregiver, women have had the opportunity of establishing stronger, more widespread networks of affectional bonds than men. It is proposed that, since men commonly rely on women to supply their social networks for them, a man is usually more psychologically isolated when his wife dies, and therefore, more physiologically vulnerable to disease or death due to spousal bereavement than a woman might be.

Marital status as an explanatory variable should be abandoned because of its gross oversimplification of human relationships, and investigation into a variety of affectionally bonded relationships should be substituted. New programs could be implemented which address the social and emotional needs of the elderly from this viewpoint. These programs would concentrate on the fostering of emotional as well as social network bonds rather than on the effects of marital status. They would be both beneficial and more applicable to the elderly in general, and the elderly bereaved in particular.

REFERENCES

APPELS, A. (1979). Myocardial infarction and depression: A cross-validation of Dreyfuss' findings. *Activitas Nervosa Superior (Praha), 21,* 65–66.

AVERILL, J. R. (1968). Grief: Its nature and significance. *Psychological Bulletin, 70,* 721–748.

BARRETT, C. J. (1981). Intimacy in widowhood. *Psychology of Women Quarterly, 5,* 473–487.

BART, P. (1971). Depression in middle-aged women. In V. Gornick & B. K. Moran (Eds.), *Woman in sexist society* (pp. 163–186). New York: Basic Books.

BECKMAN, L. (1981). Effects of social interaction and children's relative inputs on older women's psychological well-being. *Journal of Personality and Social Psychology, 4,* 1075–1086.

BELL, R. R. (1981). Friendships of women and of men. *Psychology of Women Quarterly, 5,* 402–417.

BERG, S., MELLSTROM, D., PERSSON, G., & SVANBORG, A. (1981). Loneliness in the Swedish aged. *Journal of Gerontology, 36,* 342–349.

BERARDO, F. M. (1970). Survivorship and social isolation: The case of the aged widower. *Family Coordinator, 19,* 11–25.

BLAU, Z. S. (1981). *Aging in a changing society* (2nd ed.). New York: Franklin Watts.

BOCK, E. W., & WEBBER, I. L. (1972). Suicide among the elderly: Isolating widowhood and mitigating alternatives. *Journal of Marriage and the Family, 34,* 24–31.

BOHANNON, P. (1965). *Social anthropology.* New York: Holt, Rinehart & Winston.

BOHANNON, P. (1970). The six stations of divorce. In P. Bohannon (Ed.), *Divorce and after.* Garden City, NY: Doubleday.

BOTT, E. (1957). *Conjugal roles and social networks.* London: Tavistock Publications.

BOWLBY, J. (1957). An ethological approach to research in child development. *British Journal of Medical Psychology, 30,* 230–240.

BOWLBY, J. (1961). Processes of mourning. *International Journal of Psycho-Analysis, 42,* 317–340.

BOWLBY, J. (1979). *The making and breaking of affectional bonds.* London: Tavistock Publications, 67–80.

BRAIN, R. (1977, October). Somebody else should be your own best friend. *Psychology Today,* 83–84, 120–123.

BRODY, E. M. (1981). "Women in the middle" and family help to older people. *The Gerontologist, 21,* 471–479.

BROWN, G. W., & HARRIS, T. (1978). *Social origins of depression.* New York: Free Press.

CAMPBELL, A. (1975, May). The American way of mating: Marriage si, children maybe. *Psychology Today,* 37–43.

CANNON, W. B. (1929). *Bodily changes in pain, hunger, fear and rage: An account of recent researches into the function of emotional excitement* (2nd ed.). New York: Appleton.

COBB, S. (1979). Social support and health through the life course. In M. W. Riley (Ed.), *Aging from birth to death.* AAAS Selected Symposium. Boulder, CO: Westview Press.

COE, C. L., MENDOZA, S. P., SMOTHERMAN, W. P., & LEVINE, S. (1978). Mother-infant attachment in the squirrel monkey: Adrenal response to separation. *Behavioral Biology, 22,* 256–263.

COHEN, C. I., & RAJKOWSKI, H. (1982). What's in a friend? Substantive and theoretical issues. *Gerontologist, 22,* 261–266.

CONNER, R. L., VERNIKOS-DANELLIS, J., & LEVINE, S. (1971). Stress, fighting, and neuroendocrine function. *Nature, 234,* 564–566.

DURKHEIM, E. (1951). *Suicide: A study in sociology* (John A. Spaulding & G. Simpson, Trans.). G. Simpson (Ed.). New York: Free Press. (Originally published in 1897.)

EIBL-EIBESFELDT, I. (1974). *Love and hate: The natural history of behavior patterns* (Geoffrey Strachan, Trans.). New York: Holt, Rinehart & Winston.

FARB, P. (1973). *Word play: What happens when people talk.* New York: Knopf.

FEIN, R. (1977). Examining the nature of masculinity. In A. G. Sargeant (Ed.), *Beyond sex roles.* St. Paul, MN: West Publishing Co.

FUNKENSTEIN, D. H. (1955, May). The physiology of fear and anger. *Scientific American,* 74–78, 80.

GADLIN, H. (1977). Private lives and public order: A critical view of the history of intimate relations in the United States. In G. Levinger & H. L. Raush (Eds.), *Close relationships: Perspectives on the meaning of intimacy* (pp. 33–72). Amherst: University of Massachusetts Press.

GALDIKAS-BRINDAMOUR, B. (1975, October). Orangutans, Indonesia's "people of the forest." *National Geographic, 148,* 444–473.

GOODE, W. J. (1956). *Women in divorce.* New York: Free Press.

GUNNAR, M. R., GONZALEZ, C. A., & LEVINE, S. (1980). The role of peers in modifying behavioral distress and pituitary-adrenal response to a novel environment in year-old rhesus monkeys. *Physiology and Behavior, 25,* 795–798.

HELSING, K. J., SZKLO, M., & COMSTOCK, G. W. (1981). Factors associated with mortality after widowhood. *American Journal of Public Health, 71,* 802–809.

HENDIN, H. (1964). *Suicide and Scandinavia.* New York: Grune & Stratton.

HUNT, M. M. (1966). *The world of the formerly married.* New York: McGraw-Hill.

KOMAROVSKY, M. (1950). Functional analysis of sex roles. *American Sociological Review, 15,* 508–516.

KOMAROVSKY, M. (1962). *Blue-collar marriage.* New York: Random House.

KVETNANSKY, R., & MIKULAJ, L. (1970). Adrenal and urinary catecholamines in rats during adaptation to repeated immobilization stress. *Endocrinology, 87,* 744–749.

LEVINE, S., COE, C. L., SMOTHERMAN, W. P., & KAPLAN, J. N. (1978). Prolonged cortisol elevation in the infant squirrel monkey after reunion with the mother. *Physiology and Behavior, 20,* 7–10.

LOPATA, H. Z. (1973). *Widowhood in an American city.* Cambridge, MA: Schenkman.

LORENZ, K. (1966). *On aggression.* New York: Harcourt Brace Jovanovich, Inc.

LOWENTHAL, M. (1964). Social isolation and mental illness in old age. *American Sociological Review, 29,* 54–70.

LOWENTHAL, M. F., & HAVEN, C. (1968). Interaction and adaptation: Intimacy as a critical variable. *American Sociological Review, 33,* 20–30.

MASON, J. W. (1975). Psychological stress and endocrine function. In E. J. Sachar (Ed.), *Topics in psychoendocrinology* (pp. 1–18). New York: Grune & Stratton.

McKAIN, W. (1972). A new look at older marriages. *The Family Coordinator, 21,* 61–69.

MEDALIE, J. H., & GOLDBOURT, U. (1976). Angina pectoris among 10,000 men: II. Psycholosocial and other risk factors as evidenced by a multivariate analysis of a five-year incidence study. *American Journal of Medicine, 60,* 910–921.

MELLSTROM, D., NILSSON, A., ODEN, A., RUNDGREN, A., & SVANBORG, A. (1981). Mortality in relation to marital status among the elderly in Sweden. In D. Mellstrom (Ed.), *Lifestyle, aging and health among the elderly* (pp. 1–17). Goteborg, Sweden: University of Goteborg.

MENNINGER, K. (1942). *Love against hate.* New York: Harcourt Brace Jovanovich.

PALMORE, E. B., & STONE, V. (1973). Predictors of longevity: A follow-up of the aged in Chapel Hill. *The Gerontologist, 13,* 88–90.

PARKES, C. M. (1972). *Bereavement: Studies of grief in adult life.* New York: International Universities Press.

PARKES, C. M., BENJAMIN, B., & FITZGERALD, R. G. (1969). Broken heart: A statistical study of increased mortality among widowers. *British Medical Journal, 1,* 740–743.

PARLEE, M. B., and the Editors of *Psychology Today.* (1979, October). The friendship bond. *Psychology Today,* 43–54, 113.

PAYNE, E. C. (1975). Depression and suicide. In J. G. Howell (Ed.), *Modern perspectives in the psychiatry of old age.* New York: Brunner/Mazel.

POWERS, E. A., & BULTENA, G. L. (1976). Sex differences in intimate friendships of old age. *Journal of Marriage and the Family, 38,* 739–746.

REES, W. D., & LUTKIN, S. G. (1967). Mortality of bereavement. *British Medical Journal, 4,* 13–16.

REITE, M., SHORT, R., KAUFMAN, I. C., STYNES, A. J., & PAULEY, J. D. (1978). Heart rate and body temperature in separated monkey infants. *Biological Psychiatry, 13,* 91–105.

ROSENBLATT, P. C., WALSH, R. P., & JACKSON, D. A. (1976). *Grief and mourning in a cross-cultural comparison.* New Haven, CT: Human Relations Area Files Press.

RUBIN, L. (1976). *Worlds of pain: Life in the working class family.* New York: Basic Books.

RUSSO, N. J. II, KAPP, B. S., HOLMQUIST, B. K., & MUSTY, R. E. (1976). Passive avoidance and amygdala lesions: Relationship with pituitary-adrenal system. *Physiological Behavior, 16,* 191–199.

SCHALLER, G. (1963). *The mountain gorilla: Ecology and behavior.* Chicago: University of Chicago Press.

SCHEINFELD, A. (1967). *Twins and supertwins.* Baltimore: Penguin.

SCOTT, A. F. (1970). *The southern lady: From pedestal to politics 1830–1930.* Chicago: The University of Chicago Press.

STROEBE, M. S., STROEBE, W., GERGEN, K. J., & GERGEN, M. (1981). The broken heart: Reality or myth? *Omega, 12,* 87–106.

SWEETSER, D. A. (1966). The effect of industrialization on intergenerational solidarity. *Rural Sociology, 31,* 156–170.

THOMAS, C. B., ROSS, D. C., & DUSZYNSKI, K. R. (1975). Youthful hypercholesteremia: Its associated characteristics and role in premature myocardial infarction. *Johns Hopkins Medical Journal, 136,* 193–208.

THOMPSON, W. E., & STREIB, G. F. (1961). Meaningful activity in a family context. In R. W. Kleemeier (Ed.), *Aging and leisure: A research perspective into the meaningful use of time.* New York: Oxford University Press.

TREAS, J., & VAN HILST, A. (1976). Marriage and remarriage rates among older Americans. *The Gerontologist, 16,* 132–135.

U.S. BUREAU OF THE CENSUS (1970) U.S. Census of population: 1970, General population characteristics, final report, *United States Summary, PC (1)-B1,* 31.

U.S. BUREAU OF THE CENSUS (1982) *Statistical Abstract of the United States,* 1982–1983, 103d Edition, Washington, D.C.

VAN LAWICK-GODDALL, J. (1971). *In the shadow of man.* Boston: Houghton Mifflin.

VAN LOON, G. R., SCAPAGNINI, U., MOBERG, G. P., & GANONG, W. F. (1971). Evidence for central adrenergic neural inhibition of ACTH secretion in the rat. *Endocrinology, 89,* 1464–1469.

WARD, A.W.M. (1976). Mortality of bereavement. *British Medical Journal, 1,* 700–702.

WEISS, R. S. (1973). *Loneliness: The experience of emotional and social isolation.* Cambridge, MA: The MIT Press.

WENTOWSKI, G. J. (1981). Reciprocity and the coping strategies of older people: Cultural dimensions of network building. *Gerontologist, 21,* 600–609.

WILLMOTT, P., & YOUNG, M. (1960). *Family class and generation in a London suburb.* London: Routledge and Kegan Paul.

WILSON, E. O. (1980). *Sociobiology: The abridged edition.* Cambridge, MA: The Belknap Press.

YOUNG, M., BENJAMIN. B., & WALLIS, C. (1963). Mortality of widowers. *Lancet, 2,* 454–456.

5

COGNITIVE CONTROL AND ENDORPHINS AS MECHANISMS OF HEALTH

Implications for the Relationship Between Social Support and Disease

Jerry Heckenmueller

Medical science is philosophical when the sheer power of man's reason to master his sensuous feelings by a self-imposed principle determines his manner of living. On the other hand, if medical science seeks the help of external physical means (drugs and surgery) to stimulate or ward off these sensations, it is merely empirical and mechanical.—Immanuel Kant (1798/1979)

While the general focus of all of the contributions in this book is aging and health behavior relationships, little is said about aging in the present chapter. The issue I am treating is the role of endorphins and perceived control in the relationship between social support and disease. There is a substantial literature that discusses social support and aging, disease and aging, and, to some extent, perceived control and aging (Schulz, 1980). However, experimental work on endorphin activity in the aging process is almost nonexistent. A thorough literature search located only two studies that directly investigated this relationship (Margules, 1979; Steger, Sonntag, Van Vugt, Forman, & Meites, 1980). I hope that those interested in the aging process will profit from this chapter in two ways. First, the perceived control/ endorphin mechanisms will be shown to undergo development across the life span. This suggests that any attempt to understand their role as mediating the social support/disease relationship must take into consideration the lifelong pattern of these variables starting with early infant attachment and perhaps even prenatal mother-child bonding. Second, it should be clear that there is a need for basic psychophysiological research that tests the hypothesized relationship on aged samples. The literature cited should provide adequate background to begin experimental programs.

In this chapter I first review the evidence which shows the relationship between endorphins and pain, emotional responses (especially stress reactions), social behaviors, and cognitive processes. Next I present a brief review of the literature which demonstrates the role of cognitive control in disease/health outcomes. Finally, I provide an integration along with speculations and hypotheses based on the above literature that suggests that endorphins constitute an important biological mechanism and that cognitive control is a significant psychological mechanism in the explanation of the relationship between stress and disease. In this integration I will use social support as an example of an especially pervasive source of stress and discuss its relationship to cancer.

ENDORPHINS

Endorphin is the general term (a combination of the words *endogenous* and *morphine*) used to refer to a class of naturally occurring opiatelike substances found throughout the body systems. The endorphins are a part of a long polypeptide chain of amino acids called beta-lipotropin (see Bolles & Fanselow, 1982, for a detailed discussion).

The endorphins are neuropeptides. Recently it has been shown that they function both as neurotransmitters—chemical messengers that transmit information between nerve cells at their synapses—and as hormones—chemical products released by gland cells into the circulating blood in order to influence target cells throughout the body (Bloom, 1981). Among the functionally significant kinds of endorphins that have been identified to date are alpha-, beta- and gamma-endorphins, dynorphin, and met- and leu-enkephalin.

Functions of Endorphins: Experimental Evidence

Endorphins and their receptor sites are located throughout the brain and body systems. Of special importance is their presence in the neocortex, throughout the limbic system, and in the pituitary and adrenal glands. It has long been recognized that these are the sites of cognitive processing of information, learning and memory, and of affective, emotional responses.

Looking at the literature on endorphins over the past eight years, one might be tempted to conclude that the answer to the question, What do endorphins do? is, Everything. An unending list of psychological, physiological, and behavioral effects have been attributed to the role of endorphins.

However, three current *Annual Review* articles for the disciplines of psychology, physiology, and medicine suggest extreme caution in drawing any firm conclusions regarding function (Berger, Akil, Watson, & Barchas, 1982; Bolles & Fanselow, 1982; Koob & Bloom, 1982). Holaday and Loh (1981) put it rather directly:

A common disclaimer at the conclusion of endorphin manuscripts has been, 'Of course, the physiological role of endorphins is as yet unknown.' This statement indicates the assumption that there is a single 'true' physiological function for these substances. However, it seems unlikely that complex biological systems such as the endorphins and their specific receptors would have evolved to subserve a single biological role. (p. 276)

Perhaps these cautions result from the large number of putative involvements of endorphins. Such care is well advised because of the technical and experimental difficulties associated with research on endorphins, e.g., the very low concentration required, the unreliability of assays, the similarity between various endorphins (sometimes one amino acid difference), the opioid interactions with other hormones and neurotransmitters, the confounding of psychological with physical stressors during independent variable manipulations, the use of alkaloid agonist substitutes or antagonists to infer opioid function, the great variability in sites and methods of injection, and the ubiquitous sites of occurrences (Berger et al., 1982; Koob & Bloom, 1982).

Reviews often refer to the problem of conflicting results, and attribute this to one or another experimental artifact. Sometimes there is an increase, sometimes a decrease, and sometimes no change in measured levels of endorphins under ostensibly identical experimental manipulations. Likewise, it is often observed that identical doses and controlled administration of endorphins result in an increase, decrease, or no change in some dependent variable, e.g., analgesia. However, these mixed results may reflect a failure to recognize that endorphins have the unique ability to influence hormones, neurotransmitters, and receptor sites in all of these ways (Bloom, 1981). Just as Selye was able to get *consistent* and dramatic results with his extracts because they were all so badly derived rather than because he had discovered a "new hormone" (Selye, 1976), so also it may be possible to get *inconsistent* and dramatic results because a "new peptide" has multiple effects rather than because it was badly administered. The important question may be not, What is the source of the artifact? but rather, What causes the same endorphins to behave so differently at the same sites under the same observed conditions? I hope the psychobiological control mechanisms model to be presented will begin to answer the latter question.

A selected review of endorphin function related to pain, emotion, social behavior, and cognitive processes will point to primary areas of significance to stress/disease interactions.

Pain. Ever since the discovery of opiate receptor sites (Pert & Snyder, 1973), the questions have been, Why? What are they doing there? and, What is their function? (Bolles & Fanselow, 1982). When Hughes et al. (1975) isolated and identified the enkephalins, and when Li (1976) discovered endorphin (the most potent endogenous opioid) in humans, the most direct and obvious answer to the question was that endorphins are naturally occurring analgesics. This was confirmed in a number of experiments (Bolles & Fanselow, 1982; Herz, 1978; Kosterlitz, 1976; Li, 1981; Liebeskind & Paul, 1977).

This is perhaps the total answer to the function question, and the one that is favored by some (Bolles & Fanselow, 1982). If this is the case, however, we are left with the problem of why there are times when the endorphins have this pain-control effect and why at other times they do not. Several experiments using rats and humans were described by Teschemacher (1978) in which there was no analgesic effect of endorphins under pain stress. In a recent study, Miczek, Thompson and Shuster (1982) found variability in opioid-mediated pain suppression as a function of whether bites between fighting mice had a social significance. Amir, Brown, and Amit (1980) noted that there is a separation between the sensation and perception of pain. They advanced the possibility that endorphins exert selective effects on these two components. Finally, Liebeskind and Paul (1977), in an early review chapter on endorphins, suggest that all mammals possess pain-control mechanisms that are associated with endorphins within the brain stem. They suggest that an important research goal is the discovery of how to control these pain-inhibitory resources. The implication is that there is more to endorphin function than direct pain-suppression effects.

Emotion. There is a firm empirical-theoretical history that details the involvement of the neuroendocrine system in emotions. Much of this work revolves around the issue of stress and the emotional responses to it. (For excellent treatments of this topic, see Frankenhaeuser, 1978, 1982; Henry, Chapter 2, this volume; Henry & Stephens, 1977; Mason, 1975.) The focus has been on the catecholamines secreted by the hypothalamic sympathetic adrenal-medullary system and on the corticosteroids from the pituitary adrenal-cortical system. These hormones are under the control of the limbic system.

A separate line of research has been proceeding on the relationship between emotion and endorphins. In a major review of the literature on the role of endorphins in stress, Amir et al. (1980) trace the brief but voluminous history of the experimental work done on the intimate relationships between endorphins and the major hormones involved in the stress response. They begin by demonstrating that the endorphins are located in the pituitary and in the brain areas associated with emotions, especially the limbic system, and they suggest that the endorphins may modulate the activity of endocrine systems that play a role in stress. A number of studies are cited which indicate that endorphins control catecholamine release from the adrenal medulla, and that they exercise neural control in this organ as well. Further studies show that endorphins control the hypothalamic-pituitary-adrenal cortex axis in a similar way. That is, they stimulate corticosterone synthesis and release; modulate secretion of adrenal steroids indirectly through control over ACTH; and release CRF in the hypothalamus. "Endorphin or enkephalin may modulate the function of limbic mechanisms that play a role in the elaboration of emotion" (Amir et al., 1980, p. 80).

In a more recent review, Morley (1981) essentially confirms the speculations offered by Amir et al. (1980), and further provides a direct extension of the stress model developed by the catechol and corticol researchers. He notes that some of the locations of opioids in the studies reviewed (pituitary, hypothalamus, adrenal cortex and medulla) suggest that these opioids may be the mechanism that explains Cannon's concept of flight-fight, especially as developed by Selye (1976).

All of the work reviewed by Amir et al. (1980) and Morley (1981) serves to confirm the previous studies reported on the activity of the neuroendocrine system in response to stress and adds to the development of theory that tries to present an integrated model. It provides some confirmation of an additional function of endorphins—their role in the elaboration of emotions.

Social behavior. From the discussion so far, it is evident that endorphins may play a functional role in the elaboration of pain and emotions (and their neuroendocrinological substrates). Another level of analysis suggests that a major endorphin function may be control over social behavior. Evidence for this view is presented in an important paper by Panksepp, Herman, Vilberg, and Bishop (1980), *Endogenous Opioids and Social Behavior,* which supports the hypothesis that brain-opioids mediate social affect and social attachment.

Panksepp et al. (1980) begin by noting the extensive literature which supports the notion that social motivation, and hence social behavior, is a basic biological system, rather than arising secondarily from the fulfillment of more primary needs. Referring to the literature on social isolation in young animals and humans, he notes, "Because of the vigor and ubiquity of this emotional response to social separation, it seems likely that social motivation is a direct manifestation of innate neural circuits which are as spontaneously responsive as those which govern other basic motivated behavior patterns such as feeding and drinking" (p. 473).

What brain mechanism could account for this social motive as a basic system? Panksepp et al. (1980) answer that it may be the endogenous opioid system. This system originally served a survival function through pain mediation. These same neural circuits could become involved in social attachment since such bondings are closely related to survival. "Accordingly, brain-opioid systems should be reasonable candidates for providing neurochemical mediation of social-bonding among animals" (p. 474).

Experimental evidence reviewed by Panksepp suggests that endorphins are involved in neurochemical, behavioral, and brain effects on separation distress and other social behaviors, e.g., comfort contact, proximity, maternal behaviors, and play.

The evolutionary/experimental argument provided by Panksepp suggests a developmental functional relationship for endorphins involving pain perception and control, integration of psychophysiological mechanisms of emotion, and the whole complex of organized social behavior.

Cognitive process. To what extent are endorphins correlated with neocortex function and related cognitive processes? It is often assumed that it is the highly developed neocortex that accounts for the complex form of human integration of sensation, perception, learning, motivation, and emotion into thought, awareness, consciousness, and intentionality. To be sure, humans do have by far the most cortical tissue relative to brain size, but evolution has also favored development of all the other brain systems as well, especially the limbic system. More emphasis needs to be placed on the integrated brain if we are to understand the tremendous variability of human behavior. As Trevarthen (1980) has noted, "The sensory and motor centers of the hindbrain are of supreme psychological importance because they include the core structures of communicative expression coupled to the principal regulators of bodily and emotional states. Some muscles of the head directly regulate input to olfaction, vision, hearing, and taste. They are the brain's agents for selective gating and turning off input to perceptions" (pp. 48-49). An especially interesting example is the role of the midbrain in vision. In fish, the midbrain roof (tectum) is the principal organ of sight. In humans, this area is the terminal point for axons from retinal ganglion cells before the impulse proceeds to the visual cortex (Trevarthen, 1980; Wurtz, Goldberg, & Robinson, 1982). In a well-controlled series of studies, Wurtz et al. (1982) demonstrated the neural basis of visual attention. A number of areas in the brain are involved in the visual response including the frontal eye field lateral geniculate body, superior colliculus, posterior parietal cortex, and striate cortex, reflecting an integration of sensory, motor, and motivational responses. What these researchers showed was that it is activity in the posterior parietal cortex that determines which of all objects in the visual field presently stimulating the system is the one attended to.

Thus, a psychological concept, attention, has been described in physiological terms, an integrated brain system. Somehow a shift in balance of neural activity among the brain systems determines the attention response. This notion of balance of neural activities across brain areas as being more of an effective stimulus than the total amount of neural input received by any one area is being increasingly recognized (Isaacson, 1974). Wurtz acknowledges that the neural mechanism underlying this response is not known.

Lewis, Mishikin, Bragin, Brown, Pert, and Pert (1981) provide some evidence which suggests that endorphins may constitute a mechanism that accomplishes this integration of brain activities resulting in the cognitive process of attention. They report on work which shows that opioids are involved in filtering of sensory stimuli at the cortical level and thus play a role in selective attention. They suggest that the endorphins "offer a neural mechanism whereby the limbic-mediated emotional states essential for individual and species survival could influence which sensory stimuli are selected for attention" (p. 1168). Summarizing the work in this area, Bolles and Fanselow (1982) conclude that endorphins are located in those areas and structures of the cortex which do the most advanced processing of sensory information. "It is concluded that just as the opiates gate pain information at a spinal level, so at the cortical level they gate all sorts of perceptual information. *In short, the endorphins are said to mediate attention*" (p. 97, emphasis added).

COGNITIVE CONTROL

The literature reviewed up to this point summarizes the evidence which suggests that endorphins may play a biological control role in pain perception, emotions, social behavior, and cognitive processes. Later it will be shown that these processes are significantly involved in the maintenance of health and the onset and progress of disease. However, there is also a vast literature which suggests that cognitive control is significantly implicated in health and disease. Thus there are two variables, endorphins and cognitive control, which are empirically correlated with health/disease outcomes. A question to be asked, then, is, How are these two antecedents related to each other? In preparation for an answer in this section, I first briefly review evidence which demonstrates the role of cognitive control in disease/health outcomes. Then, in an "Integration and Speculation" section, I suggest an answer to how endorphins and cognitive control are related in this process.

Helplessness: A Theoretical Account
of Perceived Control

The construct of *learned helplessness* was introduced by Seligman (1975) based on the experimental findings that animals exposed to chronic, classically conditioned shock developed an inability to later learn appropriate instrumental coping responses. The most recent, revised form of the theory is presented in detail in Garber and Seligman (1980) along with theoretical extensions and applications.

Basically, the learned helplessness hypothesis states that learning that outcomes are uncontrollable results in three deficits: (1) motivational: retarded initiation of voluntary responses because of the expectation that responding is futile; (2) cognitive: difficulty in learning that there is a connection between responses and outcomes; and (3) emotional: negative affect as a result of response-outcome independence. This is primarily a cognitive theory because the organism must come to *expect* that outcomes are not controllable, regardless of the objective circumstances that prevail. In addition, a critical cognitive component is the causal attribution that subjects infer when faced with lack of control. They ask *why* there is no relationship between responses and outcomes. The perceived answer to this question, whether veridical or not, has major implications for ensuing attempts at coping responses and ultimate well-being.

If the answer to the attributional "why" is one that leads the individual to conclude that the lack of control is due to stable and global factors that are either personal ("I am inadequate") or universal ("there is nothing anyone can do"), then the perception of noncontingency becomes an expectation that lack of control will persist, that nothing can be done to change the situation, and thus that coping responses are useless. According to Abramson, Garber, and Seligman (1980), such expectations determine the generality and chronicity of the symptoms (cognitive, motivational, and emotional) of helplessness. The result is an individual who eventually exhibits one or another negative behavioral effect, e.g., disease. If, on the other hand, the attribution leads to the conclusion that the lack of control is due to unstable and specific factors that are either personal ("I didn't try") or universal ("a chance happening occurred") then the perception of noncontingency becomes an expectation that lack of control will not persist, things can be corrected, and coping responses are appropriate. Such expectations can be expected to result in a heightened state of motivation and activity that eventually leads to enhancement of the individual's overall well-being, e.g., health.

A number of other empirical/theoretical approaches to the concept of perceived control have been advanced recently. Indeed, this topic and section could be quite extensive in coverage of these new developments. However, these are extensively reviewed by Shupe (Chapter 8, this volume), and Reker and Wong (Chapter 7, this volume) and the reader is referred to those excellent accounts. All of the accounts reviewed have the same basic theme that perceived control is health related and that lack or loss of control is associated with disease.

What is missing in all of this research is the location of perceived control in an empirical, physiological sense. A link ought to be made between the psychological process of perceived control and the physiological activities of those body systems that regulate health/disease. The remaining part of this chapter will attempt to do this. What has been shown so far is an empirically supported relationship between endorphins and pain, emotion, social behavior, and cognitions on the one hand; and cognitive control and disease on the other. In what follows it will be argued that endorphins are physiological correlates, indices, or representations of cognitive control processes.

Integration and Speculation

My thesis is that perceived control is the psychological mechanism that explains the way in which endorphins function in the cognitive control/health relationship. To demonstrate this relationship I will use stress and the psychological, physiological, and behavioral response to it. In concert with the perspectives of the neuroendocrinology of Frankenhaeuser (1978) and the cognitive psychology of Lazarus (1977), I regard stress as "a process of transactions between the individual and the environment" (Frankenhaeuser, 1978, p. 124), rather than as the more traditional "any threat to the organism" (Renner & Birren, 1980). For me, the latter implies that some kind of cognitive process/affective evaluation has already occurred, and my position is that such processing is a critical part of cognitive control. I prefer to view stress in a neutral way and use the terms *eustress* (positive stimulation) and *distress* (negative stimulation) to refer to the resultant psychological state that modulates endorphin activity after initial cognitive processing has occurred. I choose stress to discuss the psychological-perceived control/ biological-endorphin mechanisms because this represents a general framework. That is, an organism's response to stress will either lead to an overall enhancement of its well-being or threaten its survival. In general terms, the endorphins are the biological controlling/monitoring mechanisms which integrate and coordinate the activities of the various areas of the brain, especially the neocortex and the limbic system. This coordinated activity determines the quantity and quality of the outputs of the hormonal system, especially the pituitary-adrenal-cortical system and the sympathetic-adrenal-medullary system. Most important, however, is the fact that the specific nature of the activities of the endorphins varies directly with the psychological meaning of the stressor being evaluated, in terms of perceived control.

To begin with the basic endorphin-pain relationship which has been confirmed, the question can be asked, Can perceived control over pain influence the effects of endorphins on pain perception? My hypothesis is that if pain is uncontrollable, this would represent a potential threat to survival; the animal is helpless; and very basic physiological, biogrammed processes would ensue, which include direct endorphin activity to suppress pain, and related endorphin activity to control the neuroendocrine pituitary-adrenal-cortex responses associated with helplessness and loss of control. If, on the other hand, there is a response-outcome contingency, i.e., the animal can learn a relationship between an instrumental response and pain, then the animal has perceived control and there is less threat to survival. Here the role of endorphins would be to modulate cortical activities (attention to cues, problem solving, memory) and the neuroendocrine responses associated with motivation, effort, etc., that is, the sympathetic-adrenal-medullary system.

Several experiments are described by Teschemacher (1978) in which a pain stimulus was applied but there was no analgesic effect of administered endorphins. In one study, rats were exposed to escapable foot-shock. Teschemacher explains,

"The well-learned escape behavior in this experiment might have reduced the necessity for the organism of a stress-induced analgesia" (p. 118). Other studies are reported in which human subjects consented to the application of a pain stimulus with no endorphin-induced analgesia. It can be assumed that the act of consent constituted a sufficient perceived control and thus this physical stress was not seen by the subjects as in any way threatening their survival. In all of these studies, control over the pain stimulus was imparted to the subjects.

In a complementary fashion, it can be shown that "psychological" pain can produce analgesia in the absence of physical pain under conditions of lack of control. Thus Bolles and Fanselow (1982) summarize a number of studies which demonstrated that neutral stimuli which were associated with shock in a traditional classical conditioning procedure subsequently produced analgesia when these conditioned stimuli were later presented along with pain stimuli. It will be recalled that classical conditioning is a form of learning in which consequences are completely out of the control of the subjects. In these studies, then, you have endorphin activity which mimics that which occurs under uncontrollable pain, only now it occurs under uncontrollable *fear* of pain.

Taken together, these studies suggest that it is not pain per se that leads to a consistent complex of physiological responses, but rather it is the psychological meaning of pain—i.e., Is it controllable or uncontrollable?—that triggers differential endorphin activities at different sites to cause a variety of neuroendocrine responses. This makes sense in an evolutionary way. If a pain stimulus is controllable there is less threat to survival. If it is not controllable, there is more of a threat. Originally, among lower organisms, the sensation and perception of pain had a functional, survival value that triggered a whole set of biogrammed pain-motivated recuperative behaviors. However, if the source of the pain is a wound inflicted by an enemy, such behavior would be maladaptive. It would serve survival better if pain and pain-motivated behaviors were suppressed and fight-flight defensive behaviors dominated. Such is the analgesic role of endorphins according to Bolles and Fanselow (1982). As evolutionary development proceeded, along with development of the neocortex, any source of pain, physical or psychological, came to be assessed in terms of its threat to survival. If stress was seen as controllable (not a threat), then the pain led to endorphin-mediated recuperative control over physiological processes. If it was seen as uncontrollable (a threat), then the pain led to endorphin-mediated defensive responses. As a result of ever-increasing complexity of environmental stimuli, both physical and especially social, one possible outcome is that the sheer number of potentially uncontrollable threats could result in a failure to cope adequately, thus leading to the helplessness syndrome with its accompanying effects on health.

On the positive side, with the natural tendency of the brain to seek its own growth and development (Trevarthen, 1980; Wittrock, 1980), and again, with the evolutionary development of the cortex, it became possible for whole classes of stressors to be cognitively evaluated as eustress, that is, opportunities or challenges for overall enhancement of the organism. Thus, for example, neonatal attachment to the female, clearly a biogrammed survival response, also became an opportunity for enrichment of the whole organism. The confirmed high levels of endorphins present during pregnancy in the placenta and fetus and in breast milk (Holaday & Loh, 1981; Panksepp et al., 1980) suggest the possibility that during the critical periods of attachment for various species, endorphins may direct neuroendocrine activity in a way that not only accomplishes the survival function, but also in a way that results in significant others becoming a highly-valued stimulus (eustressor) for growth.

At a very basic biological level, the suggestion is that endorphins operate differently when pain represents a threat to survival as opposed to when there is no threat. At a higher level, this implies that cognitive control over and interpretation of stressors may be an important determinant of the analgesic effects of endorphins. Liebeskind and Paul (1977) hinted at this in the concluding statement of their early review chapter on endorphins:

> Thus our cognitive capacities to think, to believe, and to hope enable us, probably all of us under appropriate conditions, to find and employ our pain-inhibitory resources. The important challenge in the years to come for behavioral scientists involved in pain research will be to explore and ultimately bring under control those precise circumstances and techniques that will reliably enable people to make use of these resources when needed. (p. 54)

It would be helpful if there were studies available that implicate endorphins in the relationship between perceived control and social/emotional behaviors. I have not found any. By inference, however, three lines of research can be integrated to permit at least a logical argument that endorphins mediate the relationship between perceived control and the whole complex of responses that is referred to as socio-emotional behaviors. These are: (1) Frankenhaeuser's (1978, 1982) physiological work on perceived control over emotional responses to psychosocial stress, (2) the research by Panksepp et al. (1980; Panksepp & Bishop, 1981) which demonstrated the role of endorphins in control of the neuroendocrine system, social affect, and bonding, and (3) the psychological work of Bandura (1982), Caplan (1981), and Garber and Seligman (1980) showing the relationship between perceived control and reactions to psychosocial stress.

Frankenhaeuser (1978) offers experimental evidence in support of cognitions playing a controlling, determinant role in the quantity and quality of emotional response to environmental, and especially, psychosocial stressors. Reviewing studies that show considerable within-group variability on a number of physiological responses and subjective stress states, she concludes that these results "are consistent with the view that cognitive factors are prime determinants of emotional responses" (p. 127), and states, "Nor do our data on endogenous adrenaline and noradrenaline lend any support to the view that emotional experience would be *controlled by* the hormonal or sympathetic pattern" (p. 131). In a more recent paper Frankenhaeuser (1982) theorizes:

> The psychosocial environment reflects its emotional impact on the individual, and . . . objectively different environmental conditions may evoke the same neuroendocrine responses because they have a common psychological denominator . . . The ability to exert control over one's own activities is generally recognized as a major determinant of the stressfulness of person-environment transactions . . . A key finding is that, in general, catecholamine and cortisol secretion rates are reduced as personal control increases. (p. 3)

Panksepp has shown that: (1) the brain areas that receive and organize incoming sensory information from which the social-bond must be constructed; (2) cortical and subcortical areas that govern social interactions; and (3) brain areas which control specific social behavior patterns, are all areas rich in endorphins. In a study that manipulated the availability of social interaction among rat pups, Panksepp and Bishop (1981) confirmed that social interaction and endorphins are related. Although alternative explanations were not ruled out, the results were consistent with their hypothesis that social interaction promotes endorphin activity throughout the brain, and especially in the amygdala, the putative CNS mediator of social behaviors. If, as I suggested earlier, endorphin involvement in attentional mediation is assumed, then this selective attention may well apply to the capacity of organisms to perceive the presence of socially relevant others. Thus there is the possibility that endorphins mediate the cognitive processes involved in complex social interactions.

An appeal to a perceived control mechanism governing social stress reactions mediated by endorphins comes from a recent paper by Miczek et al. (1982). These authors report the results of a series of studies in which intruder mice were repeatedly bitten by defenders and subjected to social defeat. This defeat in a social confrontation led to pain suppression that was mediated by endorphins. This effect occurred strictly as a function of social defeat behavior and not as a result of the pain of having been bitten. A control group of animals that were artificially bitten did not show this pain suppression. The authors concluded, "Apparently, the special biological significance of the defeat experience, *and not simply the experience of* being stressed, is critical to the occurrence of opioid-like analgesia" (p. 1522, emphasis added).

From the cognitive psychology perspective, there is a vast theoretical and research literature that confirms the important determining role that perceived control plays in reaction to social stress. (For excellent reviews, see Averill, 1979; Bandura, 1982; Caplan, 1981; and Garber & Seligman, 1980.) Contrary to the earlier generalization that social support is always a eustress with positive consequences, and that loss of social support is always a distress, these recent formulations effectively show that it is the implication social stress has in terms of perceived control that determine consequences, whether it be health enhancement or physical or mental disease. These formulations are consistent with the notion that the variability observed in the social stress-endorphin response relationship can be explained by postulating a perceived control mechanism.

STRESS, DISEASE, AND SOCIAL SUPPORT

Taken together, the above research and theorizing permit a reasoned speculation that perceived control and endorphins may regulate stress reactions and related social-emotional behaviors. In this section, I use a specific and pervasive source of stress, social support, and the research on the correlates of the onset, progress, and outcome of the disease of cancer to exemplify how perceived control over social support and related endorphin functioning could determine whether health is enhanced or disease is facilitated.

Stress

Psychosomatic disorders, the diseases of adaptation, have been the object of research since the time of Galen. The basic question has been, What is the mechanism that accounts for the onset of disease in the absence of any observable trauma or infection? Two different, and until recently, largely independent lines of research developed to search for the answer. In the biological traditions, especially neurology, endocrinology, and medicine, focus has been primarily on the neuroendocrine system. In psychology, the main emphasis has been on the cognitive and affective processes of the mind. It is interesting that both of these orientations came to the same conclusion regarding the mechanism question. The answer was, *stress.*

Stress, whether broadly or narrowly defined, involves external, environmental factors, either physical or social, that place some kind of demands on the organism, either negative or positive. Experimentation in biology has favored observing the neuroendocrine responses to various sources of stress, i.e., looking at the physiological correlates of demands primarily controlled by limbic system regulators; and psychological research has emphasized understanding the perceptual/motivational/ learning/personality processes involved in the evaluation of the sources of stress and related functions of the neocortex (Averill, 1979). Both of these lines of research have made significant contributions to the reduction of disease and the enhancement of health.

Recently, there has been a multidisciplinary "getting together" of both these sources of research and theory [Jemmett and Locke (1984) provide a comprehensive review]. This psychobiological literature became the basis for my present attempt to integrate the findings from these disciplines and suggest a more general, comprehensive explanation for psychosomatic disorders. My conclusion is that stress is not the mechanism that accounts for the onset of disease. Rather it is the *perceived control* over the environmental sources of stress and the *endorphin* regulation over the physiological correlates of demands which are the mechanisms that determine whether health is enhanced or disease is facilitated.

To exemplify my thinking I will use the research literature on the relationship between social support and disease.

Disease

Stress has been implicated in practically every disease known. Except for an occasional reference to some other disorder dictated by the literature cited, I will restrict my remarks to the involvement of social support in the onset, progress, and outcome of cancer. The major reason for selecting cancer is the fact that there is considerable research evidence demonstrating a relationship between perceived control and cancer, and between social support and cancer. While there is some evidence implicating endorphins in cancer, most of what I say in this regard comes from the literature that outlines the relationship between stress, the endocrine and immune systems, and cancer, with endorphins being the inferred biological control over these systems.

The complex relationship that exists between stress and disease is demonstrated in a compelling way by Sklar and Anisman (1981) in a major review article on stress and cancer. Citing 330 studies, these authors begin their review by noting that "some investigators have reported stress-induced exacerbation of tumori-genicity, whereas others have found that stress retards tumor growth" (Sklar & Anisman, 1981, p. 370). What follows is basically a summary of the major findings that Sklar and Anisman report on the relationship between stress and cancer.

The defining characteristics of cancer cells are their abilities to proliferate uncontrollably (induction), to invade normal tissues (growth), and to travel to dif-ferent sites (metastasis).

Tumor induction is accomplished by tumor-active stimuli which can be divided into three kinds: (1) carcinogens, which produce cancer with no further host interaction; (2) procarcinogens, which produce tumors only after they have been somehow modified by the host; and (3) cocarcinogens, which do not cause cancer but enhance the effects of carcinogens and procarcinogens. There are also tumor-inhibiting stimuli that prevent tumor induction and which also can be either anticarcinogen, proanticarcinogen, or coanticarcinogen. Sklar and Anisman suggest that the physiological consequences of stress may act as either procarcinogens or cocarcinogens or as proanticarcinogens or coanticarcinogens. What we are looking for, then, is a mechanism whereby stress affects the neural, hormonal, or immune systems that either promote or inhibit tumor-active stimuli or otherwise change normal cells into neoplastic cells.

Tumor growth occurs through failure of the immune system, endocrine stimulation, and alterations in the vascular system. Since stress affects both hor-monal and immunological functioning, and since it further considerably alters the vascular system, the effects of stress on tumor growth could be accomplished through all of these pathways. Metastasis of cancer cells also involves these same systems which are intimately involved with stress reactions. At the system level, then, there is a basis for suggesting that stress can affect the induction, growth, and metastasis of tumors.

Sklar and Anisman summarize the correlational evidence available on the relationship between stress and cancer in humans. In general, they indicate that cancer is associated with psychological stress. Thus, life-stress events frequently precede cancer; cancer is particularly prevalent among individuals who have lost an important emotional relationship; cancer incidence is marked among individuals who express a sense of loss and hopelessness and inability to cope with the stress of separation. Further, psychological factors such as separation and coping failure are *predictive* of later cancer development. Finally, several studies show that diffi-culty in adjusting to illness prior to surgery is associated with relapse, whereas ability to express anger toward the disease and doctors is associated with longer survival.

Animal studies showing a relationship between stress and cancer are volumi-nous. Some selected findings reviewed by Sklar and Anisman (1981) include: Acute physical stress increases the number of tumors, whereas chronic physical stress de-creases the number and size of tumors; social stresses (e.g., isolation), both chronic and acute, increase tumor incidence; escapable shock inhibits tumor growth, in-escapable shock exacerbates growth (note that *chronic* inescapable shock inhibits growth); *change* in social condition, rather than isolation versus communal living as such, seems to be the important stimulus that promotes tumor development; and, physical stress applied *before* tumor induction inhibits tumor growth, whereas the opposite results occur when the stress is applied *after* induction. The authors summarize, "Stress may either exacerbate or inhibit tumor development, depending on the availability of coping responses, premorbid stress history, stress type, stress chronicity, and social conditions" (p. 382). They make special note of the interesting finding that *uncontrollable* stress enhances tumor growth, but that when *control* over stress is possible, tumor growth is unaffected.

With caution, Sklar and Anisman suggest that stress is related to neoplasia in humans. They contend that it is not stress that *causes* cancer, but rather that stress may affect the course of the disease. Moreover, failure to cope adequately with stress appears to be an essential element. Psychological variables might contribute to the induction of tumors or the proliferation of cancer cells following carcinogen exposure. Continued stress after induction and growth may contribute to metastasis through enhanced immuno-suppression.

In all of the studies that showed the relationship between stress and cancer, the methodology used always involved massive doses of cancer cells and the major dependent variable was the rate of cancer development. A direct test of the role of cognitive control over health/disease processes would be the ability of the organism to prevent the onset of cancer. A recent, definitive study by Visintainer, Volpicelli, and Seligman (1982) accomplished this. They "measured tumor rejection as a function of the controllability of shock by using a dose of tumor cells designed to induce tumor in only 50 percent of unshocked rats. If the shock, as a physical stressor, was sufficient to influence tumor development, then the escapable- and inescapable-shock groups would show the same rate of tumor rejection. However, if the psychological state induced by uncontrollable shock inhibited tumor rejection, then only rats exposed to inescapable shock would show a reduced ability to resist the tumor challenge" (p. 438). The results were striking. "Rats receiving inescapable shock were only half as likely to reject the tumor and twice as likely to die as rats receiving escapable shock or no shock" (p. 438). Thus, psychological control was shown to be directly related to the prevention of the onset of cancer—the maintenance of a state of health. An interesting result not discussed by Visintainer et al. was the fact that there was a trend for the stressed rats who had psychological control to be more successful in tumor rejection than the control group of rats who received no stress (63 percent rejection versus 54 percent, respectively). These data suggest that a reasonable hypothesis to test at the physiological level is to what extent exposure to stress along with psychological control may actually lead to health enhancement.

Social Support

Why social support? Earlier I argued that stress and its sources are not necessarily negative events or threats to the organism as is so often assumed. Depending on the meaning the source of stress has in terms of perceived control, it can be viewed as a positive event and an opportunity for overall enhancement of the well-being of the organism. Such is the case with social support. It is axiomatic that individuals under stress who have adequate social support do not exhibit the kind and quantity of disorders, both mental and physical, as those who lack social support. I suggest that it is not social support per se, but the meaning that it has in terms of perceived control over the sources of stress that determines the effects of social support on stress reactions. Thus I find it informative to view social support as a source of stress that could have positive or negative consequences, depending on how the organism uses it.

An equally important reason for using social support in my example is the fact that many organisms, and especially humans, are by nature social animals. The literature shows that prenatal and neonatal parent-offspring interactions are fundamental to survival. Basic attachment behaviors are biogrammed and determine not only survival but life-span adaptation. The biological and psychological literature clearly establishes that social bonding, attachment, emotional connectedness, and the use of social support is critical to well-being. Many studies reveal that there is a connection between social support, perceived control, endorphins, and disease.

What is social support? Silver and Wortman (1980) provide a summary of the numerous meanings given the term in recent research usage. Social support is: (1) expression of positive affect (e.g., information that one is cared for and loved, or that one is esteemed and respected); (2) expressing agreement with, or acknowledgment of, a person's beliefs, interpretations, or feelings; (3) encouraging the open expression of a person's beliefs and feelings; (4) provision of material aid; (5) provision of information that the person is part of a network or support system of mutual obligation or reciprocal help. It is clear from the above definitions that social support is a multidimensional construct involving cognitive, affective, and behavioral components. It might be useful to look at the function served by these various components. They all "refer to an individual's access to interpersonal resources" (Lefcourt et al., 1981). The function these resources serve is to provide the individual with information about how to cope with a stress at hand. As Caplan (1981) says, "The most important contribution of social support to a stressed individual is in the cognitive and educational areas in helping him with concrete tasks" (p. 416). This is consistent with Bandura's (1982) theory that social supports have informational implications for self-efficacy, and Averill's (1979) position on the value of information for perceived control. In emphasizing this cognitive function of social support, I do not wish to minimize the contribution of the affective and behavioral components. Rather, I see these components as augmenting the primary function of social support, which is the perceived control that information provides.

There is considerable evidence available to support the notion that social support is an important source of cognitive control. In his recent paper on the psychosocial aspects of the mastery of stress, Caplan (1981) suggests that since stress-induced shortcomings are mainly cognitive, it is in this area that an individual primarily needs assistance. Social support can add to this information. In Caplan's words, a social support group

> helps him improve his own data collection; aids him in evaluating the situation and working out a sensible plan; and assists him in implementing his plan, assessing its consequences, and replanning in line with feedback information. It reminds him of his continuing identity and bolsters his positive feelings about himself; assures him that his discomforts are expectable and, although burdensome, can usually be tolerated; and maintains his hope in some form of successful outcome of his efforts, which is a prerequisite to his continuing them. (p. 415)

Cobb's (1976) research on social support as a moderator of stress and disease favors this kind of information-leading-to-cognitive-control approach. With such diverse dependent variables as depression relief and reduced need for pain medication, Cobb shows that the value of social support in effecting these outcomes is the independence that social support information provides rather than any goods or services involved. The suggestion is that social networks without information may lead to dependency and exacerbation of symptoms. In Bandura's (1982) terms, self-efficacy is a mediator of perceived control. His research shows that social support information enhances self-efficacy in heart attack patients. Indeed, he says, "Psychological recovery from a heart attack is a social, rather than an individual, matter" (p. 131).

At the physiological level, there is a very important factor to consider regarding the meaning of social support and its effects on coping behaviors. I refer to the phenomenon known as *social facilitation* (Zajonc, 1965). For social organisms, the mere presence of others is sufficient to generate a physiological state of arousal. Whether this state of arousal is followed by positive or negative consequences is determined by the state of learning of the organism with respect to the task at hand. If the organism is in a *learned state* in a Hullian sense, the physiological arousal facilitates the emission of a *correct* response which is high in the organism's habit hierarchy leading to positive outcomes. If, on the other hand, the organism is not in a learned state with respect to the correct response, then any number of competing, incorrect responses will occur leading to negative outcomes and a weakening of the probability of emitting correct responses.

In the present context, this social facilitation principle can be applied to the presence of others as potential sources of social support during time of stress. If an individual had perceived control regarding what is to be done (i.e., is in a learned state), then the presence of others will facilitate optimal performance of appropriate coping behaviors which will reduce the effects of the stress. If, on the other hand (and this is the critical point), the individual does not have perceived control, then the presence of others will not only not have a facilitating effect, but rather, due to the accompanying increase in physiological arousal, it can be expected that dysfunctional responses will occur, and an overall increase in the negative effects of stress will result.

I suggest that such may be the case when there is a significant shift for an individual who has a history of little social support, and then experiences a significant shift in amount of social support in times of stress. The overall effect may be a debilitating state of physiological arousal.

Finally, Lefcourt (1981) reports research that individuals who are high on internality (and thus are better able to make use of problem-solving information) were the only ones to benefit from social support under stressful conditions. The upshot of these studies is that the function of social support is to provide information leading to perceived control.

Instead of looking at the presence/absence of social support, I suggest we look at *changes* in social support across the life span, and the meaning these changes have, to understand its relationship to health. As Sklar and Anisman (1981) observed, it is not the presence or absence of social support that predicts cancer induction, growth, and metastasis, but it is a change in social support that is predictive. A number of studies show that under certain conditions, the lack of social support does not lead to negative consequences whereas its presence can be deleterious (Brown, 1979; Lefcourt et al., 1981; Silver & Wortman, 1980).

Change in stressors, in general, has been shown to be more significant than the quantity or quality of stress (Amir et al., 1980; Eisdorpher & Wilke, 1977; Lefcourt et al., 1981). The question is not, What is stressing me? but, In what way and by how much does the present stressor deviate from what I am used to and hence expect? and further, What meaning does this deviation have for me especially in terms of control? Change affects the organism's physiological state. Frankenhaeuser's (1978) research confirms this. She says, "In general, stimulus conditions that are perceived as deviating from those to which a person is accustomed will induce a change in adrenaline output, whereas stimuli and events that are perceived as part of the familiar environment will not affect secretion. Novelty, change, challenge, and anticipation may be considered key components in the psychosocial conditions triggering the adrenal-medullary response" (p. 128). Note also, it is *perceived* change that counts.

This notion of change as effective stimulus is not new. A number of years ago, Fiske and Maddi (1961) presented an insightful theory of change in their text, *Functions of Varied Experience*. They presented research which supported their position that organisms seek out and are positively responsive to "optimal levels of stimulation." In a recent application of this principle, Kobasa (Kobasa, 1979; Kobasa, Hilker, & Maddi, 1979) has shown that it can apply to answering the question, Who stays healthy under stress? She shows that there are three critical variables that determine the answer—commitment, perceived control, and challenge. In her words, "Those who have sense of commitment to the various aspects of their lives, . . . who believe that they have control over their lives, . . . and *who seek novelty and challenge*, will remain relatively healthy" (p. 596, emphasis added).

To the extent that a change in social support is perceived as being within the optimal range of that which is expected, based on biological survival requirements, the organism's stage of social development, and the social learning that has occurred, to this extent it will be received as an opportunity for information leading to recovery or enhancement of perceived control. To the extent that a change in social support is unexpected, that is, outside the optimal range, to this extent it will lead to biological, psychological, and behavioral deficits (recall the Zajonc, 1965, work on social facilitation).

FUTURE DIRECTIONS

Minimally, this chapter has been a selected literature review on correlates and functions of endorphins and perceived control. Maximally, it represents the beginnings of theoretical statements regarding the role that endorphins and cognitive control play as mechanisms of health.

Clearly, a research-based theory is required. A framework to follow is provided by Panksepp (1981). In this exceptional paper he organizes the extensive work done in his laboratory and advances both an opioid theory of social attachments and a more general theoretical statement that "brain opioid systems could be major neurochemical substrates for the genesis of habits in general" (p. 163). Discussion of opioid control over pleasure, emotion, and psychiatric disorders is also included.

The major difference between Panksepp's (1981) orientation and mine is that he theorizes opioid control over behaviors (e.g., habits, social attachments) whereas I am suggesting that opioids are involved somehow in the physiological representation of cognitive processes.

A research program needs to be established that will allow for correlational and preferably direct evidence of predictable variability in endorphin effects on physiology and health as a result of the manipulation of perceived control.

An animal model would be of considerable help. In the first place, direct tests of endorphin release are being developed (Panksepp & Bishop, 1981), and these can be used with animals. Secondly, specific hypotheses about perceived control over social support as a stressor and its effects on health could be operationalized using mice and the experimental methodologies of Henry (Henry & Stephens, 1977). His studies on disruption of social order in mice could be modified to allow for the animals to either have control over the disruption or not, and resultant endorphin changes could be measured. Opioid intervention to reverse the effects could follow.

At the human level, research needs to be conducted in which social support is assessed along the lines I have indicated. That is, the quantity and quality of social support defined as the information it provides in terms of perceived control could be measured. Most importantly, an assessment could be taken of how the present levels of support are perceived in terms of changes within or outside of what the individual considers to be an optimal range (which, in my thinking, has important perceived-control implications). These measurements could be correlated with changes in endorphin levels extracted from appropriate sites (e.g., blood samples), and both of the above could be correlated with changes in health status.

My interest in aging and health is what originally led me into this field of investigation, and it occurs to me that the aged offer an especially important source of research data and theory development. Ideally, variables such as perceived control over social support should be manipulated. While we cannot and would not want to do this for ethical reasons, the environment of old people provides "natural" instances of social support as well as changes in social support. Consider such events as being isolated from children and other relations, loss of spouse, retirement from employment, either voluntary or involuntary, and entrance into a nursing home or other institution for the aged. These life events and others are natural changes in social support, and there is a wealth of literature on their effects on health including depression, cardiovascular disease, and death.

Applying my theoretical notions to the aged, it is my thesis that as a result of lifelong patterns of social support and attachment, elderly individuals are psychologically predisposed to respond to a continuation of, or changes in, social stressors in unique cognitive, affective, and behavioral ways which determine whether health is enhanced or disease is facilitated. If the above-mentioned life events are perceived by the elderly as being out of their control, then the endorphin-controlled neuroendocrine survival processes will be chronically engaged, the immune system suppressed, and disease will result. A combination of cognitive control therapy and pharmacological endorphin treatment (both yet to be developed) could be tested for ameliorative effects.

These are not easy tasks, and serious ethical and medical questions must certainly be answered, but the potential payoff in length and quality of life seem to indicate that the necessary multidisciplinary collaboration is warranted.

REFERENCES

ABRAMSON, L. Y., GARBER, J., & SELIGMAN, M.E.P. (1980). Learned helplessness in humans: An attributional analysis. In J. Garber & M.E.P. Seligman (Eds.), *Human helplessness: Theory and application* (pp. 3-34). New York: Academic Press.

AKIL, H., MADDEN, J. IV, PATRICK, R. L., & BARCHAS, J. D. (1976). Stress-induced increase in endogenous opiate peptides: Concurrent analgesia and its partial reversal by nalozone. In *Opiates and endogenous opioid peptides: Proceedings of the International Narcotics Research Club Meeting, Aberdeen, United Kingdom, July 19-22, 1976* (pp. 63-70). Amsterdam: Elsevier/North Holland Biomedical Press.

AMIR, S., BROWN, Z. W., & AMIT, Z. (1980). The role of endorphins in stress: Evidence and speculations. *Neuroscience and Biobehavioral Review, 4,* 77-86.

AVERILL, J. R. (1979). A selective review of cognitive and behavioral factors involved in the regulation of stress. In R. A. Depue (Ed.), *The psychobiology of the depressive disorders: Implications for the effects of stress* (pp. 365-387). New York: Academic Press.

BAMMER, K., & NEWBERRY, B. H. (Eds.). (1981). *Stress and cancer.* Toronto: C. J. Hogrefe, Inc.

BANDURA, A. (1982). Self-efficacy mechanism in human agency. *American Psychologist, 37,* 122-147.

BERGER, P. A., AKIL, H., WATSON, S. J., & BARCHAS, J. D. (1982). Behavioral pharmacology of the endorphins. In W. P. Cregger, C. H. Coggins, & E. W. Hancoc (Eds.), *Annual review of medicine: Selected topics in the clinical sciences* (Vol. 33, pp. 397-415). Palo Alto, CA: Annual Reviews, Inc.

BLOOM, F. E. (1981). Neuropeptides. *Scientific American, 245,* 148-168.

BOLLES, R. C., & FANSELOW, M. S. (1982). Endorphins and behavior. In M. R. Rosenzweig & L. W. Porter (Eds.), *Annual review of psychology* (Vol. 33, pp. 87-101). Palo Alto, CA: Annual Reviews, Inc.

BROWN, G. W. (1979). The social etiology of depression—London studies. In R. A. Depue (Ed.), *The psychobiology of the depressive disorders: Implications for the effects of stress* (pp. 263-289). New York: Academic Press.

CAPLAN, G. (1981). Mastery of stress: Psychosocial aspects. *American Journal of Psychiatry, 138,* 413-420.

COBB, S. (1976). Social support as a moderator of life stress. *Psychosomatic Medicine, 38,* 300-314.

EISDORPHER, C., & WILKE, F. (1977). Stress, disease, aging, and behavior. In J. E. Birren & K. W. Schaie (Eds.), *Handbook of the psychology of aging* (pp. 251-275). New York: Van Nostrand Reinhold Co.

FISKE, D. W., & MADDI, S. R. (Eds.). (1961). *Functions of varied experience.* Homewood, IL: Dorsey Press, Inc.

FRANKENHAEUSER, M. (1978). Psychoneuroendocrine approaches to the study of emotion as related to stress and coping. In H. E. Howe, Jr. & R. A. Dienstbier (Eds.), *1978 Nebraska symposium on motivation, Vol. 26* (pp. 123-161). Lincoln, NB: University of Nebraska Press.

FRANKENHAEUSER, M. (1981, June). *The sympathetic-adrenal and pituitary-adrenal response to challenge: Comparison between the sexes.* Paper prepared for the German Conference on Coronary Prone Behavior, Altenbert, F. R. G.

GARBER, J., & SELIGMAN, M.E.P. (Eds.), (1980). *Human helplessness: Theory and application.* New York: Academic Press.

HENRY, J. P., & STEPHENS, P. M. (1977). *Stress, health, and the social environment: A sociobiological approach to medicine.* New York: Springer-Verlag.

HERZ, A. (Ed.). (1978). *Developments in opiate research.* New York: Marcel and Dekker, Inc.

HOLADAY, J. W., & LOH, H. H. (1981). Neurobiology of β-endorphin and related peptides. In C. H. Li (Ed.), *Hormonal proteins and peptides, Vol. X, β-endorphin* (pp. 204-291). New York: Academic Press.

HUGHES, J., SMITH, T. W., KOSTERLITZ, H. W., FOTHERGILL, L. A., MORGAN, B. A., & MORRIS, H. R. (1975). Identification of two related pentapeptides from the brain with potent opiate agonist activity. *Nature, 258,* 577-579.

ISAACSON, R. L. (1974). *The limbic system.* New York: Plenum Press.

JEMMETT, J. B. III, & LOCKE, S. E. (1984). Psychosocial factors, immunologic mediation, and human susceptibility to infectious diseases: How much do we know? *Psychological Bulletin, 95,* 78-108.

KANT, I. (1979). On the power of the mind to master its morbid feelings by sheer resolution. In M. J. Gregor (Trans. and Intro.), *Immanuel Kant: The conflict of the faculties.* New York: Abaris Books, Inc. (Original work published 1798.)

KOBASA, S. C. (1979). Stressful life events, personality, and health: An inquiry into hardiness. *Journal of Personality and Social Psychology, 37,* 1-11.

KOBASA, S. C., HILKER, R. R., JR., & MADDI, S. R. (1979). Who stays healthy under stress? *Journal of Occupational Medicine, 21,* 595-598.

KOOB, G. F., & BLOOM, F. E. (1982). Behavioral effects of neuropeptides: Endorphins and vasopressin. In I. S. Edelman (Ed.), *Annual review of physiology, Vol. 44* (pp. 571-582). Palo Alto, CA: Annual Reviews, Inc.

KOSTERLITZ, H. W. (Ed.). (1976). *Opiates and endogenous opioid peptides: Proceedings of the International Narcotics Research Club Meeting, Aberdeen, United Kingdom, July 19-22, 1976.* Amsterdam: Elsevier/North Holland Biomedical Press.

LAZARUS, R. S. (1977). Cognitive and coping processes in emotion. In A. Monat & R. S. Lazarus (Eds.), *Stress and coping.* New York: Columbia University Press.

LEFCOURT, H. M., MARTIN, R. A., & EBERS, K. (1981). Coping with stress: A model for clinical psychology. *Academic Psychology Bulletin, 3,* 355-364.

LEWIS, W. E., MISHIKIN, M., BRAGIN, E., BROWN, R. M., PERT, C. B., & PERT, A. (1981). Opiate receptor gradients in monkey cerebral cortex: Correspondence with sensory processing hierarchies. *Science, 211,* 1166-1169.

LI, C. H. (Ed.). (1981). *Hormonal proteins and peptides, Vol. X, β-endorphin.* New York: Academic Press.

LIEBESKIND, J., & BAUL, I. (1977). Psychological and physiological mechanisms of pain. In M. R. Rosenzweig & L. W. Porter (Eds.), *Annual review of psychology* (Vol. 28, pp. 41-60). Palo Alto, CA: Annual Reviews, Inc.

MacLENNON, A. J., DRUGAN, R. C., HYSON, R. L., MAIER, S. F., MADDEN, J. IV, & BARCHAS, J. D. (1982). Corticosterone: A critical factor in an opioid form of stress-induced analgesia. *Science, 215,* 1530–1532.

MANDENOFF, A., FUMERON, F., APFELBAUM, M., & MARGULES, D. L. (1982). Endogenous opiates and energy balance. *Science, 215,* 1536–1538.

MARGULES, D. L. (1979). The obesity of middle age: A common variety of Cushing's syndrome due to a chronic increase in adrenocorticotrophin (ACTH) and beta-endorphin activity. *Advances in Experimental Medical Biology, 116,* 279–290.

MASON, J. W. (1975). A historical view of the stress field: Part II. *Journal of Human Stress, 1,* 22–36.

MASON, J. W., MAHER, J. T., HARTLEY, L. H., MORIGEY, E. H., PERLOW, M. J., & JONES, L. G. (1976). Selectivity of corticosteroid and catecholamine responses to various natural stimuli. In G. Serban (Ed.), *Psychopathology of human adaptation* (pp. 147–171). New York: Plenum.

MATARAZZO, J. D. (1982). Behavioral health's challenge to academic, scientific, and professional psychology. *American Psychologist, 37,* 1–14.

McCARTY, R., HORBALY, W. G., BROWN, M. S., & BAUCOM, K. (1981). Effects of handling during infancy on the sympathetic-adrenal medullary system of rats. *Developmental Psychobiology, 14,* 533–539.

MICZEK, K. A., THOMPSON, M. L., & SHUSTER, L. (1982). Opioid-like analgesia in defeated mice. *Science, 215,* 1520–1522.

MILLER, S. M. (1980). Why having control reduces stress: If I can stop the roller coaster, I don't want to get off. In J. Garber & M.E.P. Seligman (Eds.), *Human helplessness: Theory and application* (pp. 71–95). New York: Academic Press.

MILLER, S. M. (1981). Predictability and human stress: Toward a clarification of evidence and theory. In L. Berkowitz (Ed.), *Advances in experimental social psychology* (Vol. 14, pp. 203–256). New York: Academic Press.

MOORE, M. (1982). Endorphins and exercise: A puzzling relationship. *The Physician and Sportsmedicine, 10,* 111–114.

MORLEY, J. E. (1981). The endocrinology of the opiates and opioid peptides. *Metabolism, 30,* 195–209.

MORLEY, J. E., & LEVINE, A. S. (1980). Stress-induced eating is mediated through endogenous opiates. *Science, 209,* 1259–1261.

PANKSEPP, J. (1981). Brain opioids—A neurochemical substrate for narcotic and social dependence. In S. J. Cooper (Ed.), *Theory in psychopharmacology* (pp. 149–175). London: Academic Press.

PANKSEPP, J., & BISHOP, P. (1981). An autoradiographic map of (^{3}H) diprenorphine binding in rat brain: Effects of social interaction. *Brain Research Bulletin, 7,* 405–410.

PANKSEPP, J., HERMAN, B. H., VILBERG, T., BISHOP, P., & DE ESKINAZI, F. G. (1980). Endogenous opioids and social behavior. *Neuroscience and Biobehavioral Reviews, 4,* 473–487.

PERT, C. B., & SNYDER, S. H. (1973). Opiate receptor: Demonstration in nervous tissue. *Science, 179,* 1011–1014.

RENNER, V. J., & BIRREN, J. E. (1980). Stress: Physiological and psychological mechanisms. In J. E. Birren & R. B. Sloane (Eds.), *Handbook of mental health and aging* (pp. 310–336). Englewood Cliffs, NJ: Prentice-Hall.

RIVIER, C., BROWNSTEIN, M., SPIESS, J., RIVIER, J., & VALE, W. (1982). *In vivo* corticotropin-releasing factor-induced secretion of adrenocorticotropin, β-endorphin, and corticosterone. *Endocrinology, 110,* 272–274.

RUDA, M. A. (1982). Opiates and pain pathways: Demonstration of enkephalin synapses on dorsal horn projection neurons. *Science, 215,* 1523-1525.

SCHULZ, R. (1980). Aging and control. In J. Garber & M.E.P. Seligman (Eds.), *Human helplessness: Theory and application* (pp. 261-277). New York: Academic Press.

SELIGMAN, M.E.P. (1975). *Helplessness: On depression development and death.* San Francisco: W. H. Freeman.

SELYE, H. (1976). *The stress of life* (rev. ed.). New York: McGraw-Hill.

SHOCK, N. W. (1977). Systems integration. In C. E. Finch & L. Hayflick (Eds.), *Handbook of the biology of aging* (pp. 639-665). New York: Van Nostrand Reinhold Company.

SILVER, R. L., & WORTMAN, C. B. (1980). Coping with undesirable life events. In J. Garber & M.E.P. Seligman (Eds.), *Human helplessness: Theory and application* (pp. 279-340). New York: Academic Press.

SKLAR, L. S., & ANISMAN, H. (1981). Stress and cancer. *Psychological Bulletin, 89,* 369-406.

SMITH, A. P., & LOH, H. H. (1981). The opiate receptor. In C. H. Li (Ed.), *Hormonal proteins and peptides, Vol. X, β-endorphin* (pp. 89-170). New York: Academic Press.

STEGER, R. W., SONNTAG, W. E., VAN VUGT, D. A., FORMAN, L. J., & MEITES, J. (1980). Reduced ability of naloxone to stimulate LH and testosterone release in aging male rats: Possible relation to increase in hypothalamic met5-enkephalin. *Life Sciences, 27,* 747-753.

TESCHEMACHER, H. (1978). Endogenous ligands of opiate receptors (endorphins). In A. Herz (Ed.), *Developments in opiate research* (pp. 67-151). New York: Marcel and Dekker, Inc.

TIMIRAS, P. S. (1978). Biological perspectives on aging. *American Scientist, 66,* 605-613.

TREVARTHEN, C. (1980). Functional organization of the human brain. In M. C. Wittrock (Ed.), *The brain and psychology* (pp. 33-91). New York: Academic Press.

VISINTAINER, M. A., VOLPICELLI, J. R., & SELIGMAN, M.E.P. (1982). Tumor rejection in rats after inescapable or escapable shock. *Science, 216,* 437-439.

WILKINSON, M., & BHANOT, R. (1982). A puberty-related attenuation of opiate peptide-induced inhibition of LH secretion. *Endocrinology, 110,* 1046-1049.

WITTROCK, M. C. (Ed.). (1980). *The brain and psychology.* New York: Academic Press.

WURTZ, R. H., GOLDBERG, M. E., & ROBINSON, D. L. (1982). Brain mechanisms of visual attention. *Scientific American, 246,* 124-135.

WURTZMAN, R. J. (1982). Nutrients that modify brain function. *Scientific American, 246,* 50-59.

ZAJONC, R. B. (1965). Social facilitations. *Science, 149,* 269-274.

6

VOODOO DEATH IN THE AMERICAN AGED

How Beliefs about Health and Aging Can Affect the Health of Older People

Deborah D. Newquist

How is aging constructed in the dominant American society? Obviously, a multitude of factors is involved in this process. The purpose of this chapter is to examine one of these factors as an influence on health in the later years. Focusing on the ideational component of culture, this chapter will explore how beliefs about aging and health in American society can affect the health of people as they grow old. An overriding concern which guides this discussion is that of the potentially toxic effects of negative beliefs about aging on old age as manifested in our society. Can negative beliefs about aging impair health in old age? And, if so, how?

This chapter is divided into four parts: (1) a description of how aging is variously constructed in different societies; (2) a presentation of instances where beliefs can be seen to affect physical functioning; (3) a discussion of the physiological and behavioral mechanisms which could lead to these health outcomes; and (4) a consideration of health and aging as fashioned by our society.

AGING IN CROSS-CULTURAL PERSPECTIVE

Human aging is a cultural as well as a biological construct. Although aging entails processes intrinsic to the organism, universal functions imposed by genetic dictates, it is also a process which is shaped by culture. Biological aging involves regular changes in the organism with the passage of time which make the organism less likely to survive. Cultural customs and practices, such as dietary patterns, habitation modes, group structures, and economic pursuits, collaborate with these biological processes to fashion the aging experience of a particular group. Moreover, culture as an ideational system participates in the construction of aging. The physiological changes of aging are interpreted by culture and those interpretations, or ideas and beliefs, give rise to behavior in response to the changes. Interpretations or beliefs about aging affect what is done or not done, felt or not felt, expected or not expected in regard to it, on both an individual and a group level. In this way, culture as ideas comes to shape the process of aging, not only to react to it. The particular way in which old age is manifested in a given society, then, is the outcome of the interplay of biological and cultural forces. Thus, while intrinsic aging can be said to be panhuman, manifested aging differs across cultures.

Definitions of old age, for example, vary cross-culturally. In preliterate societies old age is often defined *functionally*: It is only when a person can no longer perform assigned roles that he or she is considered old. Observed declines in physical condition mark the onset of old age in these societies. The Chipewyan of northern Canada use this definition of old age (Sharp, 1981); so do the residents of Etal Island in Micronesia (Nason, 1981). Other societies use *formal* definitions. In these societies the commencement of old age corresponds with a change in social status, such as when a person becomes a grandparent (Clark, 1967; Clark & Anderson, 1967) or when a man's age set moves into a new age grade, as among the Latuka of southern Sudan (Kertzer & Madison, 1981). Some societies use a combination of criteria. For example, among the Annang of Nigeria people are considered old when they become grandparents and when they have gray hair (Brink, personal communication, 1982).

In contemporary Western societies, old age is formally defined, and increasingly *temporally* or *chronologically* defined. To be old is to have lived a certain number of years, commonly at least 60 to 65. The definition of old age in these societies becomes further removed from functional physiological statuses (Clark, 1967; Clark & Anderson, 1967).

Conceptions of the aging experience also vary across cultures. In some societies views of aging emphasize decline and loss. Our society would be an example. Others, such as the Kirghiz of Afghanistan, primarily regard aging as progress toward achieving greater wisdom, respect, and privilege, as a process of growth and attainment. The Kirghiz language, in fact, lacks such negative descriptions of aging as "declining years" (Shahrani, 1981, p. 190).

Views of health in old age also vary. Among the Asmat of New Guinea all illnesses of young and middle-aged people are believed to be unnatural, to be caused by either soul loss, object intrusion, or spirit intervention. Certain ailments of the elderly (those aged about 45 or older), however, are seen as natural, as inexorable concomitants of aging, and as inevitably and immediately leading to death. (Interestingly, the Asmat sometimes in these instances begin mourning rituals before the older person is actually dead; and, occasionally, older people thought to be close to death are abandoned. See Van Arsdale, 1981.) Other societies, like the Kirghiz, recognize physical decline with age but do not acknowledge mental declines. The Kirghiz vocabulary has no words equivalent to *senility,* for example (Shahrani, 1981). Among many primitive societies the aged were believed to possess magical strength and power. Some viewed them as invulnerable to disease-causing agents, as invincible in combating illnesses, as spiritual mediators of life and death forces (Simmons, 1945). These views contrast markedly with those in our society, which regard the aged as more vulnerable than younger persons.

The role and status of the elderly, their position in the social group, and the treatment they are accorded differs by society. As Simmons (1945) first described, the experience of aging varies quite dramatically. In some societies, the elderly hold positions of power and respect, are instrumental in group activities, and have enhanced access to economic, social and political resources. In other societies, however, their position in the group is tenuous; they lack resources, respect, or power; and they depend heavily upon the goodwill of others for their continued survival.

Finally, the number of people who live to old age also varies cross-culturally. Although all societies have a category of persons they define as "old," in undeveloped societies fewer people survive into chronologically defined old age than in developed societies. The life span potential of these people is relatively the same. What differs is their particular person-environment fit and, importantly for our purposes here, the interplay between their biological potential and their cultural patterns—the mediation of biology by their culture.

As this chapter is concerned with the ideational aspects of culture and the bearing which these symbolic elements can have on health outcomes in old age, we will now turn to a discussion of belief/health relationships.

THE IMPACT OF BELIEFS ON HEALTH

Numerous investigators have noted adverse effects which beliefs can render on the health or physiological functioning of individuals. These relationships can take three forms: direct, indirect, or a combination of direct and indirect impacts.

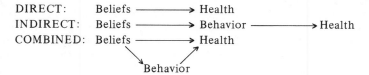

Accounts in the psychological/psychiatric literature yield several examples of direct impact relationships. Often these involve instances where a person was "frightened to death." Notable in regard to these cases is the person's absolute belief in the reality, inevitability, and immutability of his or her life circumstance. It is this belief which gives rise to the lethal response.

The case of the 27-year-old woman, described by Goodfriend and Wolpert (1976), who died from psychological fright is one example. This woman was a hospitalized psychiatric patient who died a sudden, unexpected death. Before her death the woman had appeared to be in good physical health and an autopsy revealed no pathologically explainable cause for her death, nor any signs of lethal catatonia or "exhaustion death." Prior to her death this patient had expressed fears of impending demise to her therapist. These fears followed the uncovering of repressed hostile fantasy material. Goodfriend and Wolpert explain that the patient died before therapeutic attempts to "detoxify"[1] the fantasies could be made. They state that through detoxification "she would learn that these fantasies were products of her imagination and that while there were good reasons for the form the fantasies took, they did not have anything to do with the real world, and she would not be allowed to act on them" (Goodfriend & Wolpert, 1976, pp. 353-354). In other words, detoxification would alter this woman's beliefs about the nature of her fantasies. Prior to her death this patient was in extreme emotional distress, was afraid she was going to die, and felt hopeless, alienated, and lost. Goodfriend and Wolpert postulate that this state set off a physiological reaction leading to death; they conclude that this patient was frightened to death by her fantasies.

Engel (1971) discusses the phenomenon of sudden death during emotionally intense experiences. He reports on 170 such cases and notes a pattern in their occurrence: they are characterized by an extreme emotional context wherein the person fears a loss of control over the situation and feels hopeless about changing the situation; in other words, the person believes he or she is incapable of altering its course. Saul (1966) found similar features in his examination of three cases of persons who could no longer endure their present life situation but believed no alternative existed. These patients felt hopeless. He concludes that they reacted to their circumstances by death secondary to myocardial infarct. Barker (1965) describes the case of a middle-aged man who presented himself at a hospital exclaiming, "I am going to die, please don't let me die." This man died one-half hour after admission despite medical attempts to save him. The autopsy report was negative. Barker concludes that this man died of fright; his belief in his imminent, impending demise scared him to death. Coolidge (1969) presents the case of unexpected sudden death from ventricular fibrillation leading to cardiac arrest in a middle-aged female patient. This woman saw herself as being in an intolerable yet irremediable situation. She saw death as her only escape. Finally, Mathis (1964) describes a 53-year-old man who died following a death threat made on him by his mother. In his last interview before his death, this man discussed the threat, his fear of his mother's power, and his belief that he was "allergic" to his mother.

Indirect belief/health relationships are exemplified by accounts of the self-imposed waning demise of concentration camp prisoners described by Viktor Frankl (1962). Frankl argues that hope and meaning in life are crucial for survival—they motivate and structure life-sustaining behaviors. For Frankl, one could say that hope is the wind which fills the sails of life, it powers action. Meaning, on the other hand, is life's tiller, guiding purposeful activity. Without hope and meaning, the individual flounders, and ultimately dies. As Frankl describes:

> The prisoner who had lost faith in the future—his future—was doomed. With his loss of belief in the future, he also lost his spiritual hold; he let himself decline and become subject to mental and physical decay. . . . Usually it began with the prisoner refusing one morning to get dressed and wash or to go out on the parade grounds. . . . He just lay there, hardly moving. If this crisis was brought about by an illness, he refused to be taken to the sick-bay or to do anything to help himself. He simply gave up. There he remained, lying in his own excreta, and nothing bothered him any more. (Frankl, 1962, p. 74)

[1]It should be noted that "detoxify" is used here in a metaphorical sense, referring to attempts to remove or nullify the fearful components of the fantasy material.

Milton (1973) describes cancer patients who upon learning their diagnosis assume a demeanor of hopelessness and die. They do not die from the cancer, though; rather, they die before the cancer has become fatal. Finally, Engel (1968) discusses life settings and mental states which he argues are conducive to illness. These states he has labeled the *giving-up—given-up* complex.

Combined direct-indirect relationships involve situations where the individual's beliefs and behavior together affect health outcomes. The most striking example of this is voodoo death. Cannon (1942) expertly describes and analyzes these phenomena. Reporting from accounts in the ethnographic literature dating back to the sixteenth century, and from personal communications with medical specialists who had personally witnessed such events, he describes instances of voodoo death in vivid detail. Some excerpts from his descriptions would be useful here to convey the powerful nature of these occurrences. He presents this description of voodoo death in a tribe in the Lower Niger, quoting Leonard's 1906 account:

> I have seen more than one hardened old Haussa soldier dying steadily and by inches because he believed himself to be bewitched; no nourishment or medicines that were given to him had the slightest effect either to check the mischief or to improve his condition in any way, and nothing was able to divert him from a fate which he considered inevitable. In the same way, and under very similar conditions, I have seen Kru-men and others die in spite of every effort that was made to save them, simply because they had made up their minds, not (as we thought at the time) to die, but that being in the clutch of malignant demons they were bound to die. (Leonard as cited by Cannon, p. 169)

In another example he reports on the experience of Dr. P. S. Clarke who worked among the Kanakas in North Queensland:

> One day a Kanaka came to his hospital and told him he would die in a few days because a spell had been put upon him and nothing could be done to counteract it. The man had been known to Dr. Clarke for some time. He was given a very thorough examination, including an examination of the stool and the urine. All was found normal, but as he lay in bed he gradually grew weaker. Dr. Clarke called upon the foreman of the Kanakas to come to the hospital to give the man assurance, but on reaching the foot of the bed, the foreman leaned over, looked at the patient, and then turned to Dr. Clarke saying, "Yes, doctor, close up him he die" (i.e., he is nearly dead). The next day, at 11 o'clock in the morning, he ceased to live. A postmortem examination revealed nothing that could in any way account for the fatal outcome. (p. 171)

Finally, he quotes Dr. Herbert Basedow who in his 1925 book, *The Australian Aboriginal,* vividly describes the effects of bone pointing on a native victim:

> The man who discovers that he is being boned by any enemy is, indeed, a pitiable sight. He stands aghast, with his eyes staring at the treacherous pointer, and with his hands lifted as though to ward off the lethal medium, which he imagines is pouring into his body. His cheeks blanch and his eyes become glassy and the expression of his face becomes horribly distorted. . . .

He attempts to shriek but usually the sound chokes in his throat, and all that one might see is froth at his mouth. His body begins to tremble and the muscles twist involuntarily. He sways backwards and falls to the ground, and after a short time appears to be in a swoon: but soon after he writhes as if in mortal agony, and, covering his face with his hands, begins to moan. After a while he becomes very composed and crawls to his wurley. From this time onwards he sickens and frets, refusing to eat and keeping aloof from the daily affairs of the tribe. Unless help is forthcoming in the shape of a counter-charm administered by the hands of the Nangarri, or medicine-man, his death is only a matter of a comparatively short time. If the coming of the medicine-man is opportune he might be saved. (Basedow as quoted by Cannon, p. 172)

The power of these "hexes," of the impact of native beliefs on the functioning and, indeed, very survival, of tribe members cannot be denied. Cannon's investigation disproved the possibility of poisons or outside "unnatural" substances as precipitating voodoo deaths. He documented their reality. Significantly, he also traced their etiology to the "fatal power of the imagination" (Cannon, 1942, p. 170). In all the cases reported, it was the victim's absolute belief in the lethal efficacy of a native symbol which triggered the fatal process.

Cannon's analysis revealed voodoo death to be the outcome of a destructive blending of biological, psychological, and sociocultural forces. His analysis was significant in several respects. First, as described above, he identified the symbolic trigger to the process. Secondly, he recognized the social group's powerful role in the event. The group served to reinforce and confirm the veracity of the belief system to the stricken individual. Moreover, they ostracized the victim, withdrew their support, and disengaged from him, in effect, pronounced him socially dead. They placed him in a different social category and viewed him as more closely connected to the realm of the sacred, as removed from the ordinary concerns of community life. The victim's social status thus became liminal. Later, when the victim was near death, the group returned, not to rescue the individual, but to bury him ritually, to pay him last respects as it were, to mourn his death before him. This final social act cut the doomed individual off entirely from his or her community. Physical death followed.

Sudnow (1967) has labeled this group response *social death.* Based on his research in two hospital settings over a period of 1½ years, during which time he observed approximately 200 to 250 deaths, he describes social death as the group's behavioral response to the perception that an individual is dying. Social death behavior commenced once the individual was labeled as "dying." It entailed treating the patient as if he or she were already dead, making death arrangements, such as preparation for autopsies, funerals, and donations of body parts, withdrawing socially, and undertaking new social involvements which excluded the patient. Sudnow reports:

A typical instance of "social death" involved a male patient who was admitted to the Emergency Unit with a sudden perforation of a duodenal ulcer. He was operated upon, and, for a period of six days, remained in quite critical condition. His wife was informed that his chances of survival were poor, whereupon she stopped her visits to the hospital. After two weeks, the man's condition improved markedly and he was discharged in ambulatory condition. The next day he was readmitted to the hospital with a severe coronary. Before he died, he recounted his experience upon returning home. His wife had removed all of his clothing and personal effects from the house, had made preliminary arrangements for his burial with the mortuary establishment (she had written a letter which he discovered on his bureau, requesting a brochure on their rates), she no longer wore his wedding ring, and was found with another man, no doubt quite shocked at her husband's return. He reported that he left the house, began to drink heavily, and had a heart attack. (p. 77)

That social death can encourage biological death is strongly suggested in this account.

Glascock (1983) goes a step further and argues that the group selects out individuals who have become a burden and directs *death-hastening behavior* towards those individuals. Rather than *react* to the symbolic trigger then, it is the group which pulls that trigger according to Glascock. Death-hastening behavior can include forsaking the individual both socially as well as economically, abandoning the individual, or outright killing the individual. Furthermore, Glascock has demonstrated that these behaviors are often directed at the elderly.

In addition to the group's social response, Cannon also identified and described the important role played by the individuals' behavioral responses in voodoo deaths. The victims experienced terror followed by a state of apathy and hopelessness similar to that described by Frankl. They refused food and drink and totally withdrew from involvement in group activities. Some made no effort to live, to counteract the curse. They all viewed their fate as doomed and hopeless, as inevitable. They slowly grew weak and sickened. They "pined away" as their strength dissipated. In a day or two, they succumbed. Cannon cites as highly significant these behavioral responses. They contribute directly to the victim's physiological decline.

Lastly, Cannon explored the psychophysiological mechanisms by which voodoo death can result. He first questioned whether "an ominous and persistent state of fear can end the life of a man" (Cannon, 1942, p. 176). He then traced the physiological pathways which could lead to this end. These pathways center in the sympathetic-adrenal system which exercises control over the blood vessels and internal organs. He showed that, through lasting and intense action of this system, death can indeed result through a state of prolonged shock. In addition, lack of food and liquid collaborate in this fatal process by further exciting the sympathetic-adrenal system, in other words, by amplifying the body's shock response.

Subsequent research on the question of voodoo death has elaborated and extended Cannon's early findings. Most of this research has focused on identifying the mechanisms by which voodoo deaths occur. Richter (1957), in a study of rats forced to swim until they drowned, observed a state of hopelessness accompanied by parasympathetic nervous system hyperreactivity preceding death. He postulated that these same responses are present and instrumental in voodoo deaths. Lex (1977) offered another physiological explanation which involved "tuning" of the nervous system. She argued that voodoo deaths resulted when the equilibrium of the autonomic nervous system was severely and continuously disrupted by sudden or intense negatively defined stimulation. Based on work with the Aboriginal popu-

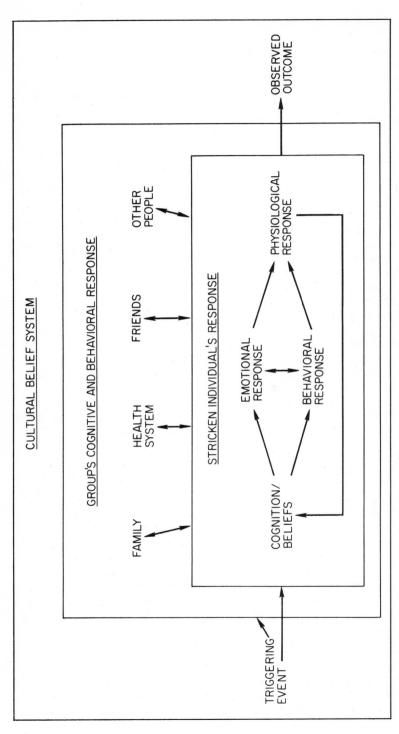

FIGURE 6-1. *The Dynamics of Voodoo Death.* This diagram illustrates how voodoo death can become a prophecy self-fulfilled. The outer circle represents the belief system which holds voodoo deaths to be real. The second, inner circle represents the group operating within the belief system, in response to a specific voodoo threat. The third, innermost circle depicts the targeted individual responding to the threat and to the group's responses and messages. The individual's responses, observed by the group, serve to influence the group's further behavior, and ultimately their belief system. If the individual dies, the efficacy of voodoo death is affirmed to the group, their beliefs are upheld.

lation in East Arnhem, Australia, Eastwell (1982) concluded that dehydration by rejection or confiscation of fluids was the mechanism of death in voodoo sequences. Furthermore, he described successful interventions by means of rehydration in two voodoo death situations. That voodoo death occurrences are triggered and reinforced by symbolic processes or that they are accompanied by group responses involving rejection of the individual while confirming the "inevitable," and that these factors are significant influences on the eventual outcome, is either explicitly or implicitly accepted by investigators in this area. A major exception would be Clune (1973), who believes, despite a lack of evidence to support his position, that poisoning is the death mechanism.

A summary of the salient features of belief/health relationships would be useful at this point. First, all the instances described above involve an *emotional response* on the part of the stricken individual. Whether fear, hopelessness, or helplessness, each occurrence is marked by an emotional component. Second, in the indirect and combined response patterns, observable *behavioral responses* are evident. The victims no longer seek food, liquid, social involvement, or help. Third, in the combined pattern there is a *social group response* which confirms and reinforces the lethal process. Fourth, the occurrences stem from the individuals' *perceptions* of a particular situation and their *belief* in the reality, inevitability, and immutability of the circumstance in which they find themselves. It is the individuals' conceptions of and belief in the situation which triggers their emotional and behavioral responses leading to their physiological decline. As fully elaborated, this relationship is diagrammed in Figure 6-1. Lastly, these occurrences have a relatively *acute character*. Although in the instances of voodoo death and the demise of the concentration camp victims, the process takes place over several days, it nonetheless is relatively brief in nature and has an intense quality.

The question now arises: Could these same outcomes result from chronic situations? If a person were repeatedly, though less intensely, threatened, could not the same or similar mechanisms operate to produce negative health outcomes? I would like to propose that they could. Using the voodoo death syndrome as a model, in the next section I will discuss the mechanisms through which these outcomes could be derived in a chronic context. This argument corresponds in part to that of Cohen and Ross (1983) who ask whether voodoo deaths do not in fact occur in modern societies; however, the approach taken here differs from theirs in that it more specifically encompasses the cultural, ideational aspects of these phenomena. It should be noted that it was Milton (1973) who first identified the voodoo principle in modern instances of self-willed death.

BELIEF-HEALTH MECHANISMS OVER TIME

A theoretical orientation which will help to guide this discussion is that of symbolic interactionism. Symbolic interactionism, originally formulated by George Herbert Mead, posits that society and individuals' actions within society are the products of expectational exchanges between those individuals. The theory rests upon the premise that humans as symbol-creating organisms have the capacity to abstract and imagine situations beyond their immediate subjective experience. This capacity enables us to produce and comprehend images of ourselves as held by others. It is these images which contribute to the formation of self-concept and to the shaping of behavior. Each of us, in turn, projects symbolic messages to our fellow group members which contribute to their conceptions of us, as well as to their own self-images and behavior. It is through this process of symbolic exchange that the human being as a social entity is created and that group norms and activities are shaped (Meltzer, 1967).

Symbolic interactionism recognizes humans as social beings highly dependent upon their group. It is their group participation which shapes their behavior and ultimately enables them to survive. Through the interaction of the group and the individual, beliefs are formulated and given reality, values and meanings are created and reinforced, knowledge is generated and transmitted, and reactions to life events are patterned. I will argue that it is also through this person/group interaction that bio-physiological processes can be shaped and that health outcomes can be influenced.

Although not labeling them as such, Cannon recognized symbolic interactionist processes as significant influences on the course of voodoo death. To quote his description:

> During the death illness which ensues, the group acts with all the outreachings and complexities of its organization and with countless stimuli to suggest death positively to the victim. . . . In addition to the social pressure upon him the victim himself . . . through the multiple suggestions which he receives, co-operates. . . . *He becomes what the attitude of his fellow tribesmen wills him to be.* Thus he assists in committing a kind of suicide. (Cannon, 1942, p. 174, emphasis added)

How can cognitive processes affect health outcomes over time? Two primary mechanisms appear relevant: stress reactions and health-related behaviors.

The Stress Model

Research in the area of stress dates back to the work of Cannon (1929) and Selye (1950). Over 50 years ago, Cannon undertook work investigating the effects of emotional excitement on physiological processes. His work on voodoo death falls within this area of investigation. While Cannon may be viewed as the grandparent of stress research, it is Hans Selye who is the recognized parent of the field. Selye's theoretical formulations mark the watershed of thinking in this area.

Stress, as defined by Selye (1974), is the nonspecific response of the body to any demand placed upon it. It involves an "unbalancing" of physiological processes necessitating increased activation of homeostatic mechanisms. Selye was primarily concerned with the effect of physical stimuli (such as temperature or exercise) upon bodily functions. Research in the area of psychoendocrinology, however, has increasingly shown that psychological and social influences are often involved in responses to physical stimuli; in other words, responses to physical stimuli are often accompanied by emotional and behavioral responses. Several studies, in fact, have shown that it is the *emotional* response to stimuli, not the physical stimuli themselves, which can activate stress responses (Mason, 1975).

Interest in the emotional component of stress has led to numerous investigations which have yielded fruitful results. Significant among these is the work of James Henry, who cites emotions as "the crucial driving force in a chain of events leading from psychosocial interaction to neuroendocrine changes" (Henry, 1982). Taking these findings one step further in a masterful integrative article, Henry demonstrates how these processes can, in time, lead to disease. Citing numerous studies, Henry first describes how emotional responses to sociocultural events can affect the sympathetic-adrenal-medullary system, the pituitary-adrenal-cortical system, and/or the pituitary-gonadotropic system. He then shows that emotions can produce changes powerful enough to override repeatedly neuroendocrine feedback mechanisms which function to restore homeostasis. These repeated overrides, he asserts, can lead to pathophysiological changes, to disease states, and eventually to death. They can do this either gradually or abruptly, as in the case of cardiac arrhythmia.

Henry's work demonstrates the link between social interaction and disease. Though centrally concerned with emotional responses to social events, he recognizes the role of cognition and learning (of cultural influences) in mediating emotional responses. To quote him:

> Disturbance of expectancies about position in the social hierarchy may lead to hippocampal arousal as a mismatch is sensed. (Henry, 1982, p. 371)

And again:

> Activation of a pattern by a perception of need can override the homeostatic hormonal feedbacks controlling the physiologist's constant internal milieu. (Henry, 1982, p. 369)

And later, when discussing our ability to defend ourselves against psychosocial stress, he notes:

> The individual's expectations depend on his or her culturally molded framework of perceptions. In a particular culture, for example, military service, common hazardous situations may be defined as not especially threatening because it is taken for granted that nothing much can be done to modify them by those involved. (Henry, 1982, pp. 376–377)

By defining situations as less hazardous, Henry argues that individuals are protected to some extent from intense stress responses. Religious beliefs, hope, and faith can also serve to reduce psychological stress. Conversely, an absence of these can render the individual more vulnerable.

The social group of the individual is also an important influence on stress reactions according to Henry. First, the group defines an event as more or less threatening. The group's assessment of the event can in this way determine the intensity of the individual's neuroendocrine response to it. This was demonstrated by Bourne (1970) who conducted an experimental study of men in combat in Vietnam. He found that despite exposure to life-threatening situations, 17-hydroxycorticosterone (17-OHCS) decreased in men who had high morale and strong motivation, leading him to conclude that the level of an individual's adrenocortical arousal to an event was modulated by the meaning ascribed to the event by the social group with whom the subject identified. Second, the group provides social and emotional support which can counterbalance stressful responses and help to enhance the individual's coping capacity. Caplan (1981), for example, describes how social supports during times of stress can assist the individual by providing affection, love, and nurturance, by helping to fortify the individual's psychosocial armature needed to master the stressful challenge. Lastly, the social group functions to assist the individual to sustain hope and motivation by helping the individual gain perspective, plan and implement a course of action, and reexperience positive feelings (Robinson & Henry, 1977).

Lack of social supports and contacts, or impoverished affiliative ties, such as ties to spouse, religion, or organizations, has been linked to increased vulnerability to various stress-related illnesses as demonstrated by several studies. Marmot and Syme (1976), for example, studied 3,809 Japanese-Americans and found that social and cultural supports were importantly related to the prevalence of coronary heart disease (CHD), more so, in fact, than observed differences in the major coronary risk factors such as diet. They state: "This study supported the suggestion that a stable society whose members enjoy the support of their fellows in closely knit groups may protect against the forms of social stress that may lead to CHD" (p. 245). Brown, Bhrolcháin, and Harris (1975) studied 458 women encountering stressful situations and found that the incidence of depression was related to the presence or absence of social supports: 41 percent of the women who encountered much stress and had little support, compared to 10 percent with much stress and much support, suffered depression. Berkman and Syme (1979), in a study of 6,928 adults in Alameda County, California, found that premature death from various causes was more likely among persons who lacked social and community ties than among those who had larger social networks. Re-examining the data of Marmot and Syme, Joseph (1980) found that current social ties were a significant independent risk factor in heart disease. Finally, Caplan (1981) reviewed nine studies on the effects of social supports and concluded: "Despite the varied settings, they uniformly support the thesis that high levels of social support protect against increased vulnerability to illness of various kinds associated with high stress" (quoted in Henry, 1982, p. 377).

Henry's summation in this discussion conjures up images of the isolation of voodoo death victims:

> If the individual is rejected and without a confidante, if he perceives himself as unloved and uncared for, if he lacks status in his social group and is a stranger to their ways and cannot call on anyone for assistance with goods and services, he then becomes vulnerable. (Henry, 1982, p. 377)

It also brings to mind descriptions of isolated elderly in this country.

It is the total of particular types of stress responses, balanced against stress reducers such as social support, which can lead to disease, according to Henry. *What begins as the body's shift in equilibrium, lasting only minutes or hours, if repeated with sufficient frequency, or if of sufficient intensity, can result in permanent alterations of physiological functioning and ultimately in pathology.* The process could be likened to a form of reverse physical conditioning. Thus, it can be seen that if a person perceived himself or herself to be repeatedly threatened, in time negative health outcomes could result.

Health Behavior Models

The relationship between negative health behaviors and negative health outcomes is taken as axiomatic in every society. To eat improperly, to fail to seek or follow health care when needed, or to forego vaccinations or other preventive health measures is viewed as a risk, as a health behavior which potentially threatens the individual and, in some societies, threatens the larger group as well. Numerous investigators have sought to understand the factors associated with health decision-making and positive health behaviors. Findings from these studies, discussed below, point to the central role of health beliefs in motivating and directing health behaviors.

The role of perceptions and beliefs in mediating patient health decisions can be seen at various stages in the illness process described by Suchman (1965). In a 1960 study of the various stages of an illness experience, Suchman interviewed 137 persons aged 21 or older who had experienced a specific illness episode during the two months prior to the interview. He identified five stages in the illness-recovery process: (1) the symptom experience stage; (2) the assumption of the sick role stage; (3) the medical care contact stage; (4) the dependent-patient role stage; and (5) the recovery or rehabilitation stage. The role of patient beliefs in decision making can be seen at several of these stages.

During the symptom experience stage, for example, the stage when the patient decides something is wrong, Suchman identified three component features contributing to the patient's decision: (1) the physical experience; (2) the cognitive aspect of the experience involving the patient's interpretation of the physical experience and the meaning ascribed to it; and (3) the emotional response that accompanies the somatic experience and the cognitive interpretation of it. He states:

> Basic to the initiation of the medical care process is the perception and interpretation of symptoms of discomfort, pain, or abnormality—the "meaning of symptoms" for the individual. (Suchman, 1965, pp. 114–115)

The role of cognitive, interpretive processes is also shown in the assumption of the sick role stage, wherein the person decides he or she is sick and needs professional care. Suchman describes that during this stage the patient begins to seek information and advice from his or her family and friends. This "lay referral structure" helps the patient to interpret the illness experience. It reacts, advises, reassures, confirms or denies, and validates or rejects the patient's experience. Through this process of symbolic exchange emerges the definition of the person as "sick" or "not sick."

In the medical care contact stage, Suchman found that the patient seeks a diagnosis and treatment prescription from an expert rather than lay source. He notes that the physician serves to legitimate the person as sick, to confirm and sanction the illness. If the individual disagrees with the physician's assessment, however, he or she may seek out another health professional. The choice of medical professional is influenced by the patient's needs and preconceptions about the illness, and by input from the patient's social group, as well as knowledge about, and availability and accessibility of services.

Finally, during the dependent-patient role stage, Suchman again shows the role of belief mechanisms in the health decision-making process. As he describes, in this stage the patient surrenders decision-making rights to the authority of the physician. The model patient becomes dependent upon the attending medical professionals. If, however, the patient and physician subscribe to different beliefs about the nature and meaning of the illness, or different conceptions of appropriate medical care, conflicts may arise between them which will interfere with the treatment process.

Other investigators have looked more closely at the initial stages of the illness process. In 1961, David Mechanic and Edmund Volkart coined the phrase *illness behavior* in reference to activities undertaken during these stages. They defined illness behavior as "the way in which symptoms are perceived, evaluated, and acted upon by a person who recognizes some pain, discomfort, or other signs of organic malfunction" (Mechanic & Volkart, 1961, p. 52). Studies in the area of illness behavior have shown that features beyond the physical experience are significant influences on whether or not individuals will define themselves as experiencing something warranting concern, in other words, as experiencing a sign of illness (Stoeckle, Zola, & Davidson, 1963).

In one such study, Zola (1966) examined the influence of culture on symptoms. He compared the presenting complaints of Irish Catholics, Italian Catholics, and Anglo-Saxon Protestants at their initial visit to an outpatient clinic. His findings revealed significant differences between the groups in their perceptions of and reactions to their illnesses. The groups differed in their descriptions of their problems, their reporting of pain associated with the problems, and their assessments of the impact of the problems. This was true even for patients who had the same diagnosed disorder.

Zola argues for a keener awareness of the role of cultural influences on illness behaviors. Symptoms and signs of illness are not exclusively objective, nor universally recognized. According to Zola, "the very labelling and definition of a bodily state as a symptom or as a problem is, in itself, part of a social process" (Zola, 1966, p. 630). What one group regards as a problem, another may not. In order for a condition to be considered symptomatic of illness, it must first be regarded as abnormal. Thus, if an aberration is widespread, it will be viewed by the group as not warranting attention. In the upper Mississippi Valley in the late nineteenth century, for example, malaria was so common it was believed to be a normal part of the acclimatization process (Ackerknecht, 1945). If a symptom is ubiquitous, then, it is regarded as natural and inevitable (albeit not pleasant or good) and as something to be ignored as inconsequential. In addition, symptoms may be overlooked if they do not deviate from group values and norms. The social context affects the meaning ascribed to a given event. So, for example, hallucinations in one society may be viewed neutrally, whereas in our society which values rationality and control, they may be regarded as a sign of disorder. Thus, the knowledge and beliefs about physiological events as evaluated within a particular social context will importantly influence the interpretation given to those events, and consequently, the emergent health behaviors.

Examinations of preventive health and patient compliance behaviors have yielded similar results indicating the central role of health beliefs in influencing patient decision making. The Health Belief Model is a dominant paradigm which has been developed out of this area of investigation. This model postulates that in order for individuals to initiate or continue positive health behaviors, the following factors must be present:

1. They must believe that they are susceptible to the particular problem;
2. They must believe that the probable consequences of the problem are serious;
3. They must believe that taking a particular health action will result in benefits to them in reducing either their susceptibility or the severity of the illness's consequences; and
4. They must perceive few if any barriers which would prevent them from taking action.

In addition, a "cue to action" must occur to trigger a health behavior. A physical symptom would be one example of a cue; so too would be an interpersonal exchange which raises the individual's level of awareness and concern about a potential health problem. Finally, demographic and sociopsychological variables are seen as indirect influences on the health decision-making process (Becker et al., 1977).

Extensive research has been conducted to test the hypotheses inherent in the Health Belief Model. Findings from these studies support the model's central focus on patients' conceptions and beliefs as critical influences on health decision-making and, ultimately, health behaviors (Becker et al., 1977).

This section has reviewed some of the key research in the area of health decision making. It reveals that patient beliefs about their health and illness states are important variables initiating and guiding their health behaviors. Beliefs about what constitutes an illness versus an ailment, about one's susceptibility to an illness, and about the efficacy of intervention can significantly affect the course of health behavior. Moreover, these beliefs originate and operate within a social context. They are part of the patient's cultural milieu. As such, they represent one feature of the ideational component of culture which serves to mediate biological functioning over time. In the next section, we will turn to an examination of health and aging in American society to illustrate how health beliefs, operating through stress reactions and health behaviors, can contribute to negative health outcomes among the aged.

THE CONSTRUCTION OF HEALTH OUTCOMES AMONG THE AGED

It is time to return to a consideration of voodoo death as a model for conceptualizing the construction (or destruction) of health in old age. As described previously, voodoo death occurrences involve culturally specific beliefs which trigger emotional, behavioral, and social responses leading to negative health outcomes for the targeted individual. Typically, these occurrences transpire over a relatively brief period of time and are acute in nature. Examination of the mechanisms involved in voodoo death—stress responses and health behaviors as fashioned through symbolic interaction—showed that these mechanisms could also operate to effect negative health outcomes over time. The question now arises as to whether these mechanisms operate in our society to contribute toward the fateful decline of health in old age.

Similarities between the voodoo death circumstance and the situation of the American aged can be observed. In the dominant American society, old age is primarily viewed as a process of decline. We emphasize losses in vigor, health, and independence; in roles and status; and in social supports, income, and power when we regard aging. We speak of the "declining years," of "the normal dependencies in aging" (Blenkner, 1969), of the need to adjust to aging and to readjust goals and expectations (Clark & Anderson, 1967). We conceive of aging as dying, as decrement and disengagement, as disease, as dependency and regression, and, occasionally, as development. The personal attributes we value in our society—achievement, status, power, self-reliance, and wealth—are the opposite of what we attribute to the aged. In a sense, old age is a form of social deviance in our society (Clark, 1973). More precisely, however, it is a liminal state. Like the voodoo death victim, the aged person in our society is placed in a different social category and is viewed as more closely associated with the sacred realm and as removed from the ordinary concerns of group life.

We define aging chronologically. This means that regardless of function, status, or capacity, an individual moves into the social category of old age after a certain period of time, usually around age 65. As individuals approach this social category, they begin to orient their self-perceptions to conform to the images of the old held in the larger society. Cultural forces gradually operate to socialize them to old age. They are expected to change their behavior, to disengage, and society is expected to change its behavior in regard to them. Slowly, the decline metaphors of aging become their own.

What are the mechanisms which contribute to this decline? I hypothesize that the same mechanisms operant in voodoo deaths are involved here. Taking beliefs about health and aging as an example, I will describe how they can contribute to health declines with aging.

Increasingly in our society, cultural conceptions of old age have become synonymous with sickness (Arluke & Peterson, 1981). To be old means to be sick. To be sick, after a certain age, means to be old. We hear reports about the increased incidence of disease in old age, about nursing home expansions, and about large health care expenditures by the elderly. Despite the fact that only 5 percent of the elderly population resides in nursing homes and the fact that illness is by no means universally experienced among the aged, on a cultural level the notion of old age is equated with sickness. More and more our beliefs about old age incorporate beliefs about illness.

On an individual level, these beliefs can act as threats. They can create an anticipatory readiness for illness which can itself be harmful. Individuals holding these beliefs feel one must *expect* sickness because one is chronologically old. This expectation can cause a person to over interpret physiological events as signs of disease and thus give rise to stress responses in the form of anxiety and fear, and either hypochondriacal behavior as the person fights for safety, or denial behavior as he or she seeks to flee from the threat. These beliefs can also cause a person to assume a sick role prior to experiencing illness, to curtail activities and involvements so as to avoid illness.

I have labeled these responses the *siege model of health.* Their effect is one of repeated stress and inappropriate health behavior. Cumulatively, their effect can be destructive to the health and functioning of the individual.

Several investigators have noted anomalies in the health behaviors of older persons which can importantly affect their health status and the nature of their health care. Hypochondriasis, for instance, is cited as a frequent pattern in old age.

This behavior is defined as an "anxious preoccupation with one's own body or a portion of one's own body which the patient believes to be either diseased or functioning improperly" (Busse & Pfeiffer, 1969, as quoted in Botwinick, 1978, p. 71). Such preoccupations can give rise to increased demands for medical services such as those noted by Haug (1981) who, in a study of medical utilization patterns of younger and older people, found that older people were more likely than younger people to overutilize services for minor complaints.

Anxiety about health can also, however, lead to a defensive denial of symptoms. This pattern was found among older, but not younger, men in a study conducted by McCrae, Bartone, and Costa (1976) on the relationship between age, anxiety, and self-reported health. They interpreted this finding to indicate that for an older person with trait anxiety, "anxiety about approaching death and increasing health problems is just too much to bear, and he resorts to denying symptoms in an effort to diminish his anxiety" (p. 49). As opposed to an overutilization of medical services, this response pattern would instead give rise to medical underutilization.

Aside from the consequences stemming from inappropriate use of medical services, the anxiety state associated with these health beliefs could in itself be harmful. Living in a state of chronic threat, or of chronic stress, could in time lead to physiological pathology, such as that described by Henry.

Negative health outcomes could also result in instances where the sick role is assumed inappropriately—in an effort to avoid sickness rather than respond to sickness. Longevity research has consistently demonstrated the important association of activity and exercise to the maintenance of health and long life (Botwinick, 1978). One could, of course, question the directionality of this relationship, but findings in the area of exercise physiology and aging strongly indicate that inactivity can be deleterious to health. Medical research corroborates these findings. Kannel (1971), for instance, found physical activity to play a significant role in coronary heart disease. He reports: "Sedentary males were more susceptible to lethal episodes of coronary heart disease . . . than were physically active males" (quoted in Botwinick, 1978, p. 36).

The beliefs which underlie these individual response patterns can be manifested at the group level as well. Thus, family members or friends will tell the individual to slow down or risk harming his or her health. They will reduce their expectations of the older individual so as to avoid stressing him or her. They will encourage medical care where it may be unwarranted.

Repeated time and again, in slow and gradual ways, the individual's and groups' expectations come to be borne out. As in the case of voodoo death, beliefs can trigger social, behavioral, and stress responses which can negatively affect health. Unlike voodoo death, however, these outcomes follow a chronic illness model—they develop over the course of time.

Viewing aging as sickness can give rise to another form of responses. This I have called the *senescence model of health.* In these instances the older person interprets physiological events as signs of aging, not illness. Here, health conditions are regarded as ailments to which one must adjust, rather than illnesses which should be treated. These beliefs result in ignoring of symptoms and in the underutilization of medical care. An example of this type of behavior is described by Curtin:

What happened is that Old Jim Crowe reached old age with a reasonably good heart. There had been no acute, sudden symptoms to send him running to the doctor. For some months he had felt "indigestion" and some pressure in his chest. But he was an old man, and didn't expect to feel good all the time. Sometimes he felt faint or short of breath . . . but he was an old man . . . or some chest pain, spreading to his arm and back . . . but he was an old man. That day on the porch, he had felt the pain begin to build in his chest. He wanted to get up and walk home to rest, but when he tried to move, the pain increased. He became dizzy and blacked out. (Curtin, 1972, p. 29)

Others have noted similar findings. DiCicco and Apple (1960), in a study of the health needs and opinions of older adults, found that older people held the conviction that aches and pains and physical limitations were normal in old age. The people in this study were generally disinclined to seek preventive services, responded inappropriately to symptoms of chronic illness, and tended not to seek care for ailments which were not yet handicapping. Shanas (1962) found similar results in her nationwide study of people aged 65 and over. She reports that the older people viewed their health problems as normal given their age. Moreover, their families expected them to experience health problems as well. In fact, it was not until the older persons experienced an acute illness episode or were stricken with a catastrophic chronic illness that their families regarded their physical complaints as signs of illness. In another study of older people in six Western societies, Shanas (1978) again found that older people "tend to accept their aches and pains and to have a low expectation of services" (Shanas, 1978, p. 197). Finally, reports from the medical literature indicate that older people often attribute various symptoms to the aging process and consequently fail to report them as problems to medical practitioners (Anderson, 1976; Steel, 1978).

While older individuals may not seek medical care because they think their problems are "just old age," physicians often hold similar beliefs, and therefore may not actively treat patients who suffer from what they also label as "just old age" (Steel, 1978, p. 3).

"When you are sixty-five, you find your complaints are no longer listened to," Sharon Curtin, R.N., testified before the Senate's Special Committee on Aging. "You meet the impenetrable barrier of glazed eyes and careless hands anxious to take care of someone younger, someone who seems to have a higher potential for complete recovery. If you have an ache or a pain, it is because you are old; if you are depressed, it is because you are senile." (Percy, 1974, p. 58)

Hence the medical profession serves to reinforce the senescence model of health; it acts to help socialize people to these beliefs.

The ramifications of the senescence model of health are clear: To the extent that older persons and their social group subscribe to this set of beliefs, the health and functioning of these older persons can be jeopardized.

The *vanquished model of health* is the final response form that the belief that aging equals sickness can take. Here sickness is recognized, unlike the senescence model which does not label problems as illnesses; however, this view holds that the old must *accept* illness. Sickness is seen as inevitable and untreatable because of one's age. Although there are certain conditions for which no cure presently exists, persons adhering to the vanquished model extend that category of untreatable problems to incorporate conditions for which treatments are available.

These responses can give rise to stress, in the form of depression and feelings of helplessness and hopelessness, and to fatalistic attitudes toward medical care where the person does not seek or follow care, or where he or she passively accepts care and does not strive to find the best treatment or does not actively participate in the treatment program. The vanquished model can give rise to behavior such as that described by Burdman and Brewer (1978) who note that older people often accept a less than adequate level of health because they believe that sickness is inevitable in old age.

The vanquished model can also be applied by medical professionals and families in responding to the health problems of an older person. As described above, these persons can discourage active pursuit of a medical remedy, advising instead acceptance and adjustment, encouraging passivity and acquiescence in the face of troubling conditions.

As can be seen, while the vanquished model of health may not contribute directly to the development of health problems in old age, its role in compounding and exacerbating existing problems, either through medical inattention or emotional stress, seems apparent. Here again then, negative health beliefs play a role in contributing toward health problems in old age.

This section has examined the effects of beliefs about aging on the health of older people. Health, in old age as in any age, rests upon a delicate balance of biological, psychological, social, and cultural forces. That balance can be tipped by any one or any combination of these forces to result in negative outcomes. In the dominant American society, beliefs which equate aging with sickness can serve as one such force. Thus, to the extent that persons subscribe to these beliefs (and it should be noted that not all persons do), their health can be jeopardized. In this way, culture as ideas comes to shape physical functioning, health in old age, the experience of aging.

RESEARCH DIRECTIONS

Heretofore little research has been conducted which examines the interplay between symbolic and biological processes as they affect aging. Recent advances within the biological sciences, yielding a better understanding of mind/body relations, now make this area of study possible. In-depth studies of aging individuals are needed which combine (1) an investigation of the beliefs and meanings associated with somatic events, (2) ethological observations of health and illness behaviors and their association to those meanings and beliefs, and (3) measurement of the physiological responses which accompany various health beliefs and behaviors. Intervention studies could also be conducted to determine whether alterations in health beliefs result in changed health behaviors and physiological responses. The results of these studies could further efforts to maintain and improve health and functioning in old age.

SUMMARY AND CONCLUSION

The purpose of this chapter was to trace the relationship between beliefs about health and aging and health outcomes to show how these beliefs can moderate and modulate the level of health in old age. My intention was to show how beliefs about aging as sickness, operant through symbolic interactional processes, can threaten the health of individuals as they grow old. Using voodoo death as an analogous model, I applied the mechanisms involved in the voodoo death phenomenon to the situation of the American aged to propose that these same mechanisms can operate over time to effect negative health consequences. In the dominant American society where old age is defined chronologically, yet is also shaded by atavistic notions of old age as synonymous with sickness, a cultural context has been established wherein conceptions and beliefs about aging, negative stereotypes if you will, can produce harmful results beyond loss of status, income, or power. It is my contention that these beliefs can actually be toxic. Their effect can be both primary and secondary: they can contribute directly toward the development of disease and illness and/or they can help to modulate illness processes once they have become evident.

Health in old age can thus be culturally constructed and not simply biologically determined. Through symbolic interaction, physiological processes and behavioral responses can be initiated, shaped, and guided. The outcome is the molding of the social *and* the biological individual. Negative beliefs about health in old age can serve to constrict the life span potential of the individual. They can give rise to harmful stress reactions, they can dampen positive health behaviors on the part of older individuals and on the part of families and health providers in regard to older individuals, and they can restrict healthful activities by fostering the assumption of sick roles when sickness is not present. Their effect can be pervasive. The magnitude of their impact is unknown.

The direct chronic effects of beliefs on health have not been adequately explored before. My analysis, therefore, drew from a variety of sources which shed light on this topic. These included the psychosomatic literature, the health belief and behavior literature, the anthropological literature, the stress literature, the literature on symbolic interaction, and the gerontological literature. Most influential among these sources was the examination of voodoo death by Cannon who identified the social, emotional, and behavioral components of these cognitively triggered phenomena. Henry's work on the psychophysiological components of stress and disease provided invaluable insights into the operation of mind/body relations. Finally, the work of Mechanic, Zola, Becker, and others has aptly demonstrated the power of beliefs as influencers of health behaviors.

This analysis represents a synthesis and integration of key findings emerging within various disciplines: anthropology, psychology, physiology, public health, and gerontology. Anthropologists have long observed the power of symbols and beliefs in illness and healing. Only recently, however, have the biological sciences come to better understand the operations of the human brain and the neuroendocrine system and hence been able to shed light on the mechanisms involved in mind/body relations. Further research in this area will help to illuminate the role of symbols in promoting health and contributing to disease. For example, it will contribute toward research on the health effects of placebos, ritual healing, or stigmatization. We are entering a new frontier of understanding, one which no longer divorces external sociocultural events from biophysiological processes. The advancement of knowledge in this area promises to further our understanding of the complex interplay of cultural and biological forces in shaping the human experience, including the experience of aging.

REFERENCES

ACKERKNECHT, E. H. (1945). Malaria in the upper Mississippi Valley, 1760–1900. *Bulletin of the History of Medicine* (Suppl. 4). Baltimore: Johns Hopkins Press.

ANDERSON, W. F. (1976). The clinical assessment of aging and problems of diagnosis in the elderly. *South African Medical Journal, 50,* 1257-1259.

ARLUKE, A., & PETERSON, J. (1981). Accidental medicalization of old age and its social control implications. In C. L. Fry and contributors, *Dimensions: Aging, culture, and health* (pp. 271-284). New York: J. F. Bergin Publishers, Inc.

BARKER, J. C. (1965). Scared to death. *British Medical Journal, 2,* 591.

BECKER, M. H., HAEFNER, D. P., KASL, S. V., KIRSCHT, J. P., MAIMAN, L. A., & ROSENSTOCK, I. M. (1977). Selected psychosocial models and correlates of individual health-related behaviors. *Medical Care, 15* (Suppl.), 27-46.

BERKMAN, L. F., & SYME, S. L. (1979). Social networks, host resistance, and mortality: A nine-year follow-up study of Alameda County residents. *American Journal of Epidemiology, 109,* 186-204.

BLENKNER, M. (1969). The normal dependencies of aging. *Mental Health Digest, 1,* 36-38.

BOTWINICK, J. (1978). *Aging and behavior: A comprehensive integration of research findings* (2nd ed.). New York: Springer Publishing Company.

BOURNE, P. G. (1970). *Men, stress, and Vietnam.* Boston: Little, Brown.

BRINK, P. (1982). Personal communication.

BROWN, G. W., BHROLCHÁIN, M. N., & HARRIS, T. (1975). Social class and psychiatric disturbance among women in an urban population. *Sociology, 9,* 225-254.

BURDMAN, G. D., & BREWER, R. M. (Eds.). (1978). *Health aspects of aging.* Portland: University of Oregon Continuing Education Books.

CANNON, W. B. (1929). *Bodily changes in pain, hunger, fear, and rage: An account of recent researches into the function of emotional excitement* (2nd ed.). New York: Appleton.

CANNON, W. B. (1942). Voodoo death. *American Anthropologist, 44,* 169-181. Excerpts reproduced by permission of the American Anthropological Association.

CANNON, W. B. (1942). Voodoo death. *American Anthropologist, 44,* 169-181.

CAPLAN, G. (1981). Mastery of stress: Psychosocial aspects. *American Journal of Psychiatry, 138,* 413-420.

CLARK, M. (1967). The anthropology of aging, a new area for studies of culture and personality. *The Gerontologist, 7*(1), 55-64.

CLARK, M. (1973). Contributions of cultural anthropology to the study of the aged. In L. Nader & T. Maretski (Eds.), *Cultural illness and health.* Washington, DC: American Anthropological Association.

CLARK, M., & ANDERSON, B. (1967). *Culture and aging: An anthropological study of older Americans.* Springfield, IL: Chas. C Thomas.

CLUNE, F. J. (1973). A comment on voodoo death. *American Anthropologist, 75,* 312.

COHEN, S. I., & ROSS, R. N. (1983). *Handbook of clinical psychobiology and pathology, 1.* Washington, DC: Hemisphere Publishing Company.

COOLIDGE, J. C. (1969). Unexpected death in a patient who wished to die. *Journal of the American Psychoanalytic Association, 17,* 413-420.

CURTIN, S. R. (1972). *Nobody ever died of old age.* Boston: Little, Brown.

DiCICCO, L., & APPLE, D. (1960). Health needs and opinions of older adults. In D. Apple (Ed.), *Sociological studies of health and sickness* (pp. 26-39). New York: McGraw-Hill.

EASTWELL, H. D. (1982). Voodoo death and the mechanism for dispatch of the dying in East Arnhem, Australia. *American Anthropologist, 84,* 5-18.

ENGEL, G. L. (1968). A life setting conducive to illness: The giving-up-given-up complex. *Bulletin of the Menninger Clinic, 32,* 355-365.

ENGEL, G. L. (1971). Sudden and rapid death during psychological stress: Folklore or folk wisdom? *Annals of Internal Medicine, 74,* 771-782.

FRANKL, V. E. (1962). *Man's search for meaning: An introduction to logotherapy.* (Revised edition of *From death-camp to existentialism.*) Boston: Beacon Press.

GLASCOCK, A. P. (1983). Death-hastening behavior: An expansion of Eastwell's thesis. *American Anthropologist, 85*(2), 417-420.

GOODFRIEND, M., & WOLPERT, E. A. (1976). Death from fright: Report of a case and literature review. *Psychosomatic Medicine, 38,* 348-356.

HAUG, M. R. (1981). Age and medical care utilization patterns. *Journal of Gerontology, 36,* 103-111.

HENRY, J. P. (1982). The relation of social to biological processes in disease. *Social Science and Medicine, 16,* 369-380.

JOSEPH, J. G. (1980). *Social affiliation, risk factor status, and coronary heart disease: A cross-sectional study of Japanese-American men* (pp. 94-105). Unpublished doctoral dissertation, University of California at Berkeley, Department of Biomedical and Environmental Health Sciences.

KERTZER, D. I., & MADISON, D.B.B. (1981). Women's age-set systems in Africa: The Latuka of southern Sudan. In C. L. Fry and contributors, *Dimensions: Aging, culture, and health* (pp. 109-130). New York: J. F. Bergin Publishers, Inc.

LEX, B. W. (1977). Voodoo death: New thoughts on an old explanation. In D. Landy (Ed.), *Culture, disease and healing: Studies in medical anthropology* (pp. 327-331). New York: Macmillan.

MARMOT, M. G., & SYME, S. L. (1976). Acculturation and coronary heart disease in Japanese-Americans. *American Journal of Epidemiology, 104,* 225-247.

MASON, J. W. (1975). A historical view of the stress field. *Journal of Human Stress, 1,* 22-36.

MATHIS, J. L. (1964). A sophisticated version of voodoo death. *Psychosomatic Medicine, 26,* 104-107.

McCRAE, R. R., BARTONE, P. T., & COSTA, P. T. (1976). Age, anxiety, and self-reported health. *International Journal of Aging and Human Development, 7,* 49-58.

MECHANIC, D., & VOLKART, E. H. (1961). Stress, illness behavior, and the sick role. *American Sociological Review, 26,* 51-58.

MELTZER, B. N. (1967). Mead's social psychology. In J. G. Manis & B. N. Meltzer

(Eds.), *Symbolic interaction: A reader in social psychology* (pp. 5-24). Boston: Allyn & Bacon.

MILTON, G. W. (1973). Self-willed death. *Lancet, 23*, 435-436.

NASON, J. D. (1981). Respected elder or old person: Aging in a Micronesian community. In P. T. Amoss & S. Harrell (Eds.), *Other ways of growing old: Anthropological perspectives* (pp. 155-174). Stanford, CA: Stanford University Press.

PERCY, C. H. (1974). *Growing old in the country of the young.* New York: McGraw-Hill.

RICHTER, C. P. (1957). On the phenomenon of sudden death in animals and men. *Psychosomatic Medicine, 19*, 190-198.

ROBINSON, D., & HENRY, S. (1977). *Self-help and health: Mutual aid for modern problems.* London: Martin Robertson.

SAUL, L. K. (1966). Sudden death at impasse. *Psychoanalytic Forum, 1*, 88-89.

SELYE, H. (1950). *The physiology and pathology of exposure to stress.* Montreal: Acta, Inc.

SELYE, H. (1974). *Stress without distress.* New York: Lippincott.

SHAHRANI, M. N. (1981). Growing in respect: Aging among the Kirghiz of Afghanistan. In P. T. Amoss & S. Harrell (Eds.), *Other ways of growing old: Anthropological perspectives* (pp. 175-192). Stanford, CA: Stanford University Press.

SHANAS, E. (1962). *The health of older people: A social survey.* Cambridge, MA: Harvard University Press.

SHANAS, E. (1978). Health status of older people: Cross-national implications. In G. Burdman & R. M. Brewer (Eds.), *Health aspects of aging.* Portland: University of Oregon Continuing Education Books.

SHARP, H. S. (1981). Old age among the Chipewyan. In P. T. Amoss & S. Harrell (Eds.), *Other ways of growing old: Anthropological perspectives* (pp. 99-110). Stanford, CA: Stanford University Press.

SIMMONS, D. (1945). *The role of the aged in primitive society.* New Haven, CT: Yale University Press.

STEEL, K. (1978). Evaluation of the geriatric patient. In W. Reichel (Ed.), *Clinical aspects of aging* (pp. 3-12). Baltimore: Williams & Wilkins.

STOECKLE, J. D., ZOLA, I. K., & DAVIDSON, G. E. (1963). On going to see the doctor: The contributions of the patient to the decision to seek medical aid. *Journal of Chronic Diseases, 16*, 975-989.

SUCHMAN, E. A. (1965). Stages of illness and medical care. *Journal of Health and Human Behavior, 6*, 114-128.

SUDNOW, D. (1967). *Passing on: The social organization of dying.* Englewood Cliffs, NJ: Prentice-Hall.

VAN ARSDALE, P. W. (1981). The elderly Asmat of New Guinea. In P. T. Amoss & S. Harrell (Eds.), *Other ways of growing old: Anthropological perspectives* (pp. 111-124). Stanford, CA: Stanford University Press.

ZOLA, I. K. (1966). Culture and symptoms—An analysis of patients' presenting complaints. *American Sociological Review, 31*, 615-630.

7

PERSONAL OPTIMISM, PHYSICAL AND MENTAL HEALTH

The Triumph of Successful Aging

Gary T. Reker and Paul T. P. Wong

You can't be optimistic if you have a misty optic.

This chapter will examine the concept of personal optimism and its influence on the physical and mental health of the individual. Following a brief introduction of behavioral health and growth models of human development, different perspectives on personal optimism and health will be evaluated. In two ensuing sections, the empirical evidence relating personal optimism to physical and mental health will be reviewed. In the final section, we shall examine the personal optimism construct in the elderly, and report on some recent studies we have conducted.

Several difficulties were faced in the development of this chapter. Foremost was the fact that very few theoretical and empirical attempts have been made to analyze concepts that *promote* physical and mental health of individuals; most of the research has focused on variables that alleviate illness or disease. Not much is known about the relationship between optimism and health in the general population; even less is known with respect to the aging population. However, despite the lack of theoretical development and empirical findings, it is generally believed

The preparation of this chapter was supported by a Leave Fellowship (No. 451-81-2093) awarded to the senior author by the Social Sciences and Humanities Research Council of Canada (SSHRC) and a SSHRC research grant to the second author.

that personal optimism is an important variable in the successful adaptation to the later years of life. For example, Palmore, Randolph, and Overholser (1979) stress four basic factors to successful aging: (1) a variety of meaningful activities; (2) good health habits; (3) sound financial planning; and (4) mental attitude—an *optimistic* outlook. Havighurst, Neugarten, and Tobin (1968) have observed that successful agers are individuals who (1) take pleasure from daily activities; (2) view life as meaningful and accept life circumstances; (3) believe they have achieved their major goals; (4) have a positive self-image; and (5) maintain happy and optimistic attitudes and moods.

BEHAVIORAL HEALTH AND GROWTH MODELS OF HUMAN DEVELOPMENT

Psychologists interested in the health field are on an exciting new frontier of inter-disciplinary collaboration in the scientific exploration of health-behavior relationships. At the first anniversary of the newly formed division of Health Psychology within the American Psychological Association, Matarazzo (1980) described the new opportunities for training, research, and practice in the fields of behavioral medicine and behavioral health. He viewed *behavioral medicine* as a broad inter-disciplinary field of inquiry concerned with health and illness or related dysfunctions (e.g., hypertension, smoking, obesity, etc.). He preferred the term *behavioral health* to describe the subspecialty concerned with the maintenance of health and the prevention of illness in currently healthy persons.

The behavioral health philosophy has emerged in response to a growing realization that the traditional illness model, with emphasis on remediation, is no longer appropriate to deal with modern stress-related problems. As well, the health system is being overburdened and the cost of health services is rising at an alarming rate each year (Ryan & Travis, 1981). Health professionals, disenchanted with the medical model, were quick to respond to the challenge by proposing new preventative approaches to health, culminating in the wellness movement (Antonovsky, 1979; Ardell, 1977; Ryan & Travis, 1981). Figure 7-1 describes the essence of the wellness model. In the medical model, health is viewed as a dichotomous construct. If disease is present, one is considered ill; if it is absent, one is considered healthy. In the wellness model, health is a continuum, anchored by premature death and a high level of wellness.

A parallel progression of events is evident in the field of life-span developmental psychology. Over the past decade, we have witnessed a shift from the deficit or decrement models of human development to growth or competence models (Albee, 1980; Bond & Rosen, 1980; Butler, 1974; McCrae, 1981). Growth models of aging give greater weight to the *adaptive processes* in the later years. The theoretical orientation of Erikson (1963), the content analysis of biographical material by Buhler (1935), and the life cycle analyses of Neugarten (1979) converge in describing the adaptive processes or developmental themes across the life span. An analysis of these themes suggests that the life span can be differentiated into three broad stages, each characterized by life experiences that differ in kind and quality (see Table 7-1).

If there are age differences in human adaptation to life events, they may be

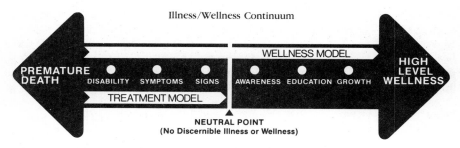

FIGURE 7-1. The Wellness Model of Health. Moving from the
center to the left shows a progressively worsening state of health.
Moving to the right of center indicates increasing levels of health
and well-being. The treatment model can bring you to the neutral
point, where the symptoms of disease have been alleviated. The
wellness model, which can be utilized at any point, directs you
beyond neutral, and encourages you to move as far to the right
as possible. It is not meant to replace the treatment model on the
left side of the continuum, but to work in harmony with it. If you
are ill, then treatment is important, but don't stop there. [From
The Wellness Workbook by Regina Sara Ryan & John W. Travis,
M.D. Copyright © 1981. Used with permission. Available from Ten
Speed Press, P.O. Box 7123, Berkeley, CA 94707.]

a function of differences in the kind and quality of experiences encountered at
different times during the life span rather than due simply to the passage of time.
The values and goals of one stage of life may become dysfunctional at another,
necessitating some reorientation. The specific set of properties that govern changes
during childhood and adolescence (e.g., biological-maturational growth) are different from the properties that govern change during adulthood and the later years
(Ager, White, Mayberry, Crist, & Conrad, 1981–82; Flavell, 1970; Lowenthal,
Thurnher, Chiriboga, & Associates, 1975). The monumental work of Lowenthal
and her associates (1975) contributes much to our understanding of adaptational
patterns at successive transition points in the life cycle. Baltes and Nesselroade
(1979) have pointed out that nonnormative events, that is, events which do not
follow a biological-maturational sequence such as illnesses, losses, marital disruptions, relocation, etc., become increasingly important later in the life span. Neugarten (1979) described the aging process as a "continually changing sense of self

TABLE 7-1   Stage of Life and Kind and Quality of Experience

STAGE	KIND AND QUALITY OF EXPERIENCE
Youth and young adulthood	Sensing, perceiving, feeling; skill acquisition; planning, developing, and testing life goals
Adulthood	Crystallization of goals; self-review of life goals; reassessment of lifestyles
Maturity	Integration, interpretation; reflection, anticipation; meaning and purpose of existence; life review; value reorientation

and a changing set of adaptations. With the passage of time, life becomes more, not less, complex; it becomes enriched, not impoverished" (p. 891).

The behavioral health approach and the growth models of life-span developmental psychology combine to provide direction to understanding the adaptive processes in the later years. Our investigation of the role of personal optimism in the health of older adults reflects the influence of these two current trends.

THEORETICAL, CONCEPTUAL, AND MEASUREMENT PERSPECTIVES

In humans, the cortex has the potential to exert complete control over the more primitive subcortex (Simeons, 1960). The ability of humans to self-reflect, to abstract, and to represent the environment symbolically has given them the power to modulate subcortical processes at the conscious level. As a result, humanity has acquired tremendous flexibility in interpreting biologically based reactions to stressful events. Such flexibility, however, can be a double-edged sword. Henry (1981) expressed the potential consequences of such flexibility when he wrote:

> The enormous complexity of human society and man's capacity through his symbol system to identify with more powerful beings—gods or chosen leaders or institutions—give him a certain invulnerability to limbic system arousal as long as he perceives himself to be socially supported here or in the hereafter. But, if as the result of early or late experience or a combination of both, he comes to perceive himself as helpless and lacking in power to control his fate, he may well become more vulnerable than an animal whose associational cortex is more limited. (p. 33)

The ability of humans to utilize symbol systems gives them the capacity to experience a wide range of emotions, such as pity, shame, guilt, hope, or optimism. It allows them to transcend the time boundaries of past, present, and future; to hold future expectations; and to give meaning to existence. Indeed, personal optimism can be considered as a "cortical elaboration" of the visceral brain (Pelletier, 1977).

The Construct of Personal Optimism

The construct of personal optimism has been most closely associated and used interchangeably with the construct of hope. It can be classified under the general heading of attitudes toward the future which also includes the concepts of future orientation, future expectation, and future time perspective.

A number of psychologists have attempted to develop a theoretical framework for the construct of hope or personal optimism. Lewin (1948) theorized about the importance of time perspective:

> The life-span of an individual, far from being limited to what he considers the present situation, includes the future, the present and also the past. Actions, emotions, and certainly the morale of an individual at any instant depend on his total time perspective. (p. 104)

The extension into future time is referred to by Lewin as the "psychological future." Hope is defined as the expectation that "sometime in the future, the real situation will be changed so that it will equal my wishes." Lewin cautions that the psychological future seldom corresponds to what actually happens later. The individual may engage in unrealistic optimism, vacillating between the extremes of hope and despair. However, "regardless of whether the individual's picture of the future is correct or incorrect at a given time, this picture deeply affects the mood and the action of the individual at that time" (p. 104). Persistence and level of aspiration depend on the value of goals and expectations of goal attainment—both considered key components of personal optimism.

Erikson (1980) places the construct of hope within his psychosocial theory of human development. Hope is based on a sense of trust (an attitude toward oneself and the world) developed during the trust-mistrust stage prior to the first year of life. For Erikson, trust implies confidence that one can cope with urges within oneself and that one can rely on the sameness and continuity of the caretaker. Successful resolution of the conflict at the trust-mistrust stage produces a sense of trust and favorable expectations of new experiences; unsuccessful resolution produces a sense of mistrust and fearful apprehension of future situations (Maier, 1969).

Farber (1967) views hope as jointly determined by personality make-up and situational demands. The critical personality factor is a sense of competence; the situational demand is the degree of threat leveled against the individual in a given culture. Examples of threats include loss of a loved one, loss of status, and the ravages of a disease. The relationship between a sense of competence and threat is described by a ratio function:

$Hope = f(C/T)$ where C = sense of competence and T = threat on a social-psychological scale of threats for a given culture, objectively determined.

Thus, the higher the sense of competence relative to a given threat, the greater the sense of hope. In addition, given a stable sense of competence, hope can vary in direct proportion to the degree of threat. Thus hope is a domain-specific construct.

In the tradition of learning theory, Mowrer (1960) equates hope with the goal event of reward and conceptualizes the mechanism of hope in terms of conditioned goal anticipatory responses, such as salivation when food is used as reward. Hope, then, may be objectively defined by various parameters of reinforcement. For example, the higher the percentage of reward, the greater the hope. The behavioral manifestation of hope is the vigor or persistence of behavior directed toward the goal event.

However, in the context of studying how organisms cope with prolonged frustration, Wong (in press) has found that goal persistence is also dependent on the availability of instrumental options. Wong has observed that for both humans and rats, the more instrumental opportunities, the greater the goal persistence, even when reinforcement parameters are kept constant. For example, given the same reinforcement history, organisms will persist longer when there are many routes leading to the goalbox than when only one route is available. By the same token, an individual should be more hopeful of achieving desired goals in life, when he or she has more instrumental options. Thus, hope may be operationally defined by the number of available alternative instrumental responses to achieve the desired goals.

In the context of developing a two-dimensional model of locus of control, Wong and Sproule (1983) argue that one's expectancy of success or hope is jointly determined by internal control and external control. An individual should have the maximum expectancy of success, when there is a high degree of internal control (in terms of competence and instrumental options) and a high degree of external control (in terms of help and support from powerful others). In other words, hope depends on both internal and external resources.

Tiger (1979), who is an anthropologist, prefers the term *optimism* to describe "a mood or attitude associated with an expectation about the social or material future—one which the evaluator regards as socially desirable, to his advantage or for his pleasure" (p. 18). For Tiger, optimism is a complex construct. It is a situation-specific state and depends on what the perceiver regards as desirable. It is also highly personal. "In essence there can be no objectively obvious optimism. It is always subjective and exists in the context of an individual's purposes as it is described or assumed by the individual" (p. 18).

Tiger argues that the role of man as a hunter-gatherer, the development of a large cerebral cortex, and the increasing complexity of social organization gives an evolutionary advantage to those who think things through, make plans, and look ahead into the future. "For social as well as economic and ecological reasons, it became useful, if not essential, to employ symbolic skills for evaluating the future" (p. 21). Thus, optimism is considered as necessary to survival as air (Tiger, 1979).

To date, Stotland (1969) has provided the most comprehensive theoretical perspective on the psychology of hope. Stotland attempts to imbed the hope construct within the experimental psychology tradition, particularly expectancy theory. He defined hope as "an expectation greater than zero of achieving a goal. The degree of hopefulness is the level of this expectation or the person's perceived probability of achieving a goal" (p. 2).

Stotland proposes seven propositions from which a number of hypotheses have been formulated. Space does not allow for a full discussion of the theory and the empirical evidence cited in support of it. Suffice it to say that the proposition that a sense of hope is a prerequisite for action is crucial to understanding the relationship between hope and health-related behaviors.

Henderson (1977) discusses hope at two levels. At level one, hope is "the expectation of something positive in the future." Hope at this level refers only to future direction. At the second level, hope is viewed as the "cognitive process of thrusting the past into the future." In elaborating, Henderson states that expectancies of something positive are to some extent determined by positive past experiences which lead to feelings of competence and mastery and which when projected into the future provide a cognitive and emotional sense of hope.

A number of clinical investigators have focused on the negative pole of the hope construct. For example, Beck, Weissman, Lester, and Trexler (1974) developed an operational measure of hopelessness defined as a system of negative expectancies concerning oneself and one's future life. Related to hopelessness is the learned helplessness construct (Garber & Seligman, 1980; Seligman, 1975). Helplessness results from the *expectation* that the outcome is independent of an individual's response. A helpless individual is one who perceives outcomes to be uncontrollable or noncontingent.

However, helplessness and hopelessness are not synonymous. One can be in a state of helplessness without feeling hopeless. Weiner and Litman-Adizes (1980) state that "even if probabilities of reward are not increased by personal responding, positive anticipation may be sustained by the knowledge that someone else is going to help or by ascribing the current noncontingency to unstable causes" (p. 52). Thus, helplessness can be viewed as a necessary but not a sufficient condition for hopelessness.

To summarize, personal optimism seems to be a multidimensional construct involving the cognitive process of expectancy of future success, the affective process of feeling happy, competent, or positive about oneself and/or the anticipated outcome, and the motivational process of pursuing the desired goals. The determinants of personal optimism include: (1) perceived competence or mastery acquired through past experience and projected into the future; (2) objectively determined probability of success (i.e., actual percentage of reinforcement); (3) availability of alternative instrumental responses; (4) availability of external resources; and (5) absence of external threats or barriers. All the above variables jointly determine one's subjective expectancies, feelings, and goal strivings—the three major components of personal optimism.

Personal optimism may be defined as a personalized, subjective system of positive expectations, feelings, and goal-directed strivings applicable to future life concerns. It should be noted that the projection into the future may be either of a short-term or long-term nature. Personal optimism is also domain-specific. That is, the level of personal optimism can vary for different life concerns for the same individual. One may be highly optimistic about future career success, but very pessimistic about one's marital life. We assume that in spite of it being domain-specific, personal optimism is additive across life concerns, making it possible to generate a global index.

The Measurement of Personal Optimism

We have developed a personal optimism measure called the Future Orientation Survey (FOS) as shown in Appendix 1. We ask respondents to list a number of desirable events to which they are currently looking forward. We also ask them to indicate the degree of their confidence that each of the desirable events will take place on a 5-point scale ranging from "not confident at all" to "extremely confident." The degree of personal optimism for each respondent is based on three measures: number of future events, average confidence ratings, and total confidence ratings. We have chosen an open-ended format because we want to know the areas of future concern as perceived by the respondents.

We have administered the FOS, along with a number of other instruments, to samples of institutionalized and community elderly. Content analysis of the responses revealed the following categories of life concerns: family life, housing/living conditions, community/social service, religion, leisure/recreation, health, friendship, personal development, finance, and miscellaneous.

In addition, we are interested in identifying the structure of free responses of optimism along three dimensions: (1) density—total number of future concerns; (2) future extension—short- versus long-term. Short-term is defined as any event that would happen within a year and/or have a duration of less than a month. Long-term is defined as any event that would happen past one year and/or have a duration longer than a month; and (3) locus of initiation—self-initiated versus other-initiated. In self-initiated optimism, the *respondent* hopes or desires to initiate, plan, and carry out some future events (equivalent to personal future commitment). In other-initiated optimism, the respondent hopes or desires that *others* will initiate, plan, and carry out events which may or may not be directly related to the respondent (i.e., others may do something to the respondent or to themselves). Others might include other individuals, government, society, nature, or God. The results of some of our findings will be described in more detail in the final section of this chapter.

Related to our FOS scale is the hopelessness (pessimism) scale developed by Beck et al. (1974). It should be noted that optimism and pessimism are opposites of the same continuum. The main differences between our scale and the hopelessness scale are that our scale is based on the wellness model rather than the disease model, and that we depend heavily on spontaneously generated life concerns about future events.

PERSONAL OPTIMISM, PHYSICAL AND MENTAL HEALTH

Much of the evidence linking personal optimism to physical and mental health has focused on the antithetical construct of hopelessness and its negative effects on the organism. This focus on the negative is a consequence of *pathogenesis,* the study of the origins of disease, which has dominated medical research for a long time. In recent years, a growing interest in *salutogenesis,* a term coined by Antonovsky (1979) for the study of the origins of health, has led to theoretical orientations and empirical research whose primary focus is on positive factors that prevent disease and promote physical and psychological well-being. It seems most sensible, then, to discuss the evidence relating personal optimism to physical and mental health within the context of the pathogenic and salutogenic orientations.

The Pathogenic Orientation

The central theme of this section is to support the assertion that negative mental attitudes and emotional states play a significant role in the susceptibility to cancer, sudden death, and suicide. The cognitive/affective states of depression, despair, hopelessness, and helplessness have been identified as the key precursors to the aforementioned life-threatening events.

Hopelessness and cancer. Simonton, Matthews-Simonton, and Creighton (1978) have proposed a mind/body model of cancer development that specifies the psychophysiological pathways which are also described more globally by the mosaic model (see Reker, Chapter 3, this volume). Their model is presented in Figure 7-2. Simonton et al. assert that cancer development is the result of coping with the stressors and strains of life with a sense of hopelessness or despair. The hopelessness response is assumed to trigger physiological reactions resulting in the suppression of the immune system, the creation of hormonal imbalances, and the generation of abnormal cells, culminating in cancerous growth. Does the literature substantiate such an assertion?

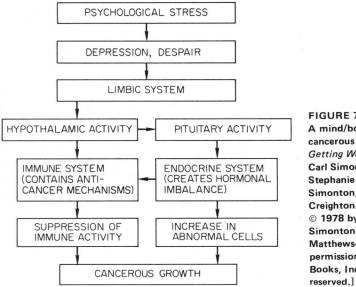

FIGURE 7-2.
A mind/body model of
cancerous growth. [From
Getting Well Again by O.
Carl Simonton, M.D.,
Stephanie Matthews-
Simonton, & James
Creighton. Copyright
© 1978 by O. Carl
Simonton & Stephanie
Matthews-Simonton. By
permission of Bantam
Books, Inc. All rights
reserved.]

The effect of stressors on cancer development in animals has been thoroughly reviewed by Friedman, Glasgow, and Ader (1969) and by LaBarba (1970) who concluded that under certain circumstances, tumorigenicity and mortality in animals can be influenced by experimental and/or environmental manipulations. Two recent studies using mice and rats report a relationship between inescapable shock (helplessness) and tumor growth, suggesting that lack of control over stressors exacerbates cancer development (Sklar & Anisman, 1979; Visintainer, Volpicelli, & Seligman, 1982).

Before we review the available human evidence, we would like to point out that we are well aware of the methodological problems that plague the research literature in this field. The majority of the studies are retrospective in their design and are subject to retrospective contamination (Brown, 1974) and interpretative problems (for a thorough critique, see Fox, 1978). Nevertheless, the results of such studies, while not conclusive, do offer suggestions and directions for prospective and/or predictive studies on the relationship between hopelessness and cancer.

One of the earliest anecdotal accounts of a relationship between psychological states and the development of cancer was given in the second century A.D. by Galen. He is reported to have found cancer to be more frequent in "melancholic" (depressed) as opposed to "sanguine" (cheerful) women (Mettler & Mettler, 1947).

In a content analysis of the writings of the eighteenth- and nineteenth-century physicians regarding the relationship between emotions and neoplastic disease, Kowal (1955) observed a characteristic pattern in the life histories of patients prior to the development of cancer. The life situation was characterized by (1) loss of a significant figure through illness, separation, or by death; (2) frustration of significant life goals; and (3) despair and hopelessness as a reaction to loss and frustration. Kowal concluded that "out of the whole range of human emotions they all [physicians], more or less, tended to select for emphasis those which reflected despair or hopelessness as the precursor of the neoplastic state. Of this relation between despair and cancer they were convinced" (p. 227). A similar pattern was reported by LeShan and Worthington (1956) in their review of the nineteenth- and twentieth-century literature.

The work of LeShan (1966) corroborated these early observations. LeShan traced the emotional life-history pattern associated with neoplastic diseases of 450 adult cancer patients and 150 controls equated by age, sex, and social class over a 12-year period. He found a specific and typical pattern of development in 72 percent of the cancer patients and in 10 percent of the equated controls. The pattern consisted of five major phases: (1) emotional disturbance in childhood, prior to the first seven years, characterized by feelings of isolation, rejection, hopelessness, and despair; (2) poor outlet for emotional discharge as an adult but a positive cathexis to spouse, job, or children that gave meaning to life; (3) loss of the cathected object; (4) feelings of isolation, hopelessness, depression, despair; and (5) discovery of cancer at some time from 6 months to 8 years following loss of the cathected object. LeShan placed primary emphasis on the feeling of despair: "The depth and intensity of this orientation is so great that it is difficult to describe. Basically, it is bleak hopelessness about ever achieving any real feelings of meaning or enjoyment in life" (p. 783). Goldfarb, Driesen, and Cole (1967) and Simonton et al. (1978) have identified similar psychological processes that precede the onset of cancer.

Thomas, Duszynski, and Shaffer (1979) shed some light on the nature of the emotional disturbance in early adulthood as described by LeShan (1966) and LeShan and Worthington (1956). In an impressive long-term prospective study of medical students (all males), Thomas et al. observed that those who perceived the relationship to their parents as one lacking in closeness (e.g., emotional distance and detachment, active hostility) were more likely to develop cancer. The father-son relationship appeared to be the most crucial; the mother-son relationship was also important but its linkage to development of cancer was less marked.

Several studies provide support for LeShan's (1966) observations that cancer patients typically have poor emotional outlets (Bahnson & Bahnson, 1966; Greer & Morris, 1975; Kissen, 1963; Kissen, Brown, & Kissen, 1969; Morris, Greer, Pettingale, & Watson, 1981; Wirsching, Stierling, Hoffman, Weber & Wirsching, 1982). Greer and Morris conducted a carefully controlled investigation of the psychological attributes of women admitted to hospital for breast tumor biopsy. Information was obtained from patients by means of detailed structured interviews and various tests on the day before the operation, without knowledge of the provisional diagnoses. Sixty-nine patients were found to have breast cancer and 91 patients, who were diagnosed as having benign breast cancer, served as controls. No differences were found between the two groups on a large number of demographic and psychological variables. However, the two groups differed significantly with respect to emotional release—a higher proportion of the cancer patients suppressed their anger and other feelings compared to controls. These results were replicated by Morris et al. (1981). Similar results were reported by Kissen (1963) and Kissen et al. (1969) who found a more restricted outlet of emotional discharge among male lung cancer patients compared to noncancerous controls. Bahnson and Bahnson (1966) found that cancer patients tended to deny and repress conflictual impulses and emotion to a significantly higher degree than normal controls.

In a recent study of the psychological profile of breast cancer patients assessed before biopsy, Wirsching et al. (1982) found that cancer patients compared to benign controls were more likely to remain aloof, suppress their emotions, rationalize, show no anxiety before the operation, show unusual altruism, avoid conflict, and to show signs of helplessness and hopelessness. This psychological profile was found in all breast cancer patients and in a quarter to a third of the patients with benign tumors. The profile led to a highly significant correct prediction of 83 percent of the cancer and 71 percent of the benign patients. Although the cancer patients were older compared to the benign controls, the age difference had no effect on the results.

A number of prospective studies linking hopelessness to the development of uterine cervical cancer in women have been reported by Schmale and Iker (1964, 1966, 1971). In one series of studies (Schmale & Iker, 1964, 1966), 51 healthy women under the age of 50 and considered equally predisposed to the disease completed an open-ended, tape-recorded interview and several psychological tests. The interview data were analyzed in terms of the extent to which feelings of hopelessness were expressed. Hopelessness was defined as "a complete sense of frustration for which the individual felt there was no solution." Cancer was *predicted,* independent of the biopsy results, as present or absent based on interview evidence of recently experienced (past 6 months) feelings of hopelessness. Of 18 women predicted to have cancer, 11 (61 percent) were actually found to have cancer; of the 33 predicted to have no cancer, 25 (76 percent) did not have cancer. These results were statistically significant. The additional predictions that cancer patients would show higher depression, lower ego strength, and lower femininity scores were not supported.

In a content analysis of the nature of the recent life events experienced by the predicted cancer versus no-cancer patients, Schmale and Iker (1966) found that while threat of loss made up the majority of the events, the threats were about equal in the two groups. Thus, it was not the life events per se, but the presence of the reported hopelessness in reaction to the experiences that differentiated the cancer from the no-cancer patients. Finally, the authors point out that the feeling of hopelessness does not predispose to cancer; it merely plays a facilitative role in an already biologically predisposed organism. These findings support earlier observations in a retrospective study conducted by Schmale (1958).

Psychological factors also play a role in the course and outcome of neoplastic disease. Greer, Morris, and Pettingale (1979) conducted a prospective 5-year study of 69 consecutive female breast cancer patients. The patients were under 70 years with no previous history of malignant disease, a breast lump less than 5 cm in diameter, and no distant metastases. Psychological responses were obtained by means of a structured interview. The responses were grouped into four mutually exclusive categories: (1) denial—active rejection of any evidence about the diagnosis, little reported emotional distress; (2) fighting spirit—a highly optimistic attitude that cancer can be beaten; (3) stoic acceptance—acknowledgment of the diagnosis, but basically ignoring it and carrying on a normal life; (4) feelings of hopelessness/helplessness—a complete engulfment by knowledge of diagnosis, preoccupation with cancer and impending death, lack of hope, obvious mental distress. The statistically significant results showed that 75 percent of the patients who were alive with no recurrence at 5 years after the operation had initially coped with denial or fighting spirit, whereas 35 percent had responded with either stoic acceptance or helplessness/hopelessness. Furthermore, of the women who subsequently died, 88 percent reacted initially with stoic acceptance or helplessness/hopelessness. Forty-six percent of the women who were alive and well showed these emotional reactions.

Horne and Picard (1979) conducted a predictive study of 110 male patients with undiagnosed subacute x-ray lesions of the lung. Ratings were made of five subscales of psychosocial risk factors selected on the basis of previous research findings: (1) childhood instability; (2) job stability; (3) marriage stability; (4) lack of plans for the future; and (5) recent significant loss. The midpoint of the composite scale score was used to *predict* patients with benign (below midpoint) or malignant (above midpoint) disease. Actual pathological diagnosis was obtained in a follow-up review at an average 26 months after the interview. The psychosocial scale correctly predicted the diagnoses of 53 (80 percent) of the 66 patients with benign disease and 27 (61 percent) of the 44 with lung cancer. Of the five subscales, recent significant loss (past 5 years), job stability, and lack of plans for the future best predicted the actual diagnoses. Although the mean age of patients with malignancy (61.6 years) was significantly greater compared to patients with benign illness (56 years), age did not account for the association between psychosocial factors and cancer. Surprisingly, the psychosocial factors were one to two times as important as smoking history (a well-established risk factor) in predicting diagnoses of lung cancer. While the Horne and Picard study did not address itself directly to hopelessness as a precursor to cancer, the findings that patients with malignant disease suffered more from recent significant loss and planned less for the future implicate hopelessness as a contributing factor.

Taken together, the anecdotal, retrospective, and prospective studies point to four key factors that influence the initiation, propagation, and spread of cancer: (1) adverse life situations involving frustration or stress; (2) inability to cope effectively with adversity; (3) inadequate emotional outlet; and (4) a cognitive/affective response of hopelessness or despair both prior to and during the course of the disease. A similar conclusion has been reached by Kissen (1969):

> Adverse life situations in an individual with poor emotional outlets, and, therefore, with diminished ability effectively to sublimate or dissipate an emotional situation, are likely to result in such effects as depression, despair, and hopelessness. It is also possible that adverse life situations may directly precipitate such effects whatever the personality, but it must be conceded that their manifestation is more likely in those with poor emotional outlets. (p. 134)

Fox (1978) has criticized the administration of psychological tests to patients who already have the disease (whether diagnosed or undiagnosed at the time) as almost tautological. He argues that while psychological differences do exist between cancer and noncancer patients, they may be due to hormonal changes associated with the disease. To address this issue, studies are required that link particular psychological states or emotions to hormonal or immunological events.

Katz, Weiner, Gallagher, and Hellman (1970) studied the effect of psychosocial coping strategies on the psychoendocrine responses of 30 patients awaiting surgery for possible breast cancer. They found that those who coped effectively with stress by means of faith, denial, pride, or hope had a lower corticosteroid response, while those who were anxious, dejected, hopeless or despairing had higher hydrocortisone rates.

In their mind/body model of cancer development (Figure 7-2), Simonton et al. (1978) describe the mechanism by which a psychological state of hopelessness or despair gets translated into malignant neoplastic disease. Several animal and human studies and review articles clearly suggest that psychological stress involves the central nervous system, particularly the hypothalamus, the neuroendocrine and the immunological systems in a complex network of mediating relationships (Cunningham, 1981). An organism's vulnerability to disease is heightened by means of cellular and humoral immunosuppression produced by central nervous system and hormonal activity. The link between psychological stress and the immune system has also been demonstrated through behaviorally conditioned immunosuppression, hypnosis, and hypothalamic lesions (Ader & Cohen, 1975; Gorczynski, MacRae, & Kennedy, 1982; Riley, cited in Holden, 1978; Rogers, Dubey, & Reich, 1979; Selye, 1956; Sklar & Anisman, 1981; Solomon, 1969; Southam, 1969; Stein, Schiavi, & Camerino, 1976).

In a unique prospective study, Bartrop, Luckhurst, Lazarus, Kiloh, and Penny (1977) investigated the effects of bereavement on the immune response of healthy adults. T and B cell numbers and function, and hormone assays were studied at two and six weeks after bereavement. The authors found the cell-mediated immune response to be significantly depressed in the bereaved group at six weeks compared to a hospital control group. No differences were found in T and B cell numbers and in hormone levels. Thus, a direct link was demonstrated between severe psychological distress and abnormality in immune function that was not mediated by hormone changes. It is worthwhile pointing out that loss of a significant other is typically accompanied by affective states, such as hopelessness, that consistently emerge in the psychosocial profile of cancer patients.

In summary, the evidence reviewed points to a fairly uniform pattern of antecedent psychosocial events having a direct as well as an indirect suppressive effect on the immunological system leading to cancer. More specifically, the construct of hopelessness or despair has been consistently identified as the primary affective precursor to the onset, development, and outcome of neoplastic disease. Certainly not all individuals with the psychological pattern described in this section develop cancer, and there are, no doubt, individuals without the pattern who do. However, the linkage of hopelessness or despair to cancer seems to have been established.

Several of the previously cited studies controlled for the effect of age and for a good reason because normal immune functions decline with age (Makinodan, 1977). In animals and humans, the thymic lymphatic mass decreases with age due to atrophy of the thymic cortex. Associated with involution of the thymus is a decline of circulation levels of natural antibodies and thymic hormones. Interestingly, the decline begins at sexual maturity (Makinodan), just about the time when mortality rates (the Gompertz curve) in the population begin to rise.

Infections, autoimmunity, and cancer increase as the normal immune functions decline with age. This relationship is most striking among the aged in both humans and animals (Makinodan, 1977; Teller, 1972). Immunoengineering through selective alteration of the immune system by the manipulation of diet, body temperature, drug treatment, and rejuvenation via injection of young donor immune cells or stored autologous immune cells has the potential to reduce the severity of various diseases associated with aging (Makinodan, 1977).

At the moment, these approaches are at a very preliminary stage of development. Furthermore, they do not directly address the question of the influence of psychological states on the growth of cancer. Since the normal immune function is already declining with age, any additional immunosuppression brought on by cognitive/affective states such as hopelessness should lead to increased susceptibility to disease in the elderly. We need an approach that will focus our attention on *positive* psychological states. Do psychological factors of a positive nature increase the efficiency of the immune system? Can a change for the better in the psychological state of a cancer patient affect the development of the tumor? What is the nature of such change? What happens physiologically and biologically when psychological states are improved? The salutogenic orientation, to be presented later, will address these issues.

Hopelessness and sudden death.   One of the mysteries of life is the sudden death phenomenon that cannot be explained in terms of pathological factors. Cannon (1957), in attempting to understand the so-called voodoo deaths occurring in primitive cultures, postulated that they were triggered by powerful emotional states that aroused the sympathicoadrenal system of the organism (see Newquist, Chapter 6, this volume). In a review of the literature on sudden death or disease, Goodfriend and Wolpert (1976) concluded that emotional states, particularly the state of hopelessness, precipitate a physiological response leading to sudden death. However, the specific physiological mechanisms could not be identified.

In a preliminary report on psychosocial factors and sudden death in 26 men predisposed to cardiovascular disease, Greene, Goldstein, and Moss (1972) reported that the majority of these men had been depressed for a week up to several months prior to sudden death. Sudden death seemed to be precipitated by acute arousal of affects such as anxiety or anger. The authors concluded that the combination of depression and acute arousal produced disharmonious responses in the hormonal and autonomic systems, although evidence for the latter conjecture was not provided.

In a now-classic study, Richter (1957) investigated the nature of this phenomenon in wild and domesticated Norway rats and attempted to identify the crucial variables. Based on some puzzling observations made in connection with another problem, Richter de-whiskered 34 wild and 12 domestic rats and placed them in an inescapable water jar. In this situation, normal control rats will swim 60 to 80 hours prior to exhaustion. He found that 3 of the 12 domesticated rats dove to the bottom of the jar and drowned within two minutes; the remaining 9 swam 40 to 60 hours. On the other hand, all 34 wild rats died within 15 minutes following immersion. Moreover, heart and respiratory rates were shown to slow down before death, indicating that the rats died as a result of overstimulation of the parasympathetic rather than the sympathicoadrenal system. Richter attributed the sudden deaths to hopelessness. "The situation of these rats scarcely seems one demanding fight or flight—it is rather one of hopelessness . . . the rats are in a situation against which they have no defense . . . they seem literally to 'give up'" (p. 196).

From the salutogenic perspective of this chapter, the more interesting finding reported by Richter is that immersion of the wild rats for a few minutes on several occasions (stress inoculation) eliminated the sudden death phenomenon. Wild rats who learned that the situation was not hopeless swam just as long as (or longer than) domestic rats. In Stotland's (1969) words, "Hope of survival is essential for action for survival" (p. 21).

In an attempt to document the sudden death phenomenon in humans, Engel (1971) analyzed a large number of newspaper accounts of sudden unexpected deaths. He identified eight life-setting categories conducive to illness or death: (1) the collapse or death of a close person; (2) during acute grief; (3) on threat of loss of a close person; (4) during mourning or on an anniversary; (5) on loss of status or self-esteem; (6) personal danger or threat of injury; (7) after a danger is over; and (8) reunion, triumph, or happy ending. Common to all of the life events is either a response to overwhelming excitation or hopelessness (giving up). Engel proposed that both the fight-flight and the conservation-withdrawal systems are provoked by the psychological stress leading to lethal cardiac events.

In another study, Engel (1968) described the common coping response leading to either illness or death as the "giving-up, given-up complex." Its characteristic feature is a sense of psychological impotence, a feeling that one cannot cope with changes in the environment and that previous coping mechanisms and resources are no longer effective or available. The "giving-up, given-up complex" is characterized by: (1) a sense of helplessness and hopelessness; (2) a depreciated image of oneself; (3) a loss of gratification from relationships or roles in life; (4) a disruption of the sense of continuity between past, present, and future; and (5) reactivation of memories of earlier periods of giving up (Engel, 1968). For Engel, the "giving-up, given-up complex" is neither a necessary nor a sufficient condition for illness or death but plays a role in *modifying* the capacity of the organism to cope with disease.

Miller and Lieberman (1965) investigated the effect of changes in the sociophysical environment on the mortality, morbidity, and psychological disability of aged persons. Forty-five women, aged 61 to 91, underwent relocation from a small state-controlled home to a large state institution. All were free from mental and physical symptoms at the initial interview. Several measures of adaptive capacity and affect were obtained at 2 weeks prior to relocation, and 6 weeks and 18 weeks after moving. At 18 weeks, 23 of the 45 women showed negative change in health (death, physical and psychological deterioration). Depressive affect at the initial interview was the only variable to differentiate the no-change from the negative-change groups. Women who had been depressed before relocation showed health declines after moving. Upon reexamination of the depression construct, however, the authors determined that meaninglessness and hopelessness were the primary components of their measure. Thus it was meaninglessness and hopelessness that modified the capacity of the women to deal with relocation stress leading to rapid physical and psychological decline.

The evidence suggests that sudden death or illness is the result of strong emotional reactions, particularly feelings of depression and hopelessness. Sudden death can occur in otherwise healthy people and is augmented in individuals predisposed to illness. The specific physiological mechanism is still unclear, although it seems to involve both the sympatheticoadrenal and the parasympathetic nervous systems.

Hopelessness and suicide. One of the most disturbing aspects of mental health and aging is the dramatic rise in the suicide rate of people 60 years and older. In 1975, Americans over 60 years of age represented 18.5 percent of the population but committed 23 percent of all suicides. Older white males are particularly vulnerable. While the suicide rate in the population has remained relatively stable at between 9 and 13 per 100,000 since 1945, the rate for older white males has ranged between 40 and 75 per 100,000. The male/female ratio during the ages 65 to 69 is 4 to 1. This increases to 12 to 1 by age 85. While females *attempt* suicide three times as often as males, males *commit* suicide three times as often as females (Miller, 1979).

Stengel (1973) has made a psychodynamic distinction between suicide attempters and suicide committers. Attempters appeal for help; committers are motivated toward self-destruction. The success of older males in committing suicide suggests that suicidal acts for appeal are not as common among older males. Suicidal behavior is often associated with an inability to cope with significant losses (Farber, 1967; Henderson, 1977; Resnik & Cantor, 1970). Losses in economic, social, physical, psychological, and emotional spheres are more common among the elderly, not necessarily because of age but because of having lived and experienced life longer.

Some elderly people experience grave tragedies throughout life, but never even think of committing suicide; others may suffer only minor fears, yet lose their desire to live. Several sociological and psychological explanations have been offered to account for suicidal behavior, including anomie, role failure, feelings of inferiority, loss of self-esteem, lack of a confidant, loneliness, dependency conflict, depression, and hopelessness (Birren, 1964; Durkheim, 1951; Farber, 1967; Henderson, 1977; Hendin, 1963; Miller, 1978, 1979; Pfeiffer, 1977; Stenback, 1980). Depression, defined as an affective disorder manifested in psychological (e.g., dysphoric mood, apathy, withdrawal) and physical (e.g., loss of appetite, sleep disturbance, constipation) ways, is the most commonly cited explanation (Stenback).

Depression may not explain why elderly white males are so much more at risk. In fact, recent evidence shows that elderly women are significantly *more* depressed compared to elderly males (Linn, Hunter, & Harris, 1980; Oltman, Michals, & Steer, 1980). Also, certain kinds of depressive disorders are episodic in nature (Pfeiffer, 1977) and, unlike hopelessness, do not necessarily imply negative future expectations. The theme to be developed in this section is that suicide in older adults, particularly in white males, can be better explained by the mental state of hopelessness or despair brought on by repeated failures to cope with various losses (Farber, 1967). As Lifton (1979) points out, "People who commit suicide may or may not be significantly depressed, but they are almost certain to be affected by despair—by a sense of radical absence of meaning and purpose, and of the impossibility of human connection" (p. 249). Given feelings of hopelessness or despair, the suicidal person can create a future only by killing himself or herself (Lifton, 1979). Thus, suicide can be viewed as an act carried out to relieve the state of hopelessness (Stenback, 1980).

The relationship between hopelessness and suicide has been investigated at the cultural level (Cecchini, 1976; Farber, 1967) and the individual level (Bjerg, 1967; Farnham-Diggory, 1964; Ganzler, 1967; Henderson, 1977; Minkoff, Bergman, Beck, & Beck, 1973; Pokorny, Kaplan, & Tsai, 1975; Stenback, 1980). Farber found Danes to view life less hopefully, to be more concerned with the present, to become more depressed, and to commit suicide more frequently than Norwegians. Bjerg found loss of hope to be the main theme in 81 percent of suicide notes. Farnham-Diggory reported that suicidal patients had a significantly constricted view of the future compared to nonsuicidal patients. Ganzler found that in comparison to nonsuicidal psychiatric outpatients and normal subjects, the suicidal group rated the future more negatively.

The importance of hopelessness as the critical variable in suicide was highlighted in a study of 68 male and female suicide attempters, age range 14 to 63 years (Minkoff et al., 1973). The patients, the majority of whom were diagnosed depressive, completed scales of hopelessness, depression, and suicidal intent within 48 hours of admission to the hospital. A highly significant correlation was found between hopelessness and seriousness of suicidal intent. Furthermore, seriousness of intent was found to be more closely related to hopelessness than to depression. In a subsequent comparison study, Pokorny et al. (1975) suggested that external support systems might lessen the impact of hopelessness as a predictor of suicide.

Feelings of hopelessness and despair were also evident in the psychophysiological profiles of severely depressed suicidal patients studied by Bunney and Fawcett (1967). These investigators identified four specific patterns of 17-hydroxy-corticosteroid (17-OHCS) excretion among 143 depressed patients. Patients with relatively stable high 17-OHCS levels and patients with periodic one-to-two-day peaks measured over an extended period of time were later found to be suicidal. None of the depressed patients with low to moderate cortisol levels showed suicidal tendencies. The suicidal patients were described as feeling utterly hopeless, suffering from intense guilt feelings, and were of the opinion that their families and friends would be better off without them. These findings have practical and theoretical implications. First, the specific pattern of biochemical changes can be used to aid in the identification of potentially suicidal individuals. Second, the relationship between behavioral manifestations of depression and biochemical changes is a complex one. Third, depression per se may not be a sufficient condition for suicidal behavior.

In a review of the evidence of possible psychosocial factors in the life history of suicidal individuals, Henderson (1977) concluded that parental loss through divorce, separation, or death early in the person's life predisposes that individual to suicidal tendencies. This individual may later develop a sense of self-worth primarily through close relationship with a significant other such as the spouse. However, when the individual again experiences a sudden disruption in the affectional relationship he or she becomes vulnerable to feelings of hopelessness, suicidal ideation, and suicidal behavior (Henderson, 1977).

Family attitudes during the early developmental period may also predispose an individual to suicide tendencies. In a prospective study of former medical students cited in an earlier section, Thomas et al. (1979) found a striking similarity between students who subsequently developed cancer and those who became suicidal/mentally ill. Both groups rated themselves significantly lower on the closeness-to-parents scale compared to their healthy classmates. While the cancer and suicidal groups were similar on some psychological variables, they differed on others. For example, the suicidal group showed significantly more evidence of depression and anger than did those who later developed cancer.

Considering Henderson's (1977) description of suicidal individuals, LeShan's (1966) life history pattern in cancer patients and the Thomas et al. (1979) study, the only apparent difference between the cancer and suicidal patients is that the former tend to suppress, whereas the latter more readily express their emotions. It may well be that faced with the same degree of hopelessness, one individual does not have the courage to commit suicide and subsequently develops cancer; whereas another individual expresses his or her anger and frustration by taking a destructive act—committing suicide.

In summary, the hopelessness-suicide relationship can be described by a specific and unique psychosocial pattern. The suicidal individual is one who has experienced early traumatic loss of an affectional relationship and/or lack of closeness to parents. In adulthood, a sense of competence, optimism, and meaningfulness is developed primarily through the spouse, the job, or the children. Later in life, disruptions through personal threats and losses lead to feelings of depression and failure. The projection of failure experiences into the future gives rise to feelings of hopelessness or despair, culminating in attempted or committed suicide.

Older white American males, particularly those from the middle or upper class, may be more vulnerable to a disruption of their goals, value orientations, and sense of competence later in life compared to either females (Thurnher, 1974) or to nonwhite male peers, fewer of whom would share the higher social status. In Farber's (1967) words:

> One possible explanation in terms of the present theory is that the upper-class person, when he becomes depressed in the face of some deprivation, is more restricted than others in psychological space of free movement, in his areas of hope. In contrast, the member of a class below in such a state can always hope for socioeconomic improvement as a possible alleviation of his difficulties. The upper-class person has everything, and still he is depressed; he knows that all the things and courses available to him are useless in his plight. In his elevated position, the world has a low ceiling . . . Suicide, then, is in the main an act of hopelessness, of despair and desperation. (p. 305)

The Salutogenic Orientation

The neologism *salutogenesis* was coined by Antonovsky (1979) to describe a new perspective on the origins of health. The salutogenic orientation embraces the question of why, in the midst of ubiquitous stressors, so many individuals are able to stay healthy most of their lives. The major consequences of a pathogenic orientation have been the overriding emphasis on negative emotional states and their influence on illness outcomes and the neglect of studying individuals who, under extremely stressful circumstances, do not become ill. It is interesting to note that in a widely referenced prospective study of life change and illness susceptibility, Holmes and Masuda (1974) found that 49 percent, 25 percent, and 9 percent of physicians with high, medium, and low life change scores, respectively, became ill 9 months later. However, not mentioned are the 51 percent in the high-risk group who do *not* report illness. Clearly, other factors are at work in the high-risk group that have not been taken into account. Kobasa (1979) used the term *hardiness* to describe a personality mediator in resistance against stress and illness; the *hardy* individual is characterized by a strong commitment to self, an attitude of vigorousness toward the environment, a sense of meaningfulness, and an internal locus of control. Antonovsky (1979) proposed the concept *sense of coherence,* an orientation that sees life as meaningful and manageable, as a psychological resource to resist stress and illness. Recently, Hutschnecker (1981) described many case studies from his practice to substantiate the theme that hope sustains life while hopelessness causes death. In the final chapter on "Hope and Cancer," Hutschnecker cites from an article produced by Hoffman-LaRoche Pharmaceutical Company:

> In a study of two hundred cancer patients, it was observed that each and every one maintained at least a little hope. People without hope see no end to their suffering but those with hope have 'confidence in the desirability of survival.' (p. 237)

In this section, we will explore the role of the salutogenic concept of personal optimism and its relationship to health-promoting behavior.

Personal optimism and cancer remission.   One of the puzzling phenomena in medical practice is the sudden regression in tumor growth for which an adequate explanation has yet to be offered. It is referred to as *spontaneous remission.* A related phenomenon, whose operation is well documented, is the so-called *placebo effect,* a positive expectation that the treatment will help, creating an expectancy of health (Beecher, 1955; Simonton et al., 1978). Simonton et al., for example, found that cancer patients with a positive attitude had better responses to treatment compared to patients with negative attitudes. Furthermore, patients with a serious prognosis but positive attitude responded better to treatment than did patients with less serious prognoses and negative attitudes. Thus attitude seems to be a better predictor of response to treatment than severity of the disease. In the Greer et al. (1979) study of breast cancer patients reported earlier, it was found that a fighting spirit, defined as a highly optimistic attitude accompanied by a search for greater information about breast cancer, proved to be an extremely effective coping response in arresting the further growth of tumors.

A mind/body model of cancer regression has been proposed by Simonton et al. (1978). The model is presented in Figure 7–3. It is based on the premise that active and positive participation in one's health can influence the onset of the disease, the outcome of treatment, and the quality of life. The model describes how the psychological state of hope or personal optimism can influence the neurophysiological systems leading to cancer regression. Strong evidence in support of such an assertion, however, is still lacking. Much of it is in the form of anecdotal accounts and case studies (Cousins, 1979; Hutschnecker, 1981; Simonton et al., 1978).

One of the most dramatic examples of the effect of positive emotions in reversing the effect of a life-threatening disease is the well-documented case study of Norman Cousins. Cousins suffered from an "incurable" collagen illness, a disease of the connective tissues that leads to a progressive disintegration of body cells. Through a regimen of good doctor-patient relationship, a strong will to live, an

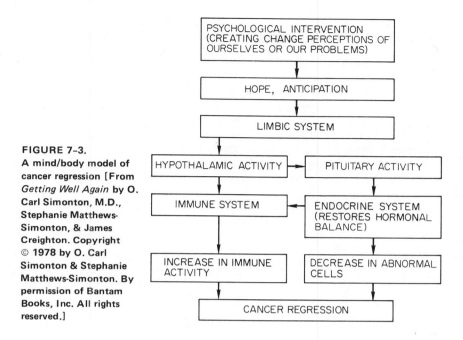

FIGURE 7–3.
A mind/body model of cancer regression [From *Getting Well Again* **by O. Carl Simonton, M.D., Stephanie Matthews-Simonton, & James Creighton. Copyright © 1978 by O. Carl Simonton & Stephanie Matthews-Simonton. By permission of Bantam Books, Inc. All rights reserved.]**

optimistic outlook, high doses of ascorbic acid (Vitamin C), and laughter, Cousins was able to mobilize his body's own natural healing resources to achieve full recovery (Cousins, 1979). The exact mechanisms in the recovery process are unknown. Suffice it to say that whatever the mediating physiological mechanism, mental attitude appears to be a powerful weapon in the war against disease.

Simonton et al. (1978) have developed a program to train cancer patients to use their minds and emotions to alter the course of their malignancies. The program was designed to be used in conjunction with traditional medical treatment for cancer. It utilized techniques for learning positive attitudes, relaxation, visualization, goal setting, pain management, exercise, and the building of emotional support systems. The visual imagery process, the core of the program, involved a period of relaxation during which the patient would mentally picture a desired goal. The cancer patient would be asked to visualize the cancer, the treatment destroying it, and the use of natural bodily defenses leading to recovery.

Over a number of years, 159 patients with a diagnosis of medically incurable malignancy took part in this program. Life expectancy for this group of patients, based on national norms, was 12 months. Sixty-three patients were still alive at the time of data reporting with an average survival time of 24.4 months; the average survival time of patients who had died was 20.3 months. In a matched control group of patients receiving only medical treatment, the average survival time was 12 months, clearly less than half that of patients still alive. Of the 63 patients in the training program who were alive, 22.2 percent showed no evidence of cancer, 46.2 percent showed tumor regression or disease stabilization, and only 31.6 percent developed new tumors. In addition, the quality of life as measured by the level of daily activity during and after treatment seemed to be almost at the same level as prior to the diagnosis.

While these results are encouraging, there is still much controversy concerning the beneficial effects of positive-attitude training. Simonton et al.'s findings need to be replicated in better-controlled investigations. The visual imagery process developed by Simonton et al. is intriguing in that it appears to be a concrete form of personal optimism; for example, it teaches patients to visualize that cancerous cells will be destroyed. Recently, the use of psychotherapy aimed at affecting the physical disease has received increasing attention (Cunningham, 1982; Feinstein, 1983). The effectiveness of this approach, however, has yet to be demonstrated. Needless to say, the relative merits of different positive-attitude training procedures for cancer patients remain an empirical question.

Dimensions of future orientation in the elderly. We have already documented the importance of a positive future orientation in health. In this section, we will attempt to identify the major dimensions of future orientation which may be importantly related to physical and mental health in the elderly.

One of the stereotypes about the elderly is that they tend to dwell disproportionately on the past (Gitelson, 1948; Lewis, 1971; Neugarten, 1964; Schuster, 1952). This widely held belief seems to make good intuitive sense, because for the elderly, the future becomes increasingly shorter, present activities become increasingly limited, but the reservoir of past events continues to increase. However, empirical support for this stereotypic belief is very weak. For example, in the Lewis (1971) study, reminiscence is defined as the frequency of talking about the past in a 30-minute interview. Cameron (1972) correctly points out that "because a person *talks* relatively more about the past does not necessarily mean he generally *thinks* more about the past" (p. 118).

By employing a consciousness-sampling technique, which consists of interrupting the subject and asking the question, "What were you just thinking about?", Cameron (1972) found that people most frequently think about the present, next most about the future, and least about the past, regardless of their age. For example, for the middle age sample, 11 percent thought about the past, 62 percent about the present, and 27 percent about the future; for the 56- to 64-year-olds, the percentages associated with thinking of the past, present, and future were 14 percent, 60 percent, and 27 percent. In subsequent studies, Cameron, Desai, Bahador, and Dremel (1977) again found that at any given moment between 8:00 a.m. and 8:00 p.m., people are most likely to think about the present, and least likely to think about the past. They also reported that for the U.S. national sample, future-oriented thinking declines with age, while present-oriented thinking increases with age, but there is no clear evidence of increase in past-oriented thinking over the life span.

However, Cameron's results may be questioned on methodological grounds. When a subject is approached by a stranger and asked the question, "What were you just thinking about?", it is highly unlikely that the subject would disclose his or her thoughts or feelings. In other words, what is reported may not be what is entertained privately by the subject. Secondly, sampling consciousness between 8:00 a.m. and 8:00 p.m. favors thinking of the present at the expense of past-oriented thinking, because daily activities typically occur during this period of time.

If consciousness sampling was taken before 8:00 a.m. and after 8:00 p.m., frequency of past-oriented thinking would have been higher because one is apt to review the day's events or to engage in reminiscing while awake in the dark.

From our point of view, the content of consciousness is much more important than temporality. It is *what* one thinks rather than *how much* one thinks about the past, present, or future that importantly affects one's well-being. Further, we hypothesize that what one thinks about in the past, the present and the future is equally important, regardless of how much time is spent in each of these three temporal orientations. The generally held belief that one spends more and more time in reminiscing but less and less time in future-oriented thinking might be true, notwithstanding Cameron's findings, but that does not necessarily mean that future-oriented thinking is less important for the elderly. What one thinks about in the future always has some consequences on the well-being of the individual, no matter how little time is devoted to prospective thinking. Even one moment's reflection on the hopelessness of the future should be sufficient to make one feel depressed. Similarly, just one glimpse of the many exciting or rewarding opportunities that lie ahead should be sufficient to spur one onward.

The issue of temporality in the elderly, while interesting in its own right, suffers from a lack of theoretical analysis. For example, what does it mean when one spends more time thinking about the future than about the past? Is this person optimistic or is he or she simply worried too much? How is temporality functionally related to emotional and health status? What are the determinants of temporality in thinking? Until these questions are answered, data on temporality have only very limited theoretical and practical implications.

Another finding relevant to the issue of future-oriented thinking among the elderly is the lack of expressed concerns or worries for the future. For example, Gurin, Veroff, and Feld (1960) in a nationwide survey of Americans found that only 6 percent of those between 21 to 34 years old reported that they "never worry" but 17 percent of those 55 years old and over claimed that. We would expect the elderly to be more worried about health problems because health generally decreases with age, but Gurin et al. found that 50 percent of those over 60 years of age expressed no worry about health, while 38 percent of middle-aged subjects (40 to 55 years) reported no health worries.

One hypothesis for the lack of future concerns is denial or avoidance (James, 1964). He found that 22 percent of 672 subjects over 60 years of age did not answer the question whether they "worry about becoming sick." This suggests that the elderly tend to avoid thinking about those threatening unpleasant events that are likely to be experienced in the future.

Heyman and Jeffers (1965) propose an alternative interpretation. They suggest that "although the mechanisms of denial may have been present, the lack of expressed concern over long-term illness appears to be based chiefly on the security these elderly persons found in family life, religion, a stable environment, financial resources and their relative good health at the time of the study" (p. 159). While these characterizations may be true of the sample of elderly investigated, it is unlikely that most of them enjoy all the benefits listed by Heyman and Jeffers.

Recently, Kulys and Tobin (1980) conducted a study to test the denial hypothesis and the security hypothesis among the elderly. They developed a measure of anticipation, planning, and preparation (APP) for future crisis in the areas of health, living arrangements, and finances. Anticipation was defined as the expectation that a crisis would occur in any one of the three areas in the next five years. For example, for health, subjects were asked: "Do you anticipate having any serious health problems in the next five years?" Subjects were also asked a "planning" question ("Have you thought about what you would do if you were faced with a serious health problem?") and a "preparation" question ("Have you made any actual preparation of how you would deal with the problems that you would have to face in the event that you were seriously ill?"). These three kinds of questions were also posed to the respondents with respect to living arrangements and finances. Thus, a total of nine APP questions were asked. For each of these questions, a "yes" response was scored 2, "uncertain," 1, and "no," 0. Therefore the maximum possible global APP score was 18.

A high APP score, then, reflects a high degree of preoccupation with possible adverse events. A low APP score indirectly reflects an optimistic outlook. Kulys and Tobin reported that APP scores are positively correlated with anxiety, but negatively correlated with the respondent's estimate of how life would be in a year's time. In other words, those who had a high APP score also had high anxiety. Further, those who expected life to be better had a lower APP score than those who expected life to remain the same. Kulys and Tobin interpreted their data as supporting the security hypothesis.

To better understand Kulys and Tobin's findings, we should consider the phenomenon of unrealistic optimism. That is, people tend to overestimate the likelihood of positive events happening to them, and underestimate the likelihood of negative events. For example, Kirscht, Haefner, Kegeles, and Rosenstock (1966) reported that those who regarded a disease as very serious were most likely to believe that their chances of suffering from the disease were less than average. Similar optimistic biases concerning disease have also been reported by Harris and Guten (1979). Recently, Weinstein (1980) found that college students rated their own chances to be above average for a wide range of positive events (well-paying job, owning a home, living past 80, marrying someone wealthy, not ill all winter, etc.) and below average for a variety of negative events (developing cancer, having a heart attack, injured in auto accident, having to take unattractive jobs, etc.).

In light of the above findings, Kulys and Tobin's results could be interpreted in terms of optimistic biases. That is, those who had a low APP score were simply optimistic. Therefore, they were hopeful that the future would be better, and they were not anxious. Their optimism might be unrealistic, but it still had the effect of reducing their anxiety and brightening their future outlook. Those who had a high APP score might be more realistic, because it is a well-established medical fact that vulnerability to disease increases with age. To be unrealistically optimistic about the future is tantamount to denial of future reality. Therefore, Kulys and Tobin's findings may not support the security hypothesis as they have claimed.

Kulys and Tobin also collected a number of demographic data, such as marital status, religion, income, occupation. The security hypothesis would be supported if a significantly high proportion of those with a low APP score were found to be religious, married, and satisfied with their income. However, the relationship between APP and the demographic variables was not established. They also failed to support the prediction that "those in poor health would be more inclined to APP than those who enjoy excellent health" (p. 113) when health was based on respondents' self-evaluation of health status as well as a clearly defined functional self-care capacity, such as the ability to go outdoors, to use stairs, to wash, etc.

In sum, the lack of future concerns may stem from a number of factors, such as denial of a threatening future, personal optimism, and security. We tend to favor the personal optimism hypothesis, because it is consistent with the many findings on optimistic biases with respect to future adverse changes.

In view of Kulys and Tobin's findings, it seems meaningless to talk about future orientation without specifying whether the anticipated future events are positive or negative. Negative future orientation is negatively related to optimism (Kulys & Tobin, 1980), while positive future orientation is positively related to optimism (Schmidt, Lamm, & Trommsdorff, 1978; Teahan, 1958). Thus, a major dimension of future orientation is *affective evaluation.* This dimension is similar to the optimism-pessimism dimension proposed by Schmidt et al. in which pessimism means the anticipation of negatively valued occurrences, and optimism means the anticipation of positive changes in the future.

A second dimension is *temporality* defined by the amount of time spent in future-oriented thinking. This dimension may not be totally orthogonal to the evaluative dimension, because people are more apt to think of the future when it promises all sorts of positive changes. But there are also individuals who seem to spend a great deal of time worrying about negative future events, both imagined and real.

Another important dimension of future orientation is *density,* first introduced by Kastenbaum (1961). It is operationally defined as the number of future events anticipated by the subject. This measure appears to be related to the temporal dimension, because the more time one spends in future-oriented thinking, the more events one may cover. However, it is also likely that one may spend a disproportionate amount of time thinking of only one or two significant events.

A fourth dimension is *extension,* defined by Wallace (1956) as "the length of the future time span which is conceptualized" (p. 240). It may be measured by the number of years or months between the subject's age and the anticipated event. Given that the elderly and younger adults may spend the same amount of time thinking about the future, they may differ vastly in the extension dimension, in that only the younger adults project into the distant future.

A fifth dimension that may be important is *locus of initiation*—it is concerned with whether the anticipated events are primarily self- or other-initiated. If one's future-oriented thinking is entirely revolved around oneself, it may indicate a very narrow scope of interest and a very limited social network.

We believe that the above multidimensional analysis of future orientation or future time perspective will help integrate past research in the area and provide new directions for future research. It will provide a theoretical framework to conduct programmatic research on future orientation. For example, one may examine what determines various dimensions, how these dimensions are interrelated, and how each dimension affects health and adjustment outcomes.

Future orientation, optimism, and successful aging.   We have already equated personal optimism with a positive future orientation. In this section, we will critically examine the few published studies that attempt to relate personal optimism to health outcomes, life satisfaction, and adjustment in the elderly.

In one of the earlier studies, Miller and Lieberman (1965) reported that a lack of future-orientation (i.e., the inability to characterize the immediate and distant future) and a negative evaluation of past life differentiated the elderly who failed to adapt to extensive changes in the sociophysical environment from those who adapted successfully. Failure to adapt was indicated by physical illness, deterioration in psychological functioning, and mortality.

Lehr (1967), as part of a larger longitudinal study, investigated the relationship between attitude towards the future and objectively rated health status. Attitudes toward the future were assessed by means of interview. The responses obtained during the interview were later judged by four or five raters on a 9-point global future-orientation rating scale. Point 1 means "completely negative attitudes toward the future, complete absence of positive expectations, and hopelessness," while point 9 means "completely positive attitudes toward the future, no fears, and expectation that the future time will bring only pleasant experiences." One hundred middle-class community elderly were divided into four groups: 60- to 65-year-old males and females, and 70- to 75-year-old males and females. Highly significant correlations between an optimistic future attitude and good health as assessed by medical examination were obtained in both groups of males and the younger female group. However, in the older female group, a negative attitude toward the future was also found in subjects rated to be in good health by the physician. The two age groups did not differ in future orientation, but men for both age groups had a more positive attitude than did their female counterparts.

Lehr (1967) also rated the subjects on six personality rating scales: activity, mood, general responsiveness, ego control, and feelings of security. These ratings were based on observations during interview sessions and informal gatherings. An optimistic attitude was related to a number of these personality ratings, but the pattern varied according to age and sex. For example, in the younger males, an optimistic attitude was significantly related to mood, general responsiveness, general adjustment, and ego control; in older males, optimism was significantly related to activity, mood, general responsiveness, and general adjustment. In younger females, optimism was significantly related to activity, mood, and general responsiveness; in older females, optimism was significantly related only to activity and feelings of security.

Ludwig and Eichhorn (1967) studied the relationship between the value orientations of farmers of different ages and self-rated health status. Optimism, defined as "faith in the future, belief in a benevolent God and control over one's own well-being" (p. 59), was one of four value orientations investigated by the authors. Farmers were divided into two age groups: 30 to 49 years and 50 to 69 years of age. Optimism was indirectly measured by respondents' answer to two questions. The first question was, "If you've got a bad disease, it's just as well you don't learn about it." Agreement with this statement implies lack of optimism about future events. Ludwig and Eichhorn reported that 23 percent of the older farmers agreed, while only 11 percent of the younger farmers did. With respect to health, 23 percent of the farmers from both age groups who reported some symptoms agreed, while 14 percent of those who reported no symptoms agreed. The second question was whether the respondents agreed with the statement, "Illness and trouble is one way God shows His displeasure." Agreement with this statement, according to the authors' reasoning, would imply lack of personal optimism because it meant a rejection of belief in a benevolent God. Results based on this question are highly similar to those based on the first question. The writers concluded that "the experiences associated with aging such as declining health led people to reject an optimistic approach to life" (p. 62). However, one may question the validity of the optimism measure used by Ludwig and Eichhorn. For example, one could dispute the assumption that benevolence and discipline are mutually exclusive. A loving father does not cease to be benevolent when he shows displeasure and disciplines his child for misbehavior. Similarly, God does not cease to be benevolent when He corrects or disciplines His children.

Several other investigators have also demonstrated that various measures of future orientation are positively related to life satisfaction and mental health (Dickie, Ludwig, & Blauw, 1979; Lewin, 1948; Sameth, 1980; Schonfield, 1973; Spence, 1968; Steuer, 1977). In one of the earliest studies, Lewin (1948) found that a sense of psychological future was positively related to morale in industrial workers. Later, Spence (1968) reported making plans for the future to be positively related to life satisfaction or morale.

Making plans for the future or future commitment seems to be most frequently used as a measure of personal optimism or positive future orientation. Schonfield (1973) investigated the relationship between future commitments and successful aging in a sample of 100 non-institutionalized elderly females. A future activity index was developed based on a 7-day future diary and a listing of activities on a "usual day." Successful aging was measured by 11 scales: happiness, financial situation, health, activities, family relationships, pleasure from companions, housing, clubs and organizations, transportation, usefulness, and a composite successful aging score. A short personality inventory was also administered. Significant associations were found between the future activity index and the composite successful aging score, ease of transportation, challenging activities, happiness, and health. Interestingly, none of the personality attributes, such as neuroticism, introversion, rigidity, aggression, and depression were significantly related to future commitments.

Dickie, Ludwig, and Blauw (1979) examined the relationship between future orientation, life satisfaction, and several measures of health in both institutionalized and non-institutionalized older adults. In both groups, the elderly who made plans for the future reported greater life satisfaction than did those without future plans.

Steuer (1977) measured both subjective time extension and future commitments. Time extension was based on subjective life expectancy (SLE) and number of good years left to live (NGL). Future commitment was measured by the number of plans made for the near and distant future. In a multiple regression analysis, Steuer found that SLE, NGL, and future commitment were all significantly correlated with life satisfaction; however, the two time extension measures accounted for most of the explained variance. More recently, Sameth (1980) also found that perceived length of future (extension) was positively associated with overall health and cognitive activity and inversely related with feelings of loneliness. Sameth also reported that perceived importance of future (quality) was positively correlated with overall happiness and negatively correlated with psychological and psychosomatic complaints and feelings of loneliness.

In sum, there is sufficient evidence demonstrating the beneficial effect of a positive future outlook on health and life satisfaction. However, most of the measures used to tap personal optimism are of the one-item variety (e.g., Cantril

& Roll, 1971) and none of the measures had proven validity or reliability. There-fore, we have attempted to construct a personal optimism scale which is based on spontaneously generated open-ended responses, and which includes both future commitments and future expectations.

ASSESSMENT OF PERSONAL OPTIMISM
IN THE ELDERLY

The Future Orientation Survey (FOS)

Our measure of personal optimism, as shown in Appendix 1, has a number of new features. It measures both the number of events anticipated, and the con-fidence that each of these events will take place. Thus, the scale provides three measures: number of future events, average confidence ratings, and total confidence ratings.

Many of the anticipated events are plans to be carried out by the respondents. These events are essentially future commitments. However, different from tradi-tional measures of future commitments, our scale also includes positive future events initiated and carried out by others, such as the birth of a grandchild, or future career success of children. These are events uncontrollable by the respon-dents. In short, the anticipated events encompass both self-initiated and other-initiated future events.

It is likely that a person may anticipate many things but is not confident at all that any of these things will materialize. The degree of confidence that each anticipated event will take place is measured by a 5-point scale, anchored at Point 1 (Not confident at all) and Point 5 (Extremely confident). The average degree of confidence over all the anticipated events can be calculated.

The most comprehensive index of personal optimism is perhaps provided by the cross-product of the number of anticipated events, and the average degree of confidence. This total confidence measure thus takes into account both the number of anticipated events and expressed confidence.

The FOS was administered to 40 community and 40 institutionalized elderly. The community group ranged from 70 to 93 years of age, with a mean age of 77.4 years. The institutionalized group ranged from 70 to 90 years of age, with a mean age of 78.2 years. The two groups did not differ significantly in terms of age. There were 28 females in the community group and 27 females in the institu-tionalized group.

The respondents were encouraged to verbalize whatever things or events they looked forward to, and the experimenter simply jotted down the responses ver-batim. The respondents were then asked to complete the confidence rating scale for each response.

The responses were content-analyzed and classified into eight categories of life concerns: family life, friendship, leisure/recreation, community/social service, health, religion, personal development, and housing/living conditions. Each re-sponse was classified as either short-term or long-term. An event was considered as short-term if it was expected to take place within a year. An event was classified as long-term, either because the event was of an enduring and protracted nature, or because its anticipated occurrence was in some distant future. In addition to the *extension* dimension, each response was also coded with respect to the *locus of initiation*. An event was considered as self-initiated if the respondent takes an active part in initiating, planning, and carrying out the event, such as visiting a friend, finishing reading a book. An event was treated as other-initiated if it is initiated, planned, and carried out by others, and over which the respondent has little or no control. Some examples of the different classifications are shown in Table 7–2.

The percentages of elderly that expressed optimism in different areas of life concerns are shown in Table 7–3. It is quite obvious that for both the community and institutionalized samples, most of the future-oriented thinking is revolved around one's own family. Since all of the elderly subjects no longer held a job at the time of the interview, how to spend their time in leisure activities became a major preoccupation. Friendship, health, voluntary service, and religious activities are also quite prominent in their minds as they think of the future. Very few people looked forward to a change in housing/living conditions. On the surface, it might appear that they were contented with where they lived.

An alternative explanation is that they were realistic about their own financial resources and the limited options they had. Therefore, most of them simply stopped hoping for any improvement in terms of accommodation.

What is most disquieting is the very low response rate in the category of personal development. Given that they have ample time on their hands, they could really develop their potentials through education and learning. They could enroll in various courses, acquire new skills, and even start a new career. They might not be aware of the learning opportunities available to senior citizens. They might also be deceived by the myth that "you cannot teach old dogs new tricks." Whatever the cause, this should be an area of concern to social gerontologists and people interested in the well-being of the elderly. The process of aging is not incompatible with growth. One can grow old and remain growing. The potentials for growth are always there, regardless of one's age, as long as there is the desire to grow.

It is worth noting that none of the elderly we interviewed anticipated financial gains. Given the fact that most of them lived on fixed incomes, it is not surprising that they did not hold out any hope for financial improvement.

We compared the number of optimistic responses for each area of life concern between the community and institutionalized elderly. The only significant difference was in the area of leisure/recreation. Community subjects made more anticipatory responses than their institutionalized counterparts (1.28 vs. 0.65), $t = 2.88$, $p < .01$. The difference seems to suggest that the community elderly have more desirable and enjoyable leisure activities to look forward to, even though institutions might provide many organized leisure activities for their residents.

When we compared the two samples in terms of the two theoretical dimensions (extension and locus of initiation), several significant differences emerged as shown in Table 7–4.

The upper half of the table is based on number of events (density). Overall, community elderly had more things to look forward to than institution subjects did. More specifically, the two groups differed in long-term rather than in short-term, and in self-initiated rather than in other-initiated events. These findings confirm that community elderly are more likely to initiate and plan long-term events than institutionalized residents are.

TABLE 7-2 Some Examples of Personal Optimism Responses in the Elderly (Age 70 and Older)

LIFE CONCERN	SELF-INITIATED		OTHER-INITIATED	
	SHORT-TERM	LONG-TERM	SHORT-TERM	LONG-TERM
Family Life	Visit my family	In future I can continue to look after my wife and home	Visit from my family	To see my youngest son get married and settled down
Leisure/Recreation	Reading good books	Visit Scotland next year. To tape my life story	Special events at the senior citizen's home	To have more recreational facilities for the seniors
Friendship	Visit my friends	Keeping good neighbors	Hearing from my friends. Visit from my friends	My friend will eventually move to the same senior's home
Community/Social Services	Help bazaar of the senior citizen's home	Continued involvement in social service	To be served by "Meals on Wheels"	That the government will not fail the elderly
Religion	To attend a church retreat. To take part in a Bible class	To get back to an active church life	Having a minister visit	God's kingdom come; Salvation of friends or relatives
Health	My eye healing completely	To maintain my health so that I can stay by myself	Health of my two friends improving	Cancer will be beaten
Housing/Living Conditions	Redecorate the room	To get out of the institution and live in my own apartment	Waiting for son to repair the verandah	My son to complete his new home
Personal Development	To attend a talk on aging	To learn a new language	My daughter has a good summer job	See my grandchildren growing up to be useful citizens

TABLE 7–3   Percentage of Elderly That Expressed Optimism in Different Areas
of Life Concerns

LIFE CONCERNS	COMMUNITY	INSTITUTION	TOTAL
	(N=40)	(N=40)	(N=80)
Family Life	85.0	87.5	86.3
Leisure/Recreation	75.0	50.0	62.5
Friendship	15.0	20.0	17.5
Health	17.5	12.5	15.0
Community/Social Service	15.0	12.5	13.7
Religion	15.0	7.5	11.3
Personal Development	7.5	10.0	8.7
Housing/Living Conditions	2.5	10.0	6.3

Average confidence ratings did not differentiate between the community and institution samples (3.74 vs. 3.76). For most of the subjects, the confidence rating was higher than Point 3 on the 5 point scale, indicating that they were fairly confident that the anticipated event would come to pass. The confidence rating suggests that the elderly are too realistic to entertain wild fantasies and that they would verbalize their expectancies only when they are fairly sure that the anticipated events are likely to materialize.

The total confidence ratings are shown in the lower half of Table 7–4. The results are very similar to those based on number of events. Since total confidence takes into account both number of events and expressed confidence, it is a more complete index of personal optimism than number of events. Therefore, we employ the total confidence measure in validating the FOS.

Subjects were also asked to complete the following instruments for purposes of concurrent validation: Beck's Depression Scale (Beck, 1967; Gallagher, Nies, & Thompson, 1982), Reker and Peacock's Life Attitude Profile (Reker & Peacock,

TABLE 7–4   Mean Differences between Community and Institution Respondents
in the Number of Events Anticipated and Total Confidence Ratings

	COMMUNITY	INSTITUTION	*T*-VALUE
	(N=40)	(N=40)	
Number of Events (Density)	3.80	2.90	2.44*
Short-term	2.93	2.48	1.31
Long-term	0.87	0.42	2.22*
Self-initiated	2.52	1.73	2.42*
Other-initiated	1.27	1.18	0.38
Total Confidence Ratings	14.20	10.90	2.06*
Short-term	10.82	9.30	0.99
Long-term	3.38	1.60	2.26*
Self-initiated	9.10	6.70	1.81
Other-initiated	5.10	4.20	0.84

*$p < .05$

1981), Reker and Wong's preliminary Perceived Well-Being Scale and Reker and Wong's Present Commitment Survey. Thirty-one community subjects and 29 institution subjects completed these additional questionnaires. Correlation coefficients between personal optimism ratings and these additional measures are shown in Table 7-5.

It is quite clear that total confidence ratings are positively related to Perceived Well-Being, Present Commitment, several subscales of the Life Attitude Profile (Life Purpose, Will to Meaning, Future Meaning to Fulfill) and negatively related to depression. However, when the total confidence ratings were broken down according to extension (short-term versus long-term) and locus of initiation (self versus other), only long-term and self-initiated events were primarily responsible for these significant correlations. These findings seem to suggest that one is more likely to experience the salutatory effects of personal optimism, when one initiates, plans, and carries out activities that extend into some distant future. Self-initiation has more beneficial effects than other-initiated probably because self-initiation enables one to maintain a sense of self-efficacy.

Long-term events, by definition, extend further into the future than short-term events. Greater optimism is required to look beyond the immediate future. Therefore, long-term events are expected to have a stronger relationship with well-being and positive life attitudes than short-term events.

The absence of significant correlations between perceived psychological well-

TABLE 7-5 The Relationship of Personal Optimism to Well-Being, Depression, Life Attitude, and Present Commitment

	PERSONAL OPTIMISM				
	TOTAL CONFIDENCE	SHORT-TERM	LONG-TERM	SELF-INITIATED	OTHER-INITIATED
Perceived Well-Being (Preliminary)					
Psychological	.15	.09	.13	.02	.19
Physical	.21*	.07	.30**	.21*	.09
Composite	.31**	.17	.32**	.30**	.14
Beck Depression	−.32**	−.29**	−.11	−.30**	−.15
Life Attitude Profile (LAP)					
Life purpose	.35***	.25*	.24*	.34**	.15
Existential vacuum	−.05	.05	−.19	−.10	.04
Life control	.10	.27*	−.30**	.15	−.02
Death acceptance	−.13	−.13	.00	−.16	−.03
Will to meaning	.25*	.14	.26*	.20	.18
Goal seeking	.02	.09	−.02	.16	−.08
Future meaning to fullfill	.36***	.20	.36***	.36***	.15
Present Commitment	.29**	.12	.36***	.25*	.15

* $p < .05$
** $p < .01$
*** $p < .001$

being and personal optimism comes as a surprise. One problem with the preliminary Perceived Well-Being Scale is that it is based on a True-False forced choice format and there are only six questions in the psychological well-being subscale. As a result, the range of the data was very limited. This problem has been corrected in the revised Perceived Well-Being Scale (Reker & Wong, 1984), which includes some new test items and employs Likert-type scales.

The Present Commitment Survey measures the number of activities to which the respondent currently devotes time and effort. It is revealing that subjects who gave more long-term optimistic responses also reported more present commitments. However, any causal relationships between long-term optimism and the degree of present commitment remains to be demonstrated.

TABLE 7-6   Means, Standard Deviations[a] and *T* Values for Community and Institutionalized Elderly on Several Dependent Variables

VARIABLES	COMMUNITY	INSTITUTION	*T* VALUES	*P*
	(N=31)	(N=29)		
Perceived Well-Being (Preliminary)				
Psychological	5.7	5.4	1.11	.270
	(.9)	(1.1)		
Physical	4.6	3.6	2.52	.01
	(1.4)	(1.7)		
Composite PWB	10.5	9.0	3.46	.001
	(1.5)	(1.9)		
Beck Depression	2.9	5.3	−3.01	.005
(short form)	(2.2)	(3.7)		
Present Commitment	21.4	17.4	2.81	.007
	(5.7)	(5.2)		
Life Purpose (LAP)	47.8	41.1	3.15	.003
	(7.0)	(9.3)		
Existential Vacuum (LAP)	20.6	24.1	−2.08	.042
	(5.5)	(7.3)		

ADDITIONAL VARIABLES	COMMUNITY	INSTITUTION	*T* VALUES	*P*
	(N=20)	(N=24)		
Perceived Well-Being (Revised)				
Psychological	36.3	31.2	3.27	.003
	(1.7)	(7.3)		
Physical	39.6	34.5	2.09	.05
	(7.4)	(8.6)		
Composite PWB	75.9	64.5	3.49	.001
	(8.4)	(13.1)		
Happiness (MUNSH)	41.1	33.0	2.81	.01
	(6.7)	(12.0)		

[a] Standard deviations are in parentheses.

TABLE 7-7   The Predictive Relationship of Personal Optimism to Happiness
and Perceived Well-Being over a Two-Month Period

	PERSONAL OPTIMISM				
	TOTAL CONFIDENCE	SHORT-TERM	LONG-TERM	SELF-INITIATED	OTHER-INITIATED
Perceived Well-Being					
Psychological	.53***	.52***	.12	.44***	.24
Physical	.18	.06	.31*	.31*	− .07
Composite	.40**	.31*	.28*	.44***	.07
Happiness					
(MUNSH)	.41**	.41**	.10	.33*	.20

N = 44
*p < .05
** p < .01
*** p < .001

The differences between the community and institution samples in various questionnaire measures are shown in the upper half of Table 7-6. It is quite impressive that the community elderly who had a more optimistic outlook also scored significantly higher in perceived well-being, present commitment, life purpose, but lower in depression and existential vacuum.

To further investigate the predictive validity of the FOS, we were able to administer two additional instruments to 20 community and 24 institution subjects from the same samples. These were the subjects who were available at the time of testing two months later, and who were willing to participate. The first additional instrument was the revised Reker and Wong's (1984) Perceived Well-Being Scale. The second additional instrument was the MUNSH Happiness Scale (Kozma & Stones, 1980). The mean differences between community and institution subjects for these two measures are shown in the lower half of Table 7-6. The most interesting aspect of our finding is that the total confidence scores obtained two months earlier are able to predict perceived well-being and happiness. These interrelationships are shown in Table 7-7. It is worth noting that personal optimism is significantly correlated with the psychological well-being subscale of the revised Perceived Well-Being Scale.

SUMMARY

The present findings replicate and extend earlier findings on the positive relationship between personal optimism and well-being. The main contribution of the FOS is that it measures three important dimensions of positive future orientation: density (number of anticipated events), extension (short-term versus long-term), and locus of initiation (self-initiated versus other-initiated). All three dimensions are importantly related to well-being. More systematic research is needed to investigate how these three dimensions are related to each other, and how they are related to different aspects of psychological and physical well-being.

Another contribution of the FOS is that it measures both the number of anticipated events and the average subjective confidence ratings. For the elderly, number of anticipated events was more important than the average confidence rating. The reverse might be true for other age groups. These two separate measures not only provide a more detailed analysis of the nature of personal optimism, but also permit a more global index in the form of total confidence ratings.

We have argued that the salutogenic approach to health care is preferable to the traditional disease model. We have also marshalled a wide range of evidence that implicates the salutary effects of personal optimism and the deleterious effects of its absence. Finally, we have developed a Future Orientation Scale that proves to be a good predictor of both physical and psychological well-being in the elderly.

According to the mosaic model (Reker, Chapter 3, this volume), successful aging is always the product of complex interactions of psychological, physiological and environmental variables. Here, we have identified personal optimism as one of the major psychological variables. Given its importance to health, and the paucity of data, systematic research on personal optimism is clearly needed.

The most fitting way to conclude this chapter is to look optimistically into the future. We foresee the development of a valid and reliable instrument to measure personal optimism. The Future Orientation Survey is a good starting point, but much work needs to be done.

Another promising direction of research is to explore the effects of personal optimism on physiological and biochemical systems. For example, it is tempting to speculate that personal optimism, as a cognitive-affective-and-a-goal-directed response, may release endorphine-like substances.

The most urgent task ahead, according to our opinion, is to identify the determinants of personal optimism. We have already alluded to a number of these determinants, such as self-efficacy, perceived instrumental options, dependence on God, etc. We anticipate that this line of research will yield a set of facts and procedures that may be used to instill hope that springs eternal.

REFERENCES

ADER, R., & COHEN, N. (1975). Behaviorally conditioned immunosuppression. *Psychosomatic Medicine, 37,* 333–340.

AGER, C. L., WHITE, L. W., MAYBERRY, W. L., CRIST, P. A., & CONRAD, M. E. (1981–82). Creative aging. *International Journal of Aging and Human Development, 14,* 67–76.

ALBEE, G. W. (1980). A competency model must replace the defect model. In L. A. Bond & J. C. Rosen (Eds.), *Competence and coping during adulthood* (pp. 75–104). Hanover: University Press of New England.

ANTONOVSKY, A. (1979). *Health, stress, and coping.* San Francisco: Jossey-Bass.

ARDELL, D. D. (1977). *High level wellness: An alternative to doctors, drugs, and disease.* Emmaus, PA: Rodale Press.

BAHNSON, C. B., & BAHNSON, M. B. (1966). Role of the ego defenses: Denial and repression of the etiology of malignant neoplasm. *Annals of the New York Academy of Sciences, 125,* 827–845.

BALTES, P. B., & NESSELROADE, J. R. (1979). History and rationale of longitudinal research. In J. R. Nesselroade & P. B. Baltes (Eds.), *Longitudi-*

nal research in the study of behavior and research (pp. 1-29). New York: Academic Press.

BARTROP, R. W., LUCKHURST, E., LAZARUS, L., KILOH, L. G., & PENNY, R. (1977). Repressed lymphocyte function after bereavement. *The Lancet, 1*, 834-836.

BECK, A. T. (1967). *Depression: Clinical, experimental, and theoretical aspects.* New York: Harper & Row.

BECK, A. T., WEISSMAN, A., LESTER, D., & TREXLER, L. (1974). The measurement of pessimism: The hopelessness scale. *Journal of Consulting and Clinical Psychology, 42*, 861-865.

BEECHER, H. K. (1955). The powerful placebo. *Journal of the American Medical Association, 159*, 1602-1606.

BIRREN, J. E. (Ed.). (1964). *The psychology of aging.* Englewood Cliffs, NJ: Prentice-Hall.

BJERG, K. (1967). The suicidal life space. In E. S. Schneidman (Ed.), *Essays in self-destruction* (pp. 475-494). New York: Science House.

BOND, L. A., & ROSEN, J. C. (1980). *Competence and coping during adulthood.* Hanover: The University Press of New England.

BROWN, G. W. (1974). Meaning, measurement and stress of life events. In B. S. Dohrenwend & B. P. Dohrenwend (Eds.), *Stressful life events: Their nature and effects* (pp. 217-243). New York: John Wiley.

BUHLER, C. (1935). The curve of life as studied in biographies. *Journal of Applied Psychology, 19*, 405-409.

BUNNEY, W. E., & FAWCETT, J. A. (1967, October). 17-Hydroxycorticosteroid excretion prior to severe suicidal behavior. In N. L. Farberow (Ed.), *Proceedings of the Fourth International Conference for Suicide Prevention* (pp. 128-139). Los Angeles, CA.

BUTLER, R. N. (1974). Successful aging. *Mental Hygiene, 58*, 6-12.

CAMERON, P. (1972). The generation gap: Time orientation. *The Gerontologist, 12*, 117-119.

CAMERON, P., DESAI, K. G., BAHADOR, D., & DREMEL, G. (1977). Temporality across the life span. *International Journal of Aging and Human Development, 8*, 229-258.

CANNON, W. B. (1957). Voodoo death. *Psychosomatic Medicine, 19*, 182-190.

CANTRIL, A. H., & ROLL, C. W. (1971). *Hopes and fears of the American people.* New York: Universe Books.

CECCHINI, SR. R. M. (1976). Women and suicide. In J. Lebra, J. Paulson, & E. Powers (Eds.), *Women in changing Japan* (pp. 263-296). Stanford, CA: Stanford University Press.

COUSINS, N. (1979). *Anatomy of an illness.* New York: Bantam Books.

CUNNINGHAM, A. J. (1981). Mind, body, and immune response. In R. Ader (Ed.), *Psychoneuroimmunology* (pp. 609-617). New York: Academic Press.

CUNNINGHAM, A. J. (1982). Should we investigate psychotherapy for physical disease, especially cancer. In S. Levy (Ed.), *Biological mediators of behavior and disease* (pp. 83-100). New York: Elsevier.

DICKIE, J. R., LUDWIG, T. E., & BLAUW, D. (1979). Life satisfaction among institutionalized and non-institutionalized older adults. *Psychological Reports, 44*, 807-810.

DURKHEIM, E. (1951). *Suicide.* New York: Free Press.

ENGEL, G. L. (1968). A life setting conducive to illness: The giving-up, given-up complex. *Annals of Internal Medicine, 69*, 293-300.

ENGEL, G. L. (1971). Sudden and rapid death during psychological stress: Folklore or folk wisdom? *Annals of Internal Medicine, 74*, 771-782.

ERIKSON, E. (1963). *Childhood and society* (2nd ed.). New York: W. W. Norton & Co., Inc.

ERIKSON, E. (1980). *Identity and the life cycle.* New York: W. W. Norton & Co., Inc.

FARBER, M. L. (1967, October). Suicide and hope: A theoretical analysis. In N. L. Farberow (Ed.), *Proceedings of the Fourth International Conference on Suicide Prevention* (pp. 297–306). Los Angeles, CA.

FARNHAM-DIGGORY, S. (1964). Self-evaluation and subjective life expectancy among suicidal and non-suicidal psychotic males. *Journal of Abnormal and Social Psychology, 69,* 628–634.

FEINSTEIN, A. D. (1983). Psychological intervention in the treatment of cancer. *Clinical Psychology Review, 3,* 1–14.

FLAVELL, J. H. (1970). Cognitive changes in adulthood. In L. R. Goulet & P. B. Baltes (Eds.), *Life-span developmental psychology: Research and theory* (pp. 247–253). New York: Academic Press.

FOX, B. H. (1978). Premorbid psychological factors as related to cancer incidence. *Journal of Behavioral Medicine, 1,* 45–133.

FRIEDMAN, S. B., GLASGOW, L. A., & ADER, R. (1969). Psychosocial factors modifying host resistance to experimental infections. *Annals of the New York Academy of Sciences, 164,* 381–393.

GALLAGHER, D., NIES, G., & THOMPSON, L. W. (1982). Reliability of the Beck Depression Inventory with older adults. *Journal of Consulting and Clinical Psychology, 50,* 152–153.

GANZLER, S. (1967). Some interpersonal and social dimensions of suicidal behavior. *Dissertation Abstracts, 28B,* 1192–1193.

GARBER, J., & SELIGMAN, M.E.P. (Eds.). (1980). *Human helplessness: Theory and applications.* New York: Academic Press.

GITELSON, M. (1948). The emotional problems of elderly people. *Geriatrics, 3,* 135–150.

GOLDFARB, O., DRIESEN, J., & COLE, D. (1967). Psychophysiologic aspects of malignancy. *American Journal of Psychiatry, 123,* 1545–1551.

GOODFRIEND, M., & WOLPERT, E. A. (1976). Death from fright: Report of a case and literature review. *Psychosomatic Medicine, 38,* 348–356.

GORCZYNSKI, R. M., MacRAE, S., & KENNEDY, M. (1982). Conditional immune response associated with allogenic skin grafts in mice. *Journal of Immunology, 129,* 704–709.

GREENE, W. A., GOLDSTEIN, S., & MOSS, A. J. (1972). Psychosocial aspects of sudden death: A preliminary report. *Archives of Internal Medicine, 129,* 725–731.

GREER, S., & MORRIS, T. (1975). Psychological attributes of women who develop breast cancer: A controlled study. *Journal of Psychosomatic Research, 19,* 147–153.

GREER, S., MORRIS, T., & PETTINGALE, K. W. (1979). Psychological response to breast cancer: Effect on outcome. *The Lancet, II,* 785–787.

GURIN, G., VEROFF, J., & FELD, S. (1960). *Americans view their mental health: A national interview study.* New York: Basic Books.

HARRIS, D. M., & GUTEN, S. (1979). Health protective behavior: An exploratory study. *Journal of Health and Social Behavior, 20,* 17–29.

HAVIGHURST, R., NEUGARTEN, B., & TOBIN, S. (1968). Disengagement and patterns of aging. In B. Neugarten (Ed.), *Middle age and aging: A reader in social psychology* (pp. 161–172). Chicago: University of Chicago Press.

HENDERSON, J. T. (1977). Hope, death and suicide. In B. K. Danto & A. H. Kutcha (Eds.), *Suicide and bereavement* (pp. 61–66). New York: Arno Press.

HENDIN, H. (1963). The psychodynamics of suicide. *Journal of Nervous and Mental Diseases, 136,* 236–244.

HENRY, J. P. (1981). *The relation of social to biological processes in disease.* Unpublished manuscript, University of Southern California, School of Medicine, Los Angeles.

HEYMAN, D., & JEFFERS, F. (1965). Observations on the extent of concern and planning by the aged for possible chronic illness. *Journal of the American Geriatric Society, 13,* 152–159.

HOLDEN, C. (1978). Cancer and the mind: How are they connected? *Science, 200,* 1363–1369.

HOLMES, T. H., & MASUDA, M. (1974). Life change and illness susceptibility. In B. S. Dohrenwend & B. P. Dohrenwend (Eds.), *Stressful life events: Their nature and effects* (pp. 45–72). New York: John Wiley.

HORNE, R. L., & PICARD, R. S. (1979). Psychosocial risk factors for lung cancer. *Psychosomatic Medicine, 41,* 503–514.

HUTSCHNECKER, A. A. (1981). *Hope: The dynamics of self-fulfillment.* New York: Putnam's.

JAMES, R. L. (1964). *Edmonton senior resident's survey report.* Edmonton Welfare Council, Edmonton, Alta.

KASTENBAUM, R. (1961). The dimensions of future time perspective: An experimental analysis. *Journal of General Psychology, 65,* 203–218.

KATZ, J. L., WEINER, H., GALLAGHER, T. F., & HELLMAN, L. (1970). Stress, distress, and ego defenses: Psychoendocrine response to impending breast tumor biopsy. *Archives of General Psychiatry, 23,* 131–142.

KIRSCHT, J. P., HAEFNER, D. P., KEGELES, S. S., & ROSENSTOCK, I. M. (1966). A national study of health beliefs. *Journal of Health and Human Behavior, 7,* 248–254.

KISSEN, D. M. (1963). Personality characteristics in males conducive to lung cancer. *British Journal of Medical Psychology, 36,* 27–36.

KISSEN, D. M. (1969). The present status of psychosomatic cancer research. *Geriatrics, 24,* 129–137.

KISSEN, D. M., BROWN, R.I.F., & KISSEN, M. (1969). A further report on personality and psychosocial factors in lung cancer. *Annals of the New York Academy of Sciences, 164,* 535–544.

KOBASA, S. C. (1979). Stressful life events, personality and health: An inquiry into hardiness. *Journal of Personality and Social Psychology, 37,* 1–11.

KOWAL, S. J. (1955). Emotions as a cause of cancer: Eighteenth and nineteenth century contributions. *The Psychoanalytic Review, 42,* 217–227.

KOZMA, A., & STONES, M. J. (1980). The measurement of happiness: Development of the Memorial University of Newfoundland Scale of Happiness (MUNSH). *Journal of Gerontology, 35,* 906–912.

KULYS, R., & TOBIN, S. S. (1980). Interpreting the lack of future concerns among the elderly. *International Journal of Aging and Human Development, 11,* 111–125.

LaBARBA, R. C. (1970). Experiential and environmental factors in cancer: A review of research with animals. *Psychosomatic Medicine, 32,* 259–276.

LEHR, U. (1967). Attitudes toward the future in old age. *Human Development, 10,* 230–238.

LeSHAN, L. L. (1966). An emotional life-history pattern associated with neoplastic disease. *Annals of the New York Academy of Sciences, 125,* 780–793.

LeSHAN, L. L., & WORTHINGTON, R. E. (1956). Personality as a factor in the pathogenesis of cancer: A review of the literature. *British Journal of Medical Psychology, 29,* 49–56.

LEWIN, K. (1948). Time perspective and morale. In K. Lewin (Ed.), *Resolving social conflicts* (pp. 103–124). New York: Harper & Row.

LEWIS, C. N. (1971). Reminiscing and self-concept in old age. *Journal of Gerontology, 26,* 240–243.

LIFTON, R. J. (1979). *The broken connection: On death and the continuity of life* (Chap. 17). New York: Simon & Schuster.

LINN, M. W., HUNTER, K., & HARRIS, R. (1980). Symptoms of depression and recent life events in the community elderly. *Journal of Clinical Psychology, 36,* 675–682.

LOWENTHAL, M. F., THURNHER, M., CHIRIBOGA, D., & ASSOCIATES. (1975). *Four stages of life: A comparative study of women and men facing transitions.* San Francisco: Jossey-Bass.

LUDWIG, E., & EICHHORN, R. L. (1967). Age and disillusionment: A study of value changes associated with aging. *Journal of Gerontology, 22,* 59–65.

MAIER, H. W. (1969). *Three theories of child development.* New York: Harper & Row.

MAKINODAN, T. (1977). Immunity and aging. In C. E. Finch & L. Hayflick (Eds.), *Handbook of the biology of aging* (pp. 379–408). New York: Van Nostrand Reinhold.

MATARAZZO, J. D. (1980). Behavioral health and behavioral medicine: Frontiers for a new health psychology. *American Psychologist, 35,* 807–817.

McCRAE, R. R. (1981). *Age differences in the use of coping mechanisms.* Paper presented at the annual meeting of the Gerontological Society of America, Toronto, Ont.

METTLER, C. C., & METTLER, F. A. (1947). *History of medicine.* Philadelphia: Blakiston Company.

MILLER, D., & LIEBERMAN, M. A. (1965). The relationship of affect state and adaptive capacity to reaction to stress. *Journal of Gerontology, 20,* 492–497.

MILLER, M. (1978). Geriatric suicide: The Arizona study. *The Gerontologist, 18,* 488–495.

MILLER, M. (1979). *Suicide after sixty: The final alternative.* New York: Springer-Verlag.

MINKOFF, K., BERGMAN, E., BECK, A. T., & BECK, R. (1973). Hopelessness, depression, and attempted suicide. *American Journal of Psychiatry, 130,* 455–459.

MORRIS, T., GREER, S., PETTINGALE, K. W., & WATSON, M. (1981). Patterns of expression of anger and their psychological correlates in women with breast cancer. *Journal of Psychosomatic Research, 25,* 111–117.

MOWRER, O. H. (1960). *Learning theory and behavior.* New York: John Wiley.

NEUGARTEN, B. (1964). *Personality in middle and late life.* New York: Atherton.

NEUGARTEN, B. L. (1979). Time, age, and the life cycle. *American Journal of Psychiatry, 136,* 887–893.

OLTMAN, A. M., MICHALS, T. J., & STEER, R. A. (1980). Structure of depression in older men and women. *Journal of Clinical Psychology, 36,* 672–674.

PALMORE, E., RANDOLPH, E., & OVERHOLSER, R. V. (1979, February 1). To enjoy old age, start now! *Family Circle,* pp. 71–73.

PELLETIER, K. R. (1977). *Mind as healer, mind as slayer.* New York: Dell Pub. Co., Inc.

PFEIFFER, E. (1977). Psychopathology and social pathology. In J. E. Birren & K. W. Schaie (Eds.), *Handbook of the psychology of aging* (pp. 650–671). New York: Van Nostrand Reinhold.

POKORNY, A. D., KAPLAN, H. B., & TSAI, S. Y. (1975). Hopelessness and attempted suicide: A reconsideration. *American Journal of Psychiatry, 132,* 954–956.

REKER, G. T., & PEACOCK, E. J. (1981). The Life Attitude Profile (LAP): A multidimensional instrument for assessing attitudes toward life. *Canadian Journal of Behavioural Science, 13,* 264–273.

REKER, G. T., & WONG, P.T.P. (1984). Psychological and physical well-being in the elderly: The Perceived Well-Being Scale (PWB). *Canadian Journal on Aging, 3,* 23–32.

RESNIK, H.L.P., & CANTOR, J. M. (1970). Suicide and aging. *Journal of American Geriatrics Society, 18,* 152–158.

RICHTER, C. P. (1957). On the phenomenon of sudden death in animals and man. *Psychosomatic Medicine, 19,* 191–198.

ROGERS, M. P., DUBEY, D., & REICH, P. (1979). The influence of the psyche and the brain on immunity and disease susceptibility: A critical review. *Psychosomatic Medicine, 41,* 147–164.

RYAN, R. S., & TRAVIS, J. W. (1981). *The wellness workbook.* Berkeley, CA: Ten Speed Press.

SAMETH, L. F. (1980). Temporal orientation and well-being in the elderly. *Dissertation Abstracts International, 40,* 5467–B.

SCHMALE, A. H. (1958). Relationship of separation and depression to disease. I. A report on a hospitalized medical population. *Psychosomatic Medicine, 20,* 259–271.

SCHMALE, A. H., & IKER, H. P. (1964). The affect of hopelessness in the development of cancer. I. The prediction of uterine cervical cancer in women with atypical cytology. *Psychosomatic Medicine, 26,* 634–635.

SCHMALE, A. H., & IKER, H. P. (1966). The psychological setting of uterine cervical cancer. *Annals of the New York Academy of Sciences, 125,* 807–813.

SCHMALE, A. H., & IKER, H. (1971). Hopelessness as a predictor of cervical cancer. *Social Science and Medicine, 5,* 95–100.

SCHMIDT, R. W., LAMM, H., & TROMMSDORFF, G. (1978). Social class and sex as determinants of future orientation (time perspective) in adults. *European Journal of Social Psychology, 8,* 71–90.

SCHONFIELD, D. (1973). Future commitments and successful aging. I. The random sample. *Journal of Gerontology, 28,* 189–196.

SCHUSTER, D. B. (1952). A psychological study of a 106-year-old man. *American Journal of Psychiatry, 109,* 112–119.

SELIGMAN, M.E.P. (1975). *Helplessness: On depression, development, and death.* San Francisco: W. H. Freeman and Company Publishers.

SELYE, H. (1956). *The stress of life.* New York: McGraw Hill.

SIMEONS, A.T.W. (1960). *Man's presumptuous brain.* New York: Dutton.

SIMONTON, O. C., MATTHEWS-SIMONTON, S., & CREIGHTON, J. L. (1978). *Getting well again.* New York: Bantam.

SKLAR, L. S., & ANISMAN, H. (1979). Stress and coping factors influence tumor growth. *Science, 205,* 513–515.

SKLAR, L. S., & ANISMAN, H. (1981). Stress and cancer. *Psychological Bulletin, 89,* 369–406.

SOLOMON, G. F. (1969). Emotions, stress, the central nervous system and immunity. *Annals of the New York Academy of Sciences, 164,* 335–343.

SOUTHAM, C. M. (1969). Emotions, immunology and cancer: How might the psyche influence neoplasia? *Annals of the New York Academy of Sciences, 164,* 473–475.

SPENCE, D. L. (1968). The role of futurity in aging adaptation. *The Gerontologist, 8,* 180–183.

STEIN, M., SCHIAVI, R. C., & CAMERINO, M. (1976). Influence of brain and behavior on the immune system. *Science, 191,* 435–440.

STENBACK, A. (1980). Depression and suicidal behavior in old age. In J. E. Birren & R. B. Sloane (Eds.), *Handbook of mental health and aging* (pp. 616–652). Englewood Cliffs, NJ: Prentice-Hall.

STENGEL, E. (1973). *Suicide and attempted suicide.* Harmondsworth: Penguin.

STEUER, J. (1977). Future time perspective, commitments and life satisfaction of retired women educators. *Dissertation Abstracts International, 37,* 5885-B.

STOTLAND, E. (1969). *The psychology of hope.* San Francisco: Jossey-Bass.

TEAHAN, J. E. (1958). Future time perspective, optimism, and academic achievement. *Journal of Abnormal and Social Psychology, 57,* 379–380.

TELLER, M. N. (1972). Age changes and immune resistance to cancer. *Advances in Gerontological Research, 4,* 25–43.

THOMAS, C. B., DUSZYNSKI, K. R., & SHAFFER, J. W. (1979). Family attitudes reported in youth as potential predictors of cancer. *Psychosomatic Medicine, 41,* 287–302.

THURNHER, M. (1974). Goals, values, and life evaluations at the preretirement stage. *Journal of Gerontology, 29,* 85–96.

TIGER, L. (1979). *Optimism, the biology of hope.* New York: Simon & Schuster.

VISINTAINER, M. A., VOLPICELLI, J. R., & SELIGMAN, M.E.P. (1982). Tumor rejection in rats after inescapable or escapable shock. *Science, 216,* 437–439.

WALLACE, M. (1956). Future time perspective in schizophrenia. *Journal of Abnormal and Social Psychology, 52,* 240–245.

WEINER, B., & LITMAN-ADIZES, T. (1980). An attributional expectancy-value analysis of learned helplessness and depression. In J. Garber & M.E.P. Seligman (Eds.), *Human helplessness: Theory and applications* (pp. 35–57). New York: Academic Press.

WEINSTEIN, N. D. (1980). Unrealistic optimism about future life events. *Journal of Personality and Social Psychology, 39,* 806–820.

WIRSCHING, M., STIERLIN, H., HOFFMAN, F., WEBER, G., & WIRSCHING, B. (1982). Psychological identification of breast cancer patients before biopsy. *Journal of Psychosomatic Research, 26,* 1–10.

WONG, P.T.P. (in press). Coping with frustrative stress: A stage model. *The Behavioral and Brain Sciences.*

WONG, P.T.P., & SPROULE, C. F. (1983). An attribution analysis of the locus of control construct and the Trent Attribution Profile. In H. M. Lefcourt (Ed.), *Research with the locus of control construct, Vol. 3: Extensions and limitations* (pp. 309–360). New York: Academic Press.

8

PERCEIVED CONTROL, HELPLESSNESS, AND CHOICE

Their Relationship to Health and Aging

Donald R. Shupe

This chapter is concerned with perceived control and some of the many related constructs and their relationship to health and aging. Perceived control may be defined as the expectation of having control over one's environment. Because this construct, measured and labelled in various ways, had been found to be associated with a large number of other variables, and hypotheses derived from it have been very fruitful, it has shown remarkable durability over the past 20 years. Becasue of its seemingly great potential, much of the research with the construct has been an attempt to refine it and give it more precision, to the point that, as Seligman and Miller (1979, p. 367) complain, "We are faced with a terminological mare's nest. In this nest are such terms as *choice, control, perceived choice and control, freedom, perceived freedom, coercion, origin/pawn, internal/external, controllable/uncontrollable, incompetence/competence/helplessness, self-administration, autonomy,* and many others."

The purpose of this chapter is not to present a review of the technical difficulties of perceived control, nor to detail its many refinements, nor to delve deeply into all the theoretical ramifications (see, for example, Perlmuter & Monty, 1979) but to give an overview of how the construct has been applied with regard to health and well-being, particularly in the elderly.

One of the most fruitful measures of the construct of perceived control has been the internal-external (I-E) scale, developed by Rotter and his associates (Rotter, 1966), which has stimulated the large amount of research that continues to the present day.

According to Rotter, individuals have a belief in external control when they perceive reinforcements as due to luck, chance, fate, or powerful others outside their control. Individuals have a belief in internal control when they believe that reinforcements are contingent upon their own behavior or permanent characteristics. For Rotter, the internal-external variable is not dichotomous but a continuum which approximates a normal distribution (Rotter, 1975).

The development of the construct of perceived control and the scale itself stems from Rotter's social learning theory. In this theory there are four classes of variables: behaviors, expectancies, reinforcements, and the psychological situation. Behavior is posited as a function of the expectancy of reinforcement in a specific situation and the value of the reinforcement to the individual. Rotter emphasizes the importance of the situation in determining whether behavior will occur, and that situations perceived as similar by the individual generate similar expectancies. Generalized expectancies are a product of a past history of reinforcement, and their importance increases as the novelty and ambiguity of the situation increase. Thus in a new or ambiguous situation the individual relies on an expectancy for reinforcement that is a generalization from past experience. The construct of perceived control, or locus of control, or internal versus external control—each of these labels is used pretty much synonymously—was an attempt to refine further the relationship between expectancy and reinforcement.

Rotter (1975) has pointed out that the construct of perceived control is not the central or major concept of the theory, but it is unquestionably the most heuristic. Most researchers appear to pay little attention to the theory from which the construct emerged.

Although the I-E scale has been widely, and to a large extent deservedly, criticized, and there have been numerous other scales designed to measure the construct,[1] it is still the most widely used measure of perceived control. The fact that there are so many different attempts to measure the construct, including specialized versions for children[2] and specialized subject areas such as health locus of control,[3] testifies to the versatility and usefulness of this construct.

In a book attempting to summarize and order the "overwhelming abundance of research pertaining to the perception of control," Lefcourt (1976) came up with the following conclusions:

> Internal control expectancies about personally important events, that are to some reasonable degree controllable, will be related to signs of vitality— affective and cognitive activity which indicates an active grappling with those self-defined important events. Where fatalism or external control beliefs are associated with apathy and withdrawal, the holding of internal control expectancies presages a connection between an individual's desires and his subsequent actions. As such, locus of control can be viewed as a mediator of involved commitment in life pursuits. If one feels helpless to effect important events, then resignation or at least benign indifference should become evident with fewer signs of concern, involvement, and vitality (pp. 151–152).

[1] For instance, the Nowicki-Strickland Locus of Control Scale (Nowicki & Strickland, 1973), the Reid-Ware Three-Factor Internal-External Scale (Reid & Ware, 1974), Levenson's Internal, Chance, and Powerful Others subscales (Levenson, 1973).

[2] The Stanford Preschool Internal-External Scale (Mischel, Zeiss, & Zeiss, 1974), the Crandall Intellectual Achievement Responsibility Questionnaire (Crandall, Katkovsky, & Crandall, 1965).

[3] The Health Locus of Control Scale and the Multiple Health Locus of Control Scale (see Wallston & Wallston, 1981 for a review of research with these instruments).

It was clear from the beginning that the construct of perceived control would have implications for health, both physical and emotional. Certainly a reasonable prediction from the definition of the variable would be that internals, believing as they do in taking responsibility and in the potency of their own actions, would take steps to maintain their health and prevent illness (at least, according to Rotter's theory, if they *value* their health). An early study using a precursor of the I-E scale indicated that internal patients had more knowledge about their disease, tuberculosis, than externals (Seeman & Evans, 1962). A number of other studies have verified the finding that internals seek knowledge related to health problems or health maintenance (Wallston, Maides, & Wallston, 1976; Wallston, Wallston, Kaplan, & Maides, 1976). Reasonably, patients with more knowledge of the disease might be in a better position to obtain adequate treatment.

In terms of more active participation in health maintenance activities, the research has indicated that internals are, for instance, more likely to engage in physical exercise (Sonstroem & Walker, 1973), use seat belts, get preventative dental checkups (Williams, 1972a, 1972b), and stop smoking (e.g., Coan, 1973; James, Woodruff, & Werner, 1965). Poll and De-Nour (1980) found that internal dialysis patients compared to external dialysis patients were more likely to follow fluid and dietary restrictions and to participate in vocational rehabilitation. They also found that internals showed more acceptance of their disease.

Strickland (1978), in her excellent review of perceived control and health-related behaviors, gives many examples of research showing a connection between internality and preventative or health-maintenance behaviors. The consensus of the literature is that internals do indeed seek more information about health conditions of interest to them than do externals. That is, they become more informed about relevant health practices, and they are more apt to engage in behaviors conducive to good health than externals.

Since internals engage in more health maintenance behaviors and take more responsibility for themselves, it might be expected that perceived control would vary with health or among those with various diseases. There is some indication that this may be true for heart patients. For instance, a study by Cromwell, Butterfield, Brayfield, and Curry (1977) indicated that heart attack patients were more external than matched controls who had other illnesses comparable in severity, but more interestingly they found that when internality-externality of the patients was crossed with nursing care and patient participation which allows patients either responsibility or passivity, both internals and externals did better in congruent combinations of perceived control and actual participation. Those patients with incongruent combinations (externals with high participation and internals with low participation) showed a higher number of returns to the hospital for additional care and, indeed, a higher death rate.

Glass (1977) has offered the interesting hypothesis that coronary-prone (Type A) behavior and internal personality style are related. He suggests that the Type A behavior characterized by competitive achievement striving, sense of time urgency, and aggressiveness and hostility emerges when the individual perceives threats to control. The relationship between Type A behavior patterns as measured by the Jenkins Activity Survey (Jenkins, Rosenman, & Friedman, 1967) and Rotter's I-E measure, though significant, is weak ($r = -.17$, Glass, 1977, pp. 184–185); to some extent this calls into question the importance of perceived control in the Type A behavior pattern.

PERCEIVED CONTROL AND STRESS

There is increasing evidence that psychological factors play an important part in stress reactions. Both Lazarus (1966) and Mason (1968, 1971) have given psychological factors a key place in their theories of stress, believing that the "essential" mediator of the stress reaction is psychological (Lazarus, 1977).

Lefcourt and his associates (Lefcourt, Martin, & Ebers, 1981; Lefcourt, Miller, Ware, & Sherk, 1981) and Johnson and Sarason (1978, 1979) have suggested locus of control as a mediator or moderator of the stress reaction. Lefcourt, Miller, Ware, and Sherk (1981) found that college student subjects who were classified as externals showed a stronger relationship between negative life events and mood scores taken over four weeks than did internals who scored lower overall on mood disturbance. Thus, perceived control may be a "modifier" of the relationship between stressors and moods. Again using undergraduate students as subjects, Johnson and Sarason (1978) found a significant correlation between negative life change and depression (r = .32) and anxiety (r = .31) for externals but not for internals. Their conclusion is that "these results strongly support the original hypothesis that locus of control orientation may be a moderator variable in the relationship between negative life change and depression and anxiety and provide support for the notion that the effects of life stress may be mediated by the degree to which individuals perceive themselves as having personal control over events" (p. 207). Additional support for the role of perceived control as a mediator of stress can be found in the research of Husaini and Neff (1980) and McFarlane, Norman, Streiner, Roy, and Scott (1980) to be discussed later.

In a laboratory test of the hypothesis that internal subjects would show less reaction to stress, Houston (1972) had college-aged subjects repeat digits backward under the threat of shock. He found that internal subjects showed a significantly greater increase in heart rate than externals but did not differ in self-reported anxiety as measured by the Multiple Affect Adjective Check List. He interpreted this as a defensiveness on the part of internals. The data can be interpreted just as well, however, as due to the attempt of internals to strive for control. The heart-rate increase may not be so much a measure of anxiety experienced as a measure of the increased arousal of the internals who, when faced with potential threat, strive to gain or regain control. The externals believing that events are outside their control show less arousal because they are fatalistic about their chances of obtaining control, and therefore strive less. This hypothesis would be congruent with that of Glass and Carver (1980a, 1980b) in regard to Type A behavior discussed previously.

PERCEIVED CONTROL AND THE ELDERLY

Although there are many notable exceptions, with increasing age there is a tendency for increased reliance on others. Eyesight may fail and the individual experiencing poor vision may now need to rely on friends, family, or public transportation to get around. Health may wane, causing a person to be confined to home, dependent on others to supply food or run errands. Because of this increased reliance on others with age it has been suggested that the elderly should experience increased external locus of control (Phares, 1976). The research, however, does not bear this prediction out. Duke, Shaheen, and Nowicki (1974), for example, found their male and female sample of elderly subjects to be even more internal than research has reported for college-aged subjects. Staats (1974) found an increase in internality with age, although his oldest group was only 45 to 60, and Knoop (1981) found significantly higher internality for his 36 to 65 age group than for those 20 to 35. Ryckman and Malikiosi (1975) showed no difference between college students and the over-60 group in perceived control and Gatz and Siegler (1981) in a study using data from the Duke Adaptation Study, and unique for being an eight-year longitudinal follow-up, showed stability in internal-external scores. Nehrke, Hulicka and Morganti (1980) found no age difference in internality for their 50 to 70+ residents of a Veterans Administration Domiciliary and only a low and insignificant relationship between internality and life satisfaction. Although it is not clear whether perceived control increases with age or remains stable over time, it does not appear to decrease.

In research in which internal-external scores have been correlated with measures of well-being, the findings have generally shown a positive correlation between internality and such measures. Kuypers (1971, 1972), for instance, found that elderly internals showed a more positive coping style as well as other more favorable characteristics than externals. Palmore and Luikart (1972) found them higher in life satisfaction, especially the 60 to 71 age group as compared to the 46 to 59 group. Cox (1980) found that those who scored more external on the Rotter I-E scale among a sample of elderly from 55 to 102 were more politically discontent and more anomic and that those more internally oriented were more likely to feel useful and show greater life satisfaction in retirement. Queen and Freitag (1978) and Hamrick (1977) also found internality correlated with life satisfaction. "Higher levels of involvement, more adaptive levels of developmental task accomplishment, and more positive emotional balance in their satisfaction with life" were reported for internal elderly subjects in a study by Wolk and Kurtz (1975, p. 176).

In a follow-up study, Wolk (1976) found that the residential situation was related to perceived control. Wolk sampled residents of two different retirement settings, a "retirement-type village" which he categorized as low in situational constraint and a "retirement home" which was higher in situational constraint. He found that the internality of the residents was significantly higher in the low constraint setting. More interestingly, in this setting there were significant relationships between the internal-external variable and life satisfaction, adjustment, self-concept, and activity levels with internals scoring higher in each case. None of these correlations was significant for the more restricted retirement home (high restraint). It is impossible to know from this study whether the type of home influenced the perceived control or whether different personality types in terms of the control construct chose the different retirement settlements on the basis of their needs and personality. Since life satisfaction and adjustment were also significantly higher in the low-constraint retirement village, it may be that low constraint, that is, more freedom of choice, is conducive to well-being. There is evidence for this position which will be discussed later in the chapter. For those who are internal, living in an arrangement which does not allow them to exercise control may lead to unhappiness, which, working against the general finding that internals are more contented, may have produced the essentially zero correlations found by Wolk between perceived control and well-being variables in the high constraint residence. In tightly controlled situations in which individuals are discouraged from making any meaningful decisions or from making even minor modifications of their environment, it may indeed be the externals who are more satisfied.

This may be the reason for the findings of Felton and Kahana (1974). These researchers sampled 124 residents of three different homes for the aged. The residents were interviewed in their rooms and to measure the locus of control they were asked to give responses to nine specific problem areas. In the privacy area, for instance, they were presented with this statement: "A man feels he doesn't have enough privacy. What does he do about it?" Their responses were coded in categories of self, staff, and others who were designated as the controlling agent in their responses. The "other" category was seldom used, and Felton and Kahana report that their subjects perceived either themselves or the staff as the locus of control. In only one area was the perception of self in control as opposed to staff related to better adjustment. Thus, in general, this research comes to the conclusion that better adjustment is related to external control orientation, a finding at odds with the bulk of the research.

The locus of control measure used by Felton and Kahana is not of the same nature as the perceived control of Rotter and those who view this construct as a generalized expectancy rather than a specific response to a specific situation. For Rotter the generalized expectancy is important in situations of ambiguity and uncertainty. The specific problem areas used by Felton and Kahana may have called for specific realistic responses and therefore may not have tapped this generalized expectancy at all. It may very well be that an intelligent, rational response to these problem areas is to delineate the staff as the major source of control, as they very likely were. What the Felton and Kahana study may have shown is that adjustment is related to a veridical perception of the situation, a not unlikely outcome, and one mentioned as a likely explanation by the authors. Fawcett, Stonner, and Zepelin (1980), in their lengthy discussion of the Felton and Kahana study, make some of these same criticisms. Their own study indicated a negative relationship between external locus of control and life satisfaction, and an even stronger negative relationship ($r = -.61$) between perception of institutional constraint and life satisfaction.

In a follow-up study Kahana and Felton (reported by Reid, Hass, & Hawkings, 1977) found no relationship between morale and their control measure, and in fact, when analyzed in terms of pre- and post-changes in morale scores, found that internality was associated with a larger increase in morale on one of two problem areas that showed significant changes. What is needed to clarify these relationships is a comparison of the internal-external variable as a generalized expectancy with more situational locus of control problems, as used by Felton and Kahana.

Reid et al. (1977) also measured a more specific locus of control. These researchers asked their elderly subjects not only if they could engage in or cause certain things to happen, but also whether such events were important or desirable to them. They asked, for instance, whether the residents could place their possessions where they wanted, or whether they could give themselves privacy. A four-choice response, from, in the case of the latter item, "never" to "always" was used.

For the "desire"-for-control portion of the scale they asked, as an example, "How important is it for you to be able to find privacy from others?", again with four choices ranging from "not desirable" to "very desirable." Their locus of control score was a product of the desire-for-control and perceived-control ratings. Contrary to the Felton and Kahana (1974) study, Reid et al. found a positive correlation between self-concept and internality, and between nurses' ratings of happiness and internality. The relationship between self-concept and internality was higher for men, and particularly for those who lived in the homes for the aged, "suggesting that somehow having a sense of control is more relevant to a man's adjustment and that this relationship is amplified in institutionalized settings where it is likely that fewer avenues of personal control are available" (p. 450).

Reid and his associates have continued to work on the Desired Control Scale and a summary of their findings, the scale itself, and its characteristics can be found in Reid and Ziegler (1981). Over a series of studies, their measure of desired control has correlated well with life satisfaction (.32 to .54), positive self-concept (.40 to .54), rated vitality (.36 to .46), and negative physical health ($-.20$ to $-.38$). What is more important, their correlations of desired control measured at one time correlates from .23 to .44 with life satisfaction measured from 6 to 18 months later. Correlations with desired control and later measures of physical health, self-concept, and vitality were equally supporting of their contention that those elderly "who feel they have control over desired outcomes are more content, happy, and generally satisfied with their lives" (Reid & Ziegler, 1981, p. 151).

Positive relationships were also found by Hulicka, Morganti, and Cataldo (1975) between their Locus and Range of Activities Checklist, designed to assess "perceived latitude of choice in activities of daily living," and measures of self-concept and life satisfaction. The instrument measured the degree of free choice available and how much personal importance was assigned to such activities as the time of meals, what TV program to watch, what clothes to wear, with whom to spend free time, etc. These authors found a significant difference between their institutionalized and noninstitutionalized elderly samples in the rated latitude of choice, with considerably more perceived choice, as one might guess, in the non-institutionalized group. Self-concept and life satisfaction scores were also higher for this group. Although, as the authors point out, causation cannot be assigned, this research also fails to support the Felton and Kahana study.

In summary, the research supports the conclusion that good adjustment and well-being are associated with an internal sense of control. The major exception was the study by Felton and Kahana, which because of their follow-up remains ambiguous. The reason for the general finding of a positive relationship between perceived control and well-being is far less clear, however. Prospective studies in this area are rare and one cannot be sure whether institutionalization may create both the externality and poorer adjustment or whether the internal person simply copes better. Most researchers either explicitly or implicitly seem to favor the latter.

RELATED CONSTRUCTS

Health and well-being have been examined from a variety of viewpoints that are related to the construct of locus of control. The fact that these concepts are in many ways so similar gives additional evidence that perceived control is indeed a useful and important cognitive construct. Some of the following constructs are so similar to locus of control or to one another that they seem little more than synonyms for the same thing.

Helplessness

During the course of using what later became one of the more famous paradigms in psychology, Martin Seligman (1975) discovered that dogs can be made helpless and passive by the application of unavoidable shock. The paradigm was to restrain the animal in a hammock and apply unavoidable shock on a noncontingent basis. There was nothing that the dog could do to avoid or escape the shock. Seligman found that this treatment produced an animal which would not avoid or escape shock in a simple shuttle box situation where the animal had to jump over a barrier to a "safe" side. It took a great deal of patience and many trials of hauling the helpless dogs across to the other side to retrain them to escape.

Seligman quickly saw the possible ramifications of this paradigm to the lives of people brought up in conditions with plenty of aversive stimulation but little opportunity to avoid it. The small child beaten by a mentally ill or alcoholic parent for no apparent reason and unable to escape or avoid such continual and noncontingent beatings would be a tragic human example of the laboratory paradigm.

For Seligman, most depression can be viewed as "learned helplessness." The total disability of depression with its passivity and hopelessness is for Seligman (1975) the result of exposure to uncontrollable and unavoidable events, that is,

> the depressed patient believes or has learned that he cannot control those elements of his life that relieve suffering, bring gratification, or provide nurture—in short, he believes that he is helpless (p. 93)

Like the locus of control construct, the learned helplessness model is primarily cognitive. It is not enough for the organism to simply experience helplessness but it must come to expect it, that is, it must expect that outcomes are beyond behavioral control. This is much like the generalized expectancy of externality that events are beyond the control of the individual and rest in the hands of fate, chance, or powerful others. In fact, Hiroto (1974) found that externals were more easily made helpless than internals. Rotter's I-E construct may be a measure of the resistance to feelings of helplessness.

A number of studies have shown that learned helplessness can be induced in humans rather easily in the laboratory situation (Hiroto, 1974; Krantz, Glass, & Snyder, 1974). In Krantz et al., subjects were given either escapable or inescapable noise of two different intensities (to form a high- versus low-stress condition). Subjects in the inescapable noise condition not only reported feeling more helpless and less in control, but also showed a significant decrement in their performance on another task in which they could escape from stressful noise. Interestingly, subjects in the inescapable condition rated themselves as significantly more incompetent, passive, and hostile than did those subjects who could escape the noise. If a short-term experimental manipulation in the laboratory can produce such differences so quickly, one wonders what the effects of long-term lack of control and helplessness does to the elderly who find themselves unable to do more than be passive responders in situations in which family, nursing home, or hospital constrain them and leave them unable to influence the environment. Consider older persons, perhaps with daily pain, who are totally dependent (or have been made this way by well-meaning friends or family, or a nursing home) on the care and help of others, and who in addition can get little verbal control over the situation as others either ignore or patronize them. These individuals have indeed been made helpless and may be expected to give up all striving, with depression a possible result.

Because Seligman has made a connection between learned helplessness and depression and because depression is a frequent illness among the elderly, we should pursue this connection in both research and treatment. In a test of Seligman's hypothesis, Hanes and Wild (1977) found positive correlations between locus of control and depression (externals were more depressed) for their sample of elderly aged 60 to 80. They suggest that the higher correlation obtained for males (r = .46) than for females (r = .22) may be due to the increased saliency of control for men because of traditional sex roles. Evans and Dinning (1978) found that locus of control scores were not related to depression in their sample of psychiatric inpatients but that their measure of reduced control over life events prior to hospitalization was. They found that neurotic depressives reported greater reduced control over life events than did either schizophrenics or personality disordered nondepressed patients. The authors interpreted their findings as support for the learned helplessness model, and, although it can be criticized because of its retrospective nature (that is, depressives may report more loss of control because of their depressed attitudes but may not have experienced more than other groups), it is consistent with other literature which indicates that control is a mediator of stress.

Helplessness has also been implicated in Type A behavior and thereby with heart disease. Glass and Carver (1980b) believe that "Type A behavior is a strategy for coping with potentially uncontrollable stress; enhanced performance reflects an attempt to assert and maintain control after its loss has been threatened" (p. 236). These authors believe that if the Type A individual cannot regain control, then the individual will tend to give up and "display *hyporesponsiveness* to uncontrollable events"—that is, learned helplessness. Greene, Goldstein, and Moss (1972) report that sudden death due to coronary disease is common in depressed men. Does the scenario run like this? The Type A individual is constantly fighting for control and at some point in his life (perhaps the stress of middle age which has recently received so much attention) he no longer can maintain control over important life events, and depression, then heart disease, set in. That it is the giving up rather than the striving which leads the Type A to heart disease is an interesting hypothesis. Since the learned helplessness model is a cognitive model, it matters little from the standpoint of the model whether the lack of control experienced is real or imagined, the outcome would be the same.

To the extent that helplessness is implicated in depression, it might be implicated in mortality and morbidity from surgery. Kimball (1968, 1969) found that the highest morbidity occurred in the depressed patients, and Tufo and Ostfeld (1968) found among several variables that preoperative depression was the only one related to operative death. Greer, Morris, and Pettingale (1979), however, found that recurrence-free survival five years after simple mastectomy, though related to helplessness, was unrelated to depression. They found survival to be significantly more common among patients who showed either denial or a fighting spirit three months after the operation than those who were either stoical or had feelings of helplessness/hopelessness.

Although the two constructs, locus of control and learned helplessness, have obvious similarities, they are not identical. I have suggested above that the I-E measure may be a measure of the ability of an individual to withstand helplessness in the face of the inability to control events, i.e., during an operation or illness or confinement.

The laboratory paradigm of an inoculation against helplessness is to submit the animal to loss of control and then to regained control in small repeated doses. A classic example which fits this model is Richter's (1957) study in which he found that holding and constraining wild rats, eliminating all chance of escape, immediately before their immersion in water resulted in a high number of deaths, some even while being held in the hand. But if the rats were repeatedly held briefly and then freed, and if they were immersed in water for a few minutes on several occasions, the rats would later swim for hours. The rats seemed to learn from this procedure that all was not hopeless.

To the extent that such a repeated exposure to brief periods of uncontrollable events give an individual a sense of internality then the I-E measure may be related to this "inoculation." But if an internal is simply a person who has always had control over situations and has never suffered any events over which he or she might generally have control that could not be controlled, then such an individual might very well succumb to a state of helplessness. Rotter suggests this when he says that "many people may already feel that they have more control than is warranted by reality, and they may be subject in the future . . . to strong trauma when they discover that they cannot control such things as automobile accidents, corporate failures, diseases, etc." (Rotter, 1975, p. 61).

Locus of control is a generalized expectancy about the individual's sense of control over events, but learned helplessness is a more specific cognitive state of the individual. Locus of control as measured by the various scales seems to correlate with a number of personality and health variables, but helplessness seems to lead behaviorally to direct deficits in learning, emotion, and motivation. A reformulation of the helplessness model (Abramson, Garber, & Seligman, 1980; Abramson, Seligman, & Teasdale, 1978) to overcome its inadequacies specifically incorporates an internal-external dimension (subtly different from Rotter's construct) along with dimensions of stable-unstable and global-specific as attributions for the cause of the helplessness. The incorporation, however, ends up by denying the general relationship between the two concepts. According to Abramson et al. (1980), locus of control and helplessness are orthogonal and the attribution made by individuals for their helplessness can be either internal or external. Only further research will clarify the similarities and differences in the two constructs.

Giving-Up–Given-Up Complex

In the course of studying the psychological factors in disease, the Medical-Psychiatric Liaison Group of the University of Rochester have come up with the concept of the *giving-up–given-up complex* (Engel, 1968; Schmale, 1972). It is called a complex because "the process goes beyond what is usually considered as an unpleasant feeling and includes a disruption in key relationships, a loss of motivation with the thought that there is no solution, plus remembered past occasions when similar reactions were experienced" (Schmale, 1972, p. 25).

The process is more complex than either a loss of control or learned helplessness, containing as it does the notion that the giving up is in part related to a disturbance in key relationships and a re-evocation of similar past experiences. Aspects of both locus of control and learned helplessness are incorporated, however, within this complex. Engel (1968) describes the complex as having five essential features, the most characteristic of which "is a sense of psychological impotence, a feeling that for briefer or longer periods of time one is unable to cope with changes in the environment; the psychological or social devices utilized in the past seem no longer effective or available" (p. 296). This giving up is labelled help-lessness or hopelessness depending on whether the cause is seen as outside the individual—that is, beyond one's help—or whether one views oneself as the cause for this failure and inability to cope. A second characteristic is a reduced self-image because of inability to control the environment or function in the usual manner. The third aspect concerns the loss of support or gratification in human relation-ships and social roles. And the fourth and fifth characteristics concern the loss of continuity between past, present, and future and the reactivation of memories of earlier periods of these same feelings of helplessness or hopelessness.

These characteristics describe, then, the *giving-up–given-up complex* which is seen as playing an important part in disease. According to the authors this complex does not cause disease, but its presence alters the physiological state of the indi-vidual and leads to an increased physical and mental vulnerability.

The interesting aspect of this complex as compared to the internal locus of control and learned helplessness is that it includes the social support variable which research is showing to be of great importance for health (Cobb, 1976; Lynch, 1978; Wilcox, 1981). Past experience with stressors and the connection of the past with the present is also included in the model which give it a more multifaceted aspect. Engel (1968) and Schmale (1972) both report anecdotal and experimental evidence for this complex as a useful conceptual tool but as yet it is too nebulous to be either proved or disproved in any rigorous way. For the present, it can only serve as a possible reference point for future research and practice, though it does again emphasize the usefulness of this control or helplessness construct in relationship to health variables.

Fatalism-Instrumentalism

Wheaton (1980) has developed the construct of fatalism-instrumentalism which is closely related to the previous concepts of internal-external control, help-lessness, and giving up, but which, in Wheaton's view, goes beyond these concepts. For Wheaton, fatalism is a "learned and persistent causal attribution tendency on the part of individuals that directs their perception of the causes of behavioral outcomes either toward external factors (e.g., task difficulty or luck), or toward internal factors (e.g., ability or effort)" (pp. 103-104). As such, it appears to be synonymous with internal-external control; but Wheaton dismisses the interchange-ability of the two constructs for two reasons. First, the internal-external control variable is the same as the Rotter I-E scale in most instances (it is not so used in the present chapter), while fatalism is not dependent on any existing measure; and secondly, the fatalism construct is conceived more broadly so as to incorporate "other internal elements such as effort and other external elements, such as task difficulty" (p. 104).

The construct is conceived as a learned and persistent (stable) characteristic of the individual. A chief mediator of this learning is the socioeconomic status (SES) of the individual. The interesting characteristic of this model as proposed by Wheaton is that it attempts to explain how SES comes to elicit psychological disorder. This model

> predicts that low SES in either childhood or adult life will socialize individuals to be more fatalistic in their causal perceptions (i.e., to emphasize environmental rather than personal causation of behavior), and that fatalism will increase one's vulnerability to psychological disorder primarily because it undermines persistence and effort in coping situations (and *not* primarily because it impairs overall coping ability). (p. 101)

Though Wheaton only considers psychological distress, the model seems directly relevant to physical and health disorders as a reaction to stress.

The model provides a nice and welcome explanation for the findings that health and socioeconomic status are negatively related. For instance, findings from the recent national health survey show that low education (a correlate of low SES) was associated with poorer self-rated health, poorer self-rated maintenance of health, more worry about health, more difficulty with physical activities, more dissatisfaction with health, less energy, having less control over health, not visiting a dentist, not having pap smears or breast examinations, smoking more cigarettes, less use of seat belts, and engaging in less dental care (Danchik, 1981). If the mediator of these poorer habits is indeed fatalism caused by the discouragement and helplessness of poor social and economic conditions, then we may have a key for improving the health of a portion of the population.

Hardiness

The constructs of fatalism, giving up, helplessness, and to some extent externality are negative qualities of the individual that, as we have seen, are generally unfavorable to the individual's well-being. There are a few investigators who have chosen to define and look at positive constructs. For instance, Caplan (1981) defines a type of response to stress which he calls *mastery,* and Kobasa (1979), more rigorously, defines a concept of *hardiness,* also in reaction to stress.

Kobasa defines the *hardy* person as having three general characteristics, the first of which is a belief that he or she has control over life events. The other two characteristics of Kobasa's model are a deep involvement or commitment to life activities and a view of change as challenging. In an experimental test of this model, Kobasa identified a high-stress/low-illness group and a high-stress/high-illness group from the middle- and upper-level executives of a large public utility. Thus both groups experienced stress, but they differed in reported illnesses. A variety of tests and instruments were mailed to the executives already classified in terms of stress and illness variables. A high rate of return was obtained (86 percent of high-stress/low-illness and 75 percent of the high-stress/high-illness returned the tests and questionnaires) and random samples from this population of returnees were drawn so that both a validation and cross-validation might be accomplished.

Kobasa found that her low-illness executives were

> distinguished by their sense of commitment to (or lack of alienation from) self, their sense of vigorousness (as opposed to vegetativeness) about life,

their sense of meaningfulness (as opposed to nihilism), and their internal (as opposed to external) locus of control (p. 8)

In addition, she found that these low-illness executives perceived the personal sphere of their lives as significantly less stressful than did the high-illness subjects.

PERCEIVED CONTROL IN SPECIFIC SITUATIONS

I wish to turn now to aspects of perceived control which are more situationally specific. Rather than looking at a generalized expectancy about being in control or being a pawn of fate and chance, what effect does it have on the individual to have the perception of being in control in specific instances? It seems reasonable that in general an individual perceiving him- or herself as having control over life events will be more apt to perceive him- or herself as having control in specific areas.

There is a vast literature on control of threat in laboratory situations, and the reader is referred to the review by Averill (1973) and Miller (1979) for a flavor of the problems and complexities of research in this area. Generalizing the laboratory studies with their relatively trivial and short-term stressors and push-button avoidance or escape mechanisms to real-life situations where stresses have life-threatening effects and long-term consequences is a problem. For this reason, the concentration in this chapter is on those studies representative of the work in this area and concerned with real-life situations. Several such studies (Felton & Kahana, 1974; Hulicka et al., 1975; Reid et al., 1977) which investigate perceived control over specific events or in specific situations have already been discussed.

In an ongoing longitudinal study by McFarlane et al. (1980) the relationship between psychosocial events and health status is under investigation. Preliminary results indicate that undesirable events over which total control is exercised did not correlate with their measure of strain, regardless of whether the person could anticipate the undesirable event or not. On the other hand, events over which the person has no control are strongly correlated with strain, again, regardless of whether they were anticipated or not. Events over which the individual has some control were more closely associated with strain when they were anticipated than when unanticipated. In general, then, not having the perception of control of undesirable events seems to strengthen the negative impact of such events.

A study by Husaini and Neff (1980) reached similar conclusions. These researchers found that life events perceived as beyond the individual's control were associated with higher scores on measures of somatic and psychological complaints and depressive symptomatology. The problem with both of these studies is the impossibility of determining whether the perception of controllability is independent of health status. Does the lack of control of a stressful event result in impaired health or does impaired health predispose an individual to rate stressful events as uncontrollable? Although there is reason to believe that the chain of causation moves from uncontrollable stress to impaired health, the alternative cannot be ruled out in either study. The McFarlane et al. (1980) study, because of its longitudinal nature, should eventually be able to tease these relationships apart and offer evidence as to the direction of causation.

If internality, hardiness, and controllability over events reduces stress, then it seems logical that to provide individuals with increased control over their environments and the events of their lives might increase health and well-being. This is exactly what Langer and Rodin (1976) did.

These researchers conducted a study using two floors of a relatively high-quality nursing home. The two floors contained residents of similar physical and psychological health and socioeconomic status. On a random basis, one floor was assigned to the experimental treatment and the other to the control treatment. The experimental treatment consisted of a lecture given to the residents by the nursing home administrator in which he stressed how much influence the residents had over their lives and the large number of decisions that they could and should make. He delineated a number of things that the residents could do and stressed that they should take the responsibility of airing their complaints and making suggestions for change. In addition, the residents were allowed to select a plant and were told they could keep and take care of the plants as they liked. Also, they were to select which night of the week they wished to see a movie.

The control treatment consisted of a talk by the same administrator which also stressed how interested and caring the home was for the residents, but in this case the weight was placed on how much the home and staff could do for the residents. Plants were also distributed, but this time the residents were each given one and were told that the nurses would water and care for the plants.

Thus, in the experimental treatment, emphasis was placed on the responsibility of the residents for themselves, while in the control condition emphasis was placed upon the staff's responsibility for the residents. Questionnaires were administered to residents and nurses one week prior to and three weeks after the administrator's talk. Generally, the results indicated improvement for the experimental group and negative changes for the control group. On the basis of self-report, the experimental group became happier and more active than the control group. Interviewer ratings of alertness showed greater positive change for the experimental (responsibility-induced) group, and nurses rated greater general improvement and an increased time spent in various social activities for this group. All of these changes were significantly different for the two groups.

An 18-month follow-up of the residents in the above study (Rodin & Langer, 1977) continued the success story with differences between the experimental and control groups continuing and significant. The follow-up allowed calculation of mortality rates for the two groups with the experimental group experiencing half of the mortality of the control group (15 percent versus 30 percent), a difference only marginally significant, however.

The study yielded impressive results, indicating that even such a mild treatment intervention as the administrator's talk could have strong positive effects on the well-being of nursing home residents. Assuming that it was this increased responsibility and the emphasis placed on the residents' control over their environment that created the differences, the study indicates very dramatically the importance of personal control over the environment. Certainly such an important study needs to be replicated and caution needs to be exercised in generalizing widely to other situations. It is possible, for instance, that the administrator who gave the two differentiating lectures to the residents, and therefore obviously understood the experimental manipulation, may have acted differently to the residents, and indeed perhaps to the staff of the two floors, creating a snowball effect. Until replications are made, we can only be impressed with the potential for intervention and positive change that this study found, regardless of its cause.

Another study (Schulz, 1976) indicates a positive result in the aged due to increased control over a small aspect of their lives. Schulz randomly assigned 42 subjects, aged 67 to 96, who resided in a private, church-affiliated retirement home, to one of four treatment conditions. In three of these conditions, the residents were visited by college undergraduates with various degrees of predictability and control exercised by the resident. One group of residents (control condition) could determine to a large extent both the occasion and duration of the visits. A second group (predict condition) had no control over the occasion or duration but was informed when the visitor would come and how long he or she would stay, so though they had no control over these variables, they were able to predict their occurrence. The third group was visited on a random basis with no control or predictability. The fourth group was a baseline comparison and received no visits. An attempt was made to keep the duration, frequency, and quality of each visit for the three groups the same. They were visited on an average of 1.3 times per week for 50 minutes each visit over a two-month period.

On various health, activity, and psychological variables, the groups who controlled and who were able to predict the visits showed positive differences or improvement when compared with the other two groups. No differences, however, were found between the control and predict group. Schulz (1976) hypothesizes that the visits had positive benefits only to the extent that the residents could look forward to them. The lack of differences obtained between the control and predict groups may be because it was the visitor's behavior that was in question. As Schulz pointed out, if it were aspects of the physical environment that were being controlled, such as when or what to eat, or when to get up, the results may have been different. It may be that under these circumstances to control the activities of visitors is less desirable than simply predicting their behavior, for the attribution that one might make in these circumstances is that one is visited *only* because one controls the visitor. This would seem less reinforcing than to have a visitor come as *they* desire but to know when and for how long they might come.

Along similar lines, Rodin (1980) reports on a study in which a sample of patients in a nursing home were given 15-minute blocks of time that a nurse would be readily available to them if they pressed the call button. The patients exercised their control extensively in the beginning but less and less as the study progressed and then developed a pattern of oscillation between use and disuse as if to reassure themselves that they still exercised control. Rodin (1980) states that

> relative to untreated controls, general health and sociability improved in the experimental patients. These data suggest that control does not have to continue to be exercised to produce beneficial effects; simply the knowledge that one has control seems to be valuable in this particular instance. This form of control appears to have provided a coping device that made a major problem in the environment appear far less stressful. Indeed we found that a reduction in perceived stress was strongly correlated with increased feelings of control. (p. 182)

Another specific situation where perceived control may play an important part in the life of the aged is in relocation. Schulz and Brenner (1977) analyzed the literature on relocation in terms of the degree of choice the individual exercised in the move and the amount of environmental change that was experienced. Since the analysis is post hoc, the authors are wisely tentative in their conclusions. Yet the data are consistent with their hypothesis that the effect of relocation will be less negative the greater the choice the individual has and the more predictable the new environment is.

Personal Causation As a Motive

The bulk of the research on perceived control as a generalized expectancy suggests that those who view themselves as in control of their fate do "better" in a variety of areas of health and well-being. As the previous section has indicated, those who see themselves as in control of certain aversive events in their lives or who are given more control over their lives seem to thrive better than those who do not experience this control. It seems, then, that believing one has control over life events is a positive asset to health and well-being. As such, could seeking for control be construed as a basic motive for humans? Richard de Charms (1968) thinks so:

> *Man's primary motivational propensity is to be effective in producing changes in his environment.* Man strives to be a causal agent, to be the primary locus of causation for, or the origin of, his behavior; he strives for personal causation. This propensity has its roots in his earliest encounters with his environment, forces him to actively engage his environment thereby testing and deriving valid personal knowledge from it, and is the basis for specific motives. His nature commits him to this path, and his very life depends on it. (p. 269)

When one gives up mastery over his or her fate, when one becomes helpless according to Seligman's paradigm or fatalistic in Wheaton's sense, or gives up according to Engel and Schmale, the stage is set for disease, illness, and even death. The possibility that this control motive may be built into the biology of the organism is suggested by a fascinating series of studies by Kavanau (1967) with white-footed mice.

Kavanau found that much of the activity of the wild white-footed mice he studied was directed toward controlling the environment and to countering the various modifications that the experimenter forced upon them. If the running wheel was turned on, the mice turned it off; if turned off, the mice turned it on. The same behavior occurred with lighting. If lighting was raised, the mice lowered it; if lowered, the mice raised it.

> When mice in experimental enclosures are disturbed during the day, they often leave the nest. Sometimes they reenter almost immediately; at others they wait until the disturbance is over. But if they are placed back in the nest by hand, they leave it again immediately (as do kittens and puppies). They persist in leaving, no matter how many times they are put back. In this relatively clear-cut case, an act or situation which is rewarding when carried

out volitionally is avoided when initiated by force—the animal responds by doing the opposite. (Kavanau, 1967, p. 1631)

As Kavanau has pointed out, the tendency to anthropomorphize is almost irresistible. It seems that these delightful creatures "would rather do it themselves."

Seligman (1975) has noticed the similarity between his work in learned helplessness, Kavanau's findings that his mice resisted outside control, and White's (1959) concept of competence as a basic motivation for behavior.

A drive for competence or to resist compulsion is, from my point of view, a drive to avoid helplessness. The existence of such a drive follows directly from the emotional premise of our theory. Since being helpless arouses fear and depression, activity that avoids helplessness thereby avoids these aversive emotional states. Competence may be a drive to avoid the fear and depression induced by helplessness. (Seligman, 1975, pp. 55)

Along similar lines Brehm (1966) proposed that people are motivated to re-establish any free behaviors that have been threatened or eliminated. Brehm labelled this motivational state that occurs in response to a reduction or threatened reduction of an individual's potential for acting as *psychological reactance,* and hypothesized that the magnitude of the reactance is a function of the importance of the behaviors eliminated or threatened, the proportion of such behaviors eliminated or threatened, and the magnitude of the threat in the case of behaviors threatened with elimination. But as the white-footed mice are inbred to become more docile and congenial for research, they lose their capability for psychological reactance and so, too, it seems, do humans, though the mechanism is not clear. Brehm's theory does not address the problem of docility and passivity in people who show little attempt to regain their threatened or lost freedoms.

IMPLICATIONS OF THE PERCEIVED CONTROL
RESEARCH FOR THE ELDERLY

The evidence seems compelling that one's sense of control over one's life is an important aspect of general well-being, both psychological and physical. It is not clear from the literature whether a sense of personal control confers positive benefits in its own right or whether it is the lack of control, a helplessness or inefficacy in the face of the environment, which diminishes well-being, or whether both are operative.

The relationship between personal control as a generalized expectancy versus personal control as a specific expectancy in a discrete situation remains unclear. Internal-external control as a measure of the generalized expectancy for control has a positive relationship with a variety of health and well-being variables but the relationship is never strong. Whether this is due to problems with the scale or the concept itself is still unclear. Personality traits like the locus of control trait always remain rather vague and perhaps the more current trend to examine specific issues of control in circumscribed environments or with specific events is a good trend, and may be more fruitful in the long run. Certainly the research in the area (e.g., Langer & Rodin, 1976; Rodin & Langer, 1977; Schulz, 1976) offers exciting possibilities for increasing the health and psychological well-being and, indeed, the longevity of the aged. More such studies need to be done to carefully delineate just which variables are operative. Is it control per se that is the contributor or is it aspects of competence, efficacy, predictability, or some unknown factors, that are important causative agents? At this point, however, the evidence suggests that to give the elderly individual control over his or her environment is conducive to good health and well-being. Personal control, a sense of competence, autonomy, efficacy, or whatever label may be used is probably a good thing for everyone to have. However, for the elderly who have suffered losses in health and function and in relationships and mobility, having residual control in some areas is even more important.

Sperbeck and Whitbourne comment that "one of the most damaging effects of institutionalization of the elderly is dependence on staff, characterized by apathy, passivity, and the eventual reduction in self-maintenance behaviors" (1981, p. 268). These authors believe that the staff, because of inaccuracy in their assessments of the abilities of older persons and stereotyped beliefs, tend to reinforce the dependent and sick role of the institutionalized elderly. Their solution is to provide the staff not only with information about the capacities of the elderly and the strong role played by situational and environmental factors in promoting dependency, but with the principles and techniques of behavior management as a means for reversing this dependency.

The staff of nursing homes and residential homes must be made aware of the importance of those small areas of control in daily activities that go far to make up the meaning of life and in Antonovsky's (1980) phrase give life a "sense of coherence." The problem has been recognized for some time: "Nursing homes must be recompensed for bringing life back to their residents. Dull as it seems, life for most of us is cleaning, cooking, dressing, working, socializing, and helping others. Of these activities, many are within the capability of many nursing home patients" (Gottesman, Quarterman, & Cohn, 1973, p. 421).

Families of the aged may be equally guilty. The all-too-common refrain of "Mother, let me do that, you deserve a rest," may not be in the best interests of Mother. As one woman told me recently: "I couldn't stand to live with my children, as much as I love them, because they always want to take over my life."

What about those elderly individuals already made passive, external, and helpless by their environment? A number of treatment programs have been suggested in the literature to reestablish a sense of control, autonomy, and efficacy. For instance, the work of Baltes and Zerbe (1976), Barton, Baltes, and Orzech (1980), Goldstein (1979), MacDonald and Butler (1974), Rodin (1980), Sperbeck and Whitbourne (1981), and the references associated with these papers suggest approaches to reverse helplessness and reactivate a sense of efficacy.

Mercer and Kane (1979), for instance, conducted an intervention in a nursing home along the lines of Langer and Rodin (1976). The administrator of the nursing home in a speech to the residents encouraged them to take responsibility for themselves and to contribute ideas or complaints. A week later, the administrator followed-up this message by visiting each resident individually. The patients were also given a plant to select and care for and invited to participate in a newly established resident council. Another comparable nursing home was selected as a control. The patients in the intervention home showed, relative to the controls, a significant decrease in hopelessness, a significant increase in activity, and significant improvement on a 16-item staff rating scale of patients' eating and sleeping behaviors, hostility, depression, social activity, etc.

Though the experimenters got pre- and post-measures and used analysis of covariance where appropriate, there are the inevitable problems of working with intact groups and the resultant lack of randomization that must make the conclusions tentative. Nevertheless, they and other researchers who have engaged in this difficult research are to be commended for doing the best they can with what seldom lends itself to strict experimental design. The accumulation of positive results in even weak studies suggests that such treatment manipulations do have an effect on the well-being of institutionalized elderly.

Starting from the learned helplessness model itself, Tickle and Davis (1982) describe an intervention procedure with disabled older adults in a day care center. These investigators believe that the declines in function, sensory loss, and social loss which the elderly have experienced result in feelings of diminished control and helplessness. As a preliminary step in their program, each patient is assessed in terms of helplessness behaviors, and a program is developed which emphasizes the successful accomplishment of various tasks such as self-care, cooking, and social interaction. Their treatment program attempts to reestablish feelings of control by providing tasks such as self-care, cooking, and social interaction at which the patients can be successful.

The research surveyed in this chapter suggests that the perception of being in control of life events is a positive asset to health and well-being, and that the elderly, who in many cases have had their freedom of choice drastically reduced, can profit from the restoration, even in small measure, of control and choice over their lives. Ten years later, we can only reiterate Bengtson's (1973) plea that

> we need to *give more responsibility to the aged themselves,* to enhance their competence. Recall that competence involves adequate performance, coping, and a *feeling* of efficacy, and that implied in this definition is doing what you want to do. How often do we as professionals allow patients to decide for themselves what they want to be doing, what therapeutic regimen makes most sense to them? How quick we are to organize activities *for* older people; how little we give such responsibility to them. In so doing, of course, we may lose some of our own power as well as some time and efficiency. We may also feel that we are not helping. Actually, as older people become more competent there is no loss, there are only gains. (p. 130)

REFERENCES

ABRAMSON, L. Y., GARBER, J., & SELIGMAN, M.E.P. (1980). Learned helplessness in humans: An attributional analysis. In J. Garber & M.E.P. Seligman (Eds.), *Human helplessness: Theory and applications.* New York: Academic Press.

ABRAMSON, L. Y., SELIGMAN, M.E.P., & TEASDALE, J. D. (1978). Learned helplessness in humans: Critique and reformulation. *Journal of Abnormal Psychology, 87,* 49–74.

ANTONOVSKY, A. (1980). *Health, stress, and coping.* San Francisco: Jossey-Bass.

AVERILL, J. R. (1973). Personal control over aversive stimuli and its relationship to stress. *Psychological Bulletin, 80,* 286–303.

BALTES, M. M., & ZERBE, M. B. (1976). Independence training in nursing-home residents. *The Gerontologist, 16,* 428–432.

BARTON, E. M., BALTES, M. M., & ORZECH, M. J. (1980). Etiology of dependence in older nursing home residents during morning care: The role of staff behavior. *Journal of Personality and Social Psychology, 38,* 423–431.

BENGTSON, V. L. (1973). Self-determination: A social-psychological perspective on helping the aged. *Geriatrics, 28(12),* 118–130.

BREHM, J. W. (1966). *A theory of psychological reactance.* New York: Academic Press.

CAPLAN, G. (1981). Mastery of stress: Psychosocial aspects. *American Journal of Psychiatry, 138,* 413–420.

COAN, R. W. (1973). Personality variables associated with cigarette smoking. *Journal of Personality and Social Psychology, 26,* 86–104.

COBB, S. (1976). Social support as a moderator of life stress. *Psychosomatic Medicine, 38,* 300–314.

COX, H. (1980). The motivation and political alienation of older Americans. *International Journal of Aging and Human Development, 11,* 1–12.

CRANDALL, V. C., KATKOVSKY, W., & CRANDALL, V. J. (1965). Children's beliefs in their own control of reinforcements in intellectual-academic situations. *Child Development, 36,* 91–109.

CROMWELL, R. L., BUTTERFIELD, E. C., BRAYFIELD, F. M., & CURRY, J. J. (1977). *Acute myocardial infarction: Reaction and recovery.* St. Louis, MO: C. V. Mosby.

DANCHIK, K. M. (1981). *Highlights from Wave I of the National Survey of Personal Health Practices and Consequences: United States, 1979.* (DHHS Publication No. (PHS) 81-1162). Washington, DC: U.S. Government Printing Office.

de CHARMS, R. (1968). *Personal causation.* New York: Academic Press.

DUKE, M. P., SHAHEEN, J., & NOWICKI, S. (1974). The determination of locus of control in a geriatric population and a subsequent test of the social learning model for interpersonal distances. *Journal of Psychology, 86,* 277–285.

ENGEL, G. L. (1968). A life setting conducive to illness: The giving-up–given-up complex. *Annals of Internal Medicine, 69,* 293–300.

EVANS, R. G., & DINNING, W. D. (1978). Reductions in experienced control and depression in psychiatric inpatients: A test of the learned helplessness model. *Journal of Clinical Psychology, 34,* 609–613.

FAWCETT, G., STONNER, D., & ZEPLIN, H. (1980). Locus of control, perceived constraint, and morale among institutionalized aged. *International Journal of Aging and Human Development, 11,* 13–23.

FELTON, B., & KAHANA, E. (1974). Adjustment and situationally bound locus of control among institutionalized aged. *Journal of Gerontology, 29,* 295–301.

GATZ, M., & SIEGLER, I. C. (August 1981). *Locus of control: A retrospective.* Paper presented at the meeting of the American Psychological Association, Los Angeles, CA.

GLASS, D. C. (1977). *Behavior patterns, stress, and coronary disease.* Hillsdale, NJ: Lawrence Erlbaum Associates.

GLASS, D. C., & CARVER, C. S. (1980a). Environmental stress and the Type A responses. In A. Baum & J. E. Singer (Eds.), *Advances in environmental psychology. Vol. 2: Applications of personal control.* Hillsdale, NJ: Lawrence Erlbaum Associates.

GLASS, D. C., & CARVER, C. S. (1980b). Helplessness and the coronary-prone personality. In J. Garber & M.E.P. Seligman (Eds.), *Human helplessness: Theory and applications.* New York: Academic Press.

GOLDSTEIN, S. E. (1979). Depression in the elderly. *Journal of the American Geriatrics Society, 27,* 38–42.

GOTTESMAN, L. E., QUARTERMAN, C. E., & COHN, G. M. (1973). Psychosocial treatment of the aged. In C. Eisdorfer & M. P. Lawton (Eds.), *The psychology of adult development and aging.* Washington, DC: American Psychological Association.

GREENE, W. A., GOLDSTEIN, S., & MOSS, A. J. (1972). Psychosocial aspects of sudden death: A preliminary report. *Archives of Internal Medicine, 129,* 725–731.

GREER, S., MORRIS, T., & PETTINGALE, K. W. (1979). Psychological response to breast cancer: Effect on outcome. *The Lancet, II,* 785–787.

HAMRICK, N. D. (1977). Learned helplessness and internal-external locus of control in the elderly. *Dissertation Abstracts International, 37,* 5812B.

HANES, C. R., & WILD, B. S. (1977). Locus of control and depression among noninstitutionalized elderly persons. *Psychological Reports, 41,* 581–582.

HIROTO, D. S. (1974). Locus of control and learned helplessness. *Journal of Experimental Psychology, 102,* 187–193.

HOUSTON, B. K. (1972). Control over stress, locus of control, and response to stress. *Journal of Personality and Social Psychology, 21,* 249–255.

HULICKA, I. M., MORGANTI, J. B., & CATALDO, J. F. (1975). Perceived latitude of choice of institutionalized and noninstitutionalized elderly women. *Experimental Aging Research, 1,* 27–39.

HUSAINI, B. A., & NEFF, J. A. (1980). Characteristics of life events and psychiatric impairment in rural communities. *Journal of Nervous and Mental Disease, 168,* 159–166.

JAMES, W. H., WOODRUFF, A. B., & WERNER, W. (1965). Effect of internal and external control upon changes in smoking behavior. *Journal of Consulting Psychology, 29,* 184–186.

JENKINS, C. D., ROSENMAN, R. H., & FRIEDMAN, M. (1967). Development of an objective psychological test for the determination of the coronary-prone behavior pattern in employed men. *Journal of Chronic Diseases, 20,* 371–379.

JOHNSON, J. H., & SARASON, I. G. (1978). Life stress, depression and anxiety: Internal-external control as a moderator variable. *Journal of Psychosomatic Research, 22,* 205–208.

JOHNSON, J. H., & SARASON, I. G. (1979). Moderator variables in life stress research. In I. G. Sarason & C. D. Spielberger (Eds.), *Stress and anxiety* (Vol. 6). Washington, DC: Hemisphere Publishing Corporation.

KAVANAU, J. L. (1967). Behavior of captive white-footed mice. *Science, 155,* 1623–1639.

KIMBALL, C. P. (1968). The experience of open heart surgery: Psychological responses to surgery. *Psychosomatic Medicine, 30,* 552.

KIMBALL, C. P. (1969). Psychological responses to the experience of open heart surgery: I. *American Journal of Psychiatry, 126,* 348–359.

KNOOP, R. (1981). Age and correlates of locus of control. *The Journal of Psychology, 108,* 103–106.

KOBASA, S. C. (1979). Stressful life events, personality, and health: An inquiry into hardiness. *Journal of Personality and Social Psychology, 37,* 1–11.

KRANTZ, D. S., GLASS, D. C., & SNYDER, M. L. (1974). Helplessness, stress level, and the coronary-prone behavior pattern. *Journal of Experimental Social Psychology, 10,* 284–300.

KUYPERS, J. (1971). Internal-external locus of control and ego functioning correlates in the elderly. *The Gerontologist, 11*(3, Part II), 39.

KUYPERS, J. A. (1972). Internal-external locus of control, ego functioning, and personality characteristics in old age. *The Gerontologist, 12,* 168–173.

LANGER, E. J., & RODIN, J. (1976). The effects of choice and enhanced personal responsibility for the aged: A field experiment in an institutional setting. *Journal of Personality and Social Psychology, 34,* 191–198.

LAZARUS, R. S. (1966). *Psychological stress and the coping process.* New York: McGraw-Hill.

LAZARUS, R. S. (1977). Cognitive and coping processes in emotion. In A. Monat & R. S. Lazarus (Eds.), *Stress and coping: An anthology.* New York: Columbia University Press.

LEFCOURT, H. M. (1976). *Locus of control: Current trends in theory and research.* Hillsdale, NJ: Lawrence Erlbaum Associates.

LEFCOURT, H. M., MARTIN, R. A., & EBERS, K. (1981). Coping with stress: A model for clinical psychology. *Academic Psychology Bulletin, 3,* 355–364.

LEFCOURT, H. M., MILLER, R. S., WARE, E. E., & SHERK, D. (1981). Locus of control as a modifier of the relationship between stressors and moods. *Journal of Personality and Social Psychology, 41,* 357–369.

LEVENSON, H. (1973). Multidimensional locus of control in psychiatric patients. *Journal of Consulting and Clinical Psychology, 41,* 397–404.

LYNCH, J. J. (1978). *The broken heart: The medical consequences of loneliness.* New York: Basic Books.

MacDONALD, M. L., & BUTLER, A. K. (1974). Reversal of helplessness: Producing walking behavior in nursing home wheelchair residents using behavior modification procedures. *Journal of Gerontology, 29,* 97–101.

MASON, J. W. (1968). Organization of psychoendocrine mechanisms. *Psychosomatic Medicine, 30,* 565–808.

MASON, J. W. (1971). A re-evaluation of the concept of "non-specificity" in stress theory. *Journal of Psychiatric Research, 8,* 323–333.

McFARLANE, A. H., NORMAN, G. R., STREINER, D. L., ROY, R., & SCOTT, D. J. (1980). A longitudinal study of the influence of the psychosocial environment on health status. *Journal of Health and Social Behavior, 21,* 124–133.

MERCER, S., & KANE, R. A. (1979). Helplessness and hopelessness among the institutionalized aged: An experiment. *Health and Social Work, 4,* 90–116.

MILLER, S. M. (1979). Controllability and human stress: Method, evidence and theory. *Behavior Research and Therapy, 17,* 287–304.

MISCHEL, W., ZEISS, R., & ZEISS, A. (1974). Internal-external control and persistence: Validation and implications of the Stanford Preschool Internal-External Scale. *Journal of Personality and Social Psychology, 29,* 265–278.

NEHRKE, M. F., HULICKA, I. M., & MORGANTI, J. B. (1980). Age differences in life satisfaction, locus of control, and self-concept. *International Journal of Aging and Human Development, 11,* 25–33.

NOWICKI, S., & STRICKLAND, B. R. (1973). A locus of control scale for children. *Journal of Consulting and Clinical Psychology, 40,* 148–154.

PALMORE, E., & LUIKART, C. (1972). Health and social factors related to life satisfaction. *Journal of Health and Social Behavior, 13,* 68–80.

PERLMUTER, L. C., & MONTY, R. A. (Eds.). (1979). *Choice and perceived control.* Hillsdale, N.J.: Lawrence Erlbaum Associates.

PHARES, E. J. (1976). *Locus of control in personality.* Morristown, NJ: General Learning Press.

POLL, I. B., & De-NOUR, A. K. (1980). Locus of control and adjustment to chronic haemodialysis. *Psychological Medicine, 10,* 153-157.

QUEEN, L., & FREITAG, C. B. (1978). A comparison of externality, anxiety, and life satisfaction in two aged populations. *The Journal of Psychology, 98,* 71-74.

REID, D. W., HAAS, G., & HAWKINGS, D. (1977). Locus of desired control and positive self-concept of the elderly. *Journal of Gerontology, 32,* 441-450.

REID, D. W., & WARE, E. E. (1974). Multidimensionality of internal versus external control: Addition of a third dimension and non-distinction of self versus others. *Canadian Journal of Behavioural Science, 6,* 131-142.

REID, D. W., & ZIEGLER, M. (1981). The desired control measure and adjustment among the elderly. In H. M. Lefcourt (Ed.), *Research with the locus of control construct. Vol. 1: Assessment methods.* New York: Academic Press.

RICHTER, C. P. (1957). On the phenomenon of sudden death in animals and man. *Psychosomatic Medicine, 19,* 191-198.

RODIN, J. (1980). Managing the stress of aging: The role of control and coping. In S. Levine & H. Ursin (Eds.), *Coping and health.* New York: Plenum.

RODIN, J., & LANGER, E. J. (1977). Long-term effects of a control-relevant intervention with the institutionalized aged. *Journal of Personality and Social Psychology, 35,* 897-902.

ROTTER, J. B. (1966). Generalized expectancies for internal versus external control of reinforcement. *Psychological Monographs, 80*(1, Whole No. 609).

ROTTER, J. B. (1975). Some problems and misconceptions related to the construct of internal versus external control of reinforcement. *Journal of Consulting and Clinical Psychology, 43,* 56-67.

RYCKMAN, R. M., & MALIKIOSI, M. X. (1975). Relationship between locus of control and chronological age. *Psychological Reports, 36,* 655-658.

SCHMALE, A. H. (1972). Giving up as a final common pathway to changes in health. In Z. J. Lipowski (Ed.), *Advances in psychosomatic medicine, Vol. 8, Psychosocial aspects of physical illness.* Basel, Switzerland: S. Karger.

SCHULZ, R. (1976). Effects of control and predictability on the physical and psychological well-being of the institutionalized aged. *Journal of Personality and Social Psychology, 33,* 563-573.

SCHULZ, R., & BRENNER, G. (1977). Relocation of the aged: A review and theoretical analysis. *Journal of Gerontology, 32,* 323-333.

SEEMAN, M., & EVANS, J. W. (1962). Alienation and learning in a hospital setting. *American Sociological Review, 27,* 772-782.

SELIGMAN, M.E.P. (1975). *Helplessness: On depression, development, and death.* San Francisco: W. H. Freeman and Company Publishers.

SELIGMAN, M.E.P. & MILLER, S.M. (1979). The psychology of power: Concluding comments. In L. C. Perlmuter & R. A. Monty (Eds.), *Choice and perceived control.* Hillsdale, N.J.: Lawrence Erlbaum Associates.

SONSTROEM, R. J., & WALKER, M. I. (1973). Relationship of attitudes and locus of control to exercise and physical fitness. *Perceptual and Motor Skills, 36,* 1031-1034.

SPERBECK, D. J., & WHITBOURNE, S. K. (1981). Dependency in the institutional setting: A behavioral training program for geriatric staff. *The Gerontologist, 21,* 268-275.

STAATS, S. (1974). Internal versus external locus of control for three age groups. *International Journal of Aging and Human Development, 5,* 7-10.

STRICKLAND, B. R. (1978). Internal-external expectancies and health-related behaviors. *Journal of Consulting and Clinical Psychology, 46,* 1192–1211.

TICKLE, L. S., & DAVIS, L. J. (1982, March). *Learned helplessness: An applied rehabilitation model for adult day care.* Paper presented at the meeting of the Western Gerontological Society, San Diego, CA.

TUFO, H. M., & OSTFELD, A. M. (1968). A prospective study of open-heart surgery. *Psychosomatic Medicine, 30,* 552–553.

WALLSTON, B. S., WALLSTON, K. A., KAPLAN, G. D., & MAIDES, S. A. (1976). Development and validation of the Health Locus of Control (HLC) Scale. *Journal of Consulting and Clinical Psychology, 44,* 580–585.

WALLSTON, K. A., MAIDES, S., & WALLSTON, B. S. (1976). Health-related information seeking as a function of health-related locus of control and health value. *Journal of Research in Personality, 10,* 215–222.

WALLSTON, K. A., & WALLSTON, B. S. (1981). Health locus of control scales. In H. M. Lefcourt (Ed.), *Research with the locus of control construct, Vol. I, Assessment methods.* New York: Academic Press.

WHEATON, B. (1980). The sociogenesis of psychological disorder: An attributional theory. *Journal of Health and Social Behavior, 21,* 100–124.

WHITE, R. W. (1959). Motivation reconsidered: The concept of competence. *Psychological Review, 66,* 297–333.

WILCOX, B. L. (1981). Social support, life stress, and psychological adjustment: A test of the buffering hypothesis. *American Journal of Community Psychology, 9,* 371–386.

WILLIAMS, A. F. (1972a). Factors associated with seat belt use in families. *Journal of Safety Research, 4,* 133–138.

WILLIAMS, A. F. (1972b). Personality characteristics associated with preventive dental health practices. *Journal of the American College of Dentists, 39,* 225–234.

WOLK, S. (1976). Situational constraint as a moderator of the locus of control-adjustment relationship. *Journal of Consulting and Clinical Psychology, 44,* 420–427.

WOLK, S., & KURTZ, J. (1975). Positive adjustment and involvement during aging and expectancy for internal control. *Journal of Consulting and Clinical Psychology, 43,* 173–178.

Appendix

FUTURE ORIENTATION SURVEY

Paul T. P. Wong and Gary T. Reker

We are interested in whether people differ in their future orientation. We are also interested in how confident people are that various future events will take place.

On the lines below, please indicate what desirable events you are looking forward to at this moment. Also, indicate the degree of your confidence or expectancy that each of these events will take place by writing down the appropriate number as indicated from the scale below.

1	2	3	4	5
not confi- dent at all	slightly confident	fairly confident	very confident	extremely confident

For example:

I look forward to my son's visit next week. (4)

I look forward to completing the book I am writing. (2)

Please note that the numbers within parentheses indicate the degree of confidence as described by the scale. For example, 4 means very confident that the event will take place.

- -

AGE: _____   SEX: _____

INDEXES

AUTHOR INDEX

SUBJECT INDEX